# How to Get Run Over by a Truck

# How to Get Run Over by a Truck

*a Memoir*

## Katie McKenna

INKSHARES

Published by Inkshares, Inc., San Francisco, California
www.inkshares.com

Edited and designed by Girl Friday Productions
www.girlfridayproductions.com

Cover design by Kathleen Lynch

ISBN: 9781941758984
e-ISBN: 9781941758991
Library of Congress Control Number: 2016931481

First edition

Printed in the United States of America

To Mom, Dad, Conor, Callie and James,

"There are darknesses in life and there are lights,
and you are one of the lights, the light of all lights."
—Bram Stoker

Thank you for being my lights.

*Do not pray for an easy life,*
*pray for the strength to endure a difficult one.*
*—Bruce Lee*

# TABLE OF CONTENTS

**PART I: GIRL MEETS TRUCK**

Chapter One: How to Get Run Over by a Truck. . . . . . . . 3
Chapter Two: More . . . . . . . . . . . . . . . . . . . . . 15
Chapter Three: In Between. . . . . . . . . . . . . . . . . . 23
Chapter Four: I Get Knocked Down . . . and I Stay There . 37
Chapter Five: "Am I Naked?" and Other Important
    Questions . . . . . . . . . . . . . . . . . . . . . . . . 45
Chapter Six: Visitors. . . . . . . . . . . . . . . . . . . . . 55
Chapter Seven: You Must Be So Grateful. . . . . . . . . . . 63
Chapter Eight: Dr. Douchebag . . . . . . . . . . . . . . . . 73
Chapter Nine: Happy Hour Hunger Strike . . . . . . . . . . 85
Chapter Ten: The Record . . . . . . . . . . . . . . . . . . 89
Chapter Eleven: Roomies . . . . . . . . . . . . . . . . . . 93
Chapter Twelve: How to Cure Nice White Girlitis . . . . .109
Chapter Thirteen: Roberto . . . . . . . . . . . . . . . . . .127
Chapter Fourteen: Pain Management. . . . . . . . . . . . .129
Chapter Fifteen: Breaking Out . . . . . . . . . . . . . . . .137

**PART II: PUTTING YOUR PIECES BACK TOGETHER**

Chapter Sixteen: Indulged . . . . . . . . . . . . . . . . . .157
Chapter Seventeen: Katie's First Steps . . . . . . . . . . . .173

Chapter Eighteen: Pennies and Ring Rosaries . . . . . . . .181
Chapter Nineteen: Physical Therapy . . . . . . . . . . . .183
Chapter Twenty: *Jeopardy* . . . . . . . . . . . . . . . . . .193
Chapter Twenty-One: Mackers . . . . . . . . . . . . . . .197
Chapter Twenty-Two: Lean On Me, When I'm Kinda
    Strong. . . . . . . . . . . . . . . . . . . . . . . . . . . . .203
Chapter Twenty-Three: Dr. Belkin. . . . . . . . . . . . . .211
Chapter Twenty-Four: Heel to Toe . . . . . . . . . . . . .223
Chapter Twenty-Five: Home . . . . . . . . . . . . . . . . .229
Chapter Twenty-Six: Removing Your Own Catheter
    (A Twentysomething's Guide). . . . . . . . . . . . . .233
Chapter Twenty-Seven: The Giving of Thanks . . . . . . .245
Chapter Twenty-Eight: Momma. . . . . . . . . . . . . . .255
Chapter Twenty-Nine: The Blame Game—Rules and
    Regulations . . . . . . . . . . . . . . . . . . . . . . . .261
Chapter Thirty: BFF . . . . . . . . . . . . . . . . . . . . . .279
Chapter Thirty-One: Jump and the Net Will Appear . . . .285
Chapter Thirty-Two: Becoming a Real Girl. . . . . . . . .289
Chapter Thirty-Three: Dance Dance Dance . . . . . . . .295
Chapter Thirty-Four: First Day of Work Mix. . . . . . . .301

PART III: OLD KATIE MEETS NEW KATIE

Chapter Thirty-Five: Miss Dependent. . . . . . . . . . . .309
Chapter Thirty-Six: Angry Little Grown-up . . . . . . . .317
Chapter Thirty-Seven: Warren. . . . . . . . . . . . . . . .323
Chapter Thirty-Eight: Baggage. . . . . . . . . . . . . . . .331
Chapter Thirty-Nine: Now . . . . . . . . . . . . . . . . . .337

Epilogue: Eff the Tee. . . . . . . . . . . . . . . . . . . . . .343

# PART I

# Girl Meets Truck

# CHAPTER ONE

# How to Get Run
# Over By a Truck

So, how do you get run over by a truck? My first recommendation is to ride a bicycle. This is specifically for their fool factor—every time I saw someone riding a bicycle it seemed so innocuous. It was low-impact exercise that was good for you. Lance Armstrong rode a bicycle, and he beat like one million kinds of cancer. What could be healthier?

Plus, I live in Brooklyn, and all the hipsters ride bicycles: they have messenger bags and wear vintage glasses, and they make riding over the Williamsburg Bridge look cool and effortless. I figured if those pasty-skinned music lovers could handle riding their bikes in Brooklyn so could I. I mean, hello! I was an all-county track champion in high school. I knew I could own that bicycle. I'm not just talking about owning it in the actual "I purchased it" kind of way—I mean own it in the frat-boy way, e.g., "We totally owned that keg last night." That was the way I was going to own that bicycle.

I actually did, for almost a year. I rode my bike for errands. I rode my bike to work. I rode my bike to my friends' apartments in the neighborhood, locking it to stop signs and feeling eco-conscious and thoughtful. In the summer I even took myself on romantic bike rides—and let me tell you, that bicycle had moves. Stopping in McCarren Park at twilight made me feel like I was in a foreign film, sitting on a park bench in a black beret and a scarf, drinking wine—when in fact I was sitting on patchy brown grass, wearing sport shorts and running shoes and drinking a Bud Light tall boy in a brown paper bag.

When I woke up early on October 2, I won't tell you that I had a premonition or that there was a hand on my shoulder that told me not to go out that day—because that would be untrue. But I did get the feeling that someone was trying to tell me something I obviously had no interest in hearing. These were signs from God. Three, in fact: 1. My bike tires were flat; 2. I almost fell down the stairs trying to get my bike out of the apartment; and—most important—3. I decided not to wear any underwear that day.

Most lazy twenty-four-year-olds, when faced with the fact that their bike tires were flat, would say, "Fuck it, I'm not going to bother." Nope, not me, not Katie can-do. I thought instead, *I'll fill up my tires and get in a workout—this is going to be the best morning ever!*

Then my bike tried to attack me as I took it down the stairs. We got out of the door just fine, but as we went down the stairs the bike started to bend and fold as if it was trying to fight me back into the apartment. I should have seen it for what it was: a cry for help. Bob the Bike knew more than I did—he didn't want to die that day either. He was trying to stop me, but I wasn't listening. I wanted to be thin, to get that endorphin rush, and on top of that I wanted to see the sunrise—I wanted it all.

And then there was the matter of the last sign that I shame-lessly ignored. As a child I was told to always wear clean underwear. My mother's reason was always the same: "What if you get into an accident?" This never made any sense to me, because I always assumed that if I got into an accident I would wind up peeing my pants anyway. But because I was a good girl I wore clean underwear nonetheless. That morning I made a conscious decision to go without and, by doing so, I now believe I tempted fate; my accident was bound to happen.

Before I continue, I need to make one point about this whole underwear thing: I had just gotten up, underwear-free, and the idea of putting on a beautifully pristine pair of undies just to get them dirty made no sense at all. I figured that on this point, God and I were on the same page. . . . I was mistaken.

It was an unbelievably beautiful day. There was the smell of fall in the air, the sky was a deep blue, and there was no one on the streets. The morning felt like a secret; it was so dark and quiet, it gave me shivers. The few trees left on my block were beginning to change from dark green into a golden yellow. Fall has always been my favorite season, a time of new beginnings, a new year of school, a new fall jacket—a chance to start over again.

I walked my bike one block up and over another to the Hess station on the corner of Metropolitan and Humboldt. I had a quarter tucked into my sock to pay for the air I was going to pump into Bob's tires. By 6:15, tires fully inflated, I was riding down Metropolitan without much of a plan. I knew I wanted to ride for forty-five minutes and just explore the neighborhood.

My roommates and I had recently moved into a new apart-ment in Williamsburg. In the most classic of New York real estate scams, our Mafia-esque landlords (I am talking gold chains nestled in a tuft of chest hair and velour Fila tracksuits) had told us that our old building was being sold, and that we had to be out in a month. In actuality the building was not being sold; they were just bringing in people who would pay more rent. We moved about ten blocks away, farther from the sweet Italian neighborhood that we had been living in and closer to the industrial part of Williamsburg.

I actually liked living closer to the factories. I thought it was cool to live in a place that was a little less gentrified, a little grittier. I loved being able to see dirty New York—the New York that had frightened me as a kid. When I was little, I was so afraid of the big bad dirty city that when my mom and I came in from Long Island to see *Peter Pan* on Broadway, I made her leave during intermission. Now that I was a big girl, I was proud I wasn't scared of the city anymore.

On this particular morning I rode past the furniture outlets and the mattress factories, past the abandoned brick buildings with the painted names of past tenants chipping off their brick façades. I wanted to take it all in. I was feeling good. I was forgetting about the fight that I had with my boyfriend the night before. I was sweating off my nerves about my new job. The world felt big, and I felt wonderfully small.

About a half hour into my ride, the sun was starting to rise over the low buildings on Vandervoort Avenue. I decided that watching the sunrise as I rode out the last fifteen minutes would be a perfect conclusion to my morning workout. I wanted to take this morning and make it mine. I wanted to see something beautiful and then be able to keep it in my pocket all day. It would be my secret to keep.

Stopping at the light at the corner of Maspeth and Vandervoort, I looked back at the car behind me, a black Mazda sedan. I waved at the driver and pointed to the right, letting them know which way I was going to turn. The truck that was next to me didn't have its indicator on, so I assumed the driver was going straight. Just in case he wasn't, I waved in his side mirror anyway. I pointed to myself and then I pointed to the right. I always communicated with truck drivers via their side-view mirrors. I spent a lot of time behind trucks on Interstate 80 on my trips from college in Ohio back to my home in New York. Every one of them had a sign that specifically said, "IF YOU CAN'T SEE MY MIRRORS, I CAN'T SEE YOU." My assumption was that the opposite was also true: "If you can see my mirrors, I can see you." I was wrong.

When the light turned green, I took my right turn wide and easy, without a thought about the eighteen-wheel vehicle to my left—because it wasn't turning, and for that matter the Mazda wasn't either. I thought I had tons of room.

I didn't.

The truck driver hadn't seen my very clear indication that I was going to turn right. He hadn't seen me at all. He hadn't seen my metallic blue bicycle with the red writing on it. He hadn't seen the long-sleeve T-shirt I was wearing—the one I got from running a 5K for a fallen Army Ranger. He hadn't seen the Denison lacrosse shorts I had owned since my senior year of college. He hadn't seen any part of me. All he saw was a green light, and he turned.

The last thing I remember before actually being run over was the hollow sound of my fist banging the side of the truck, and then I felt as though I was tumbling. I don't know where my bike had gone. I knew I was on the road, and there was this moment when I thought, *Am I in an action movie? This is the kind of shit that happens in action movies. What would Bruce Willis do? What can I do to stop this?!?*

The answer was nothing. There was nothing I could do.

Before I even really realized what was happening, I felt pressure and then heard a cracking sound. The realization that the cracking was my bones shocked me. I squeezed my eyes shut, and I felt the first four wheels of the truck run over my body. I didn't have time to process the pain. All I could think was, *Sweet Jesus, please let this man stop before the second set of wheels comes for me.*

"No, no, no, please God no," I shrieked before the second set of wheels rolled over my already crushed middle.

This time I kept my eyes open. I watched this second set of giant wheels run over my body. I heard more cracking and felt the grooves in the tires on my skin. I heard the mud flaps thwack over me. I felt gravel in my back. I was a sparrow that had lingered too long in the road, no different from every slow bird, every irresponsible squirrel, every wayward dog that just wasn't fast enough.

Then there was the sound of a horn—a one-note beep that didn't stop. This was the kind of horn-blowing you hear on the BQE during rush hour, the kind where you know the horn is being punched out of frustration. When I heard that horn, I thought to myself, *Now you beep. You couldn't have beeped before your death machine crushed my body?* Hearing something meant I was still alive. I was still here and—as long as I stayed awake—I was alive. As long as my eyes were open, I was awake. So I barely blinked.

My bike was tangled up in my legs, like a five-year-old who had just had her first spill. I remember being nine and watching my little sister, Callie, learn how to ride her bike in the street in front of our house. My dad had just removed her training wheels and was holding the seat. He was running behind her, keeping her steady, making her feel grown-up but protected. She could look back and he was there. When he thought she could do it on her own, he let go, as all parents do. She was great for about fifty feet, but then she looked back and realized he wasn't behind her anymore. Callie lost all her confidence in that moment. She forgot that she had been doing it on her own for the last few moments, and she wobbled, screamed, and fell.

As she fell, her legs kept moving. They looked like they weren't even a part of her body, as though they were working on their own, and she was unsure if she should continue to pedal or if jumping off would save her.

My body must have reacted the same way as it felt those wheels, trying to jump off, trying to go faster . . . trying, trying, trying. Flesh and metal had merged together. Bob the Bike was dead. I was left with bits of his shattered metal body embedded in my skin, his gearshift impaled in my stomach.

I never saw the driver. He didn't leave the scene of the accident, but he didn't walk back to see if I was okay either. I guess he didn't want to see the fruits of his recklessness. To be fair, I couldn't look at myself either, at where the tires had made contact with my body.

I lay there waiting for something to change, to get better or worse. I waited for a break in the silence that kept ringing in my ears. I remember looking up as the early morning sky went from that deep blue to a sunlight-pale, pale blue—the clouds looked as if they were whipped out of cotton candy.

I screamed out for someone to call my mother. If my mom was there, she could fix it. As soon as she was notified, all this could be undone. Because this was not reality. Reality was the fact that I had to get back to my apartment and iron my button-down shirt. Reality was that I had a big day at work, and I was nervous about getting really sweaty in my new suit. Reality was not that I was on the precipice of losing my life—that was not what was happening. I refused to close my eyes.

As the initial shock of impact began to wear off, my body reacted with crushing pain. It was unlike anything I could have imagined. I was confused by it. I couldn't believe there could be a sensation so horrible and intense or that it would continue to radiate out of my body—usually the pain of dropping something on your foot or running your knee into a door fades, even if just a little. This excruciating pain stayed right where it was, doing relay races up and down the length of my body. I didn't know what to do. I didn't know how to stop it. I couldn't shake it off, or massage it, or walk to a place that I thought would somehow give me relief. I had no choice but to just lie there, trying not to drown in it.

I remember a young woman who was about my age came over to me and said she would call my mom. She asked me if I knew her phone number. I did. I remembered it as a song that my mom had taught my siblings and me to help us learn all the numbers. This young woman, the one who was calling my mom now, had been in the black Mazda. Her boyfriend had been driving. He was directing traffic around me, around the accident scene. They were saving me.

He put up orange cones, and flares were lit around me. Everything changed. I watched as this woman took responsibility for calling a perfect stranger's mother to tell her that her daughter's body had just been crushed by an eighteen-wheeler. I heard her say that her name was Gisele; she sounded scared. Her voice shook as she told my family's answering machine that I had been in an accident and that whoever got this should call her back as soon as possible.

I knew then that I was broken. My mom wasn't home. She had been called and nothing was better. Plus, Gisele was so frightened—she couldn't even feign calm as she left that message. I was stricken with terror, but I couldn't give in to it. I thought that if I let myself fall into it—fall into the fear, the loneliness, the hurt—I would be lost forever. I had no cell phone, no ID, and, Jesus Christ, no underwear. If I didn't manage to stay conscious, I would become a whorish Jane Doe who rode a bicycle. I couldn't go out like that.

My one job was to stay awake. I needed to stay awake.

My brain kept whirring as I lay on that Brooklyn street: *What do these people need to know? What do I need to say?*

"I can move my toes and my fingers—if I pass out, tell the paramedics I'm not paralyzed." I spoke with the authority of someone who actually knew what they were talking about, not a theater major who could barely put on a Band-Aid. Thank God for all those TV movies I watched—you know the ones, where someone gets into an accident, and then they freak out and say, "I can't move my legs, I CAN'T MOVE MY LEGS." Well, I couldn't move my legs either. But I could move my toes, and I knew that counted for something.

"Please, can you hold my hand?" I asked Gisele. "I'm scared." I didn't want to say it. I wanted to be strong and funny and to let this just roll off me. I wanted to believe that this wasn't a big deal—that I could put a Band-Aid on this one, all by myself. But after telling another person I was frightened, it became clear to me that I wasn't tough enough to do this on my own. My mom wasn't there, and I was surrounded by strangers. So I did what made me feel like I was close to my family: I began to pray.

I asked Gisele, the stranger holding my hand, if she would pray with me. Without knowing if she was Catholic, Protestant, Jewish, or Muslim—I began to pray the Hail Mary. I prayed to Mary to not let me die. I really didn't want to die.

"Hail Mary, full of grace, the Lord is with thee, blessed art thou among women, and blessed is the fruit of your womb, Jesus. Holy Mary, mother of God, pray for us sinners now and at the hour of our death." My voice usually quivered at the hour-of-death part when I said this prayer out loud—this time it felt as if the words were shaking my entire body. Was this it? Seriously? Was I going to die, here on this street in Brooklyn, because of a wrong turn on a fucking bike ride?

I always thought I might die young. When I was a little kid, I would watch the five o'clock news, and whenever there was a news report about a young girl, with everything to live for, who had been killed in a freak accident, I would think, *That's going to be me in about ten years.* Then I would think about what my news report was going to be like. I wondered what they would say about me. Would they talk about my family? My friends? Or would the focus be on my athletic accomplishments? I hoped they used good pictures. I even told my parents the song I wanted played at my funeral: "Solsbury Hill" by Peter Gabriel. Of course, they would tell me how morbid I was and how it was wrong to talk like that. I understood what they were saying, but part of me just wanted everyone to be prepared, plus that song would be killer during the procession.

As I held desperately on to the hand of my new best friend, a man in khaki cargo shorts, a plaid short-sleeve shirt, and a New York Yankees hat stepped out of his Toyota Camry and walked toward my spot on the asphalt.

With no hesitation he slipped his rough hand into mine, looked into my eyes, and with a Spanish accent and a confident tone said, "Listen to me, I am a pastor—I have spoken to God, and he has told me you are not going to die today. Okay?"

I needed for him to be right. I wanted him to be my prophet. "Do you promise?" I asked, with the sincerity of a six-year-old.

"Yes," he promised. If I could have lifted my hand, I would have made him pinkie swear.

He took Gisele's hand and said, "Let us say the Lord's Prayer," and I said the Our Father with my new congregation of three. I realize now that I had never said the Our Father with such fear—I really prayed that God would forgive me my trespasses! I had trespassed a lot. Like the time in third grade when I broke my date to the SCA fair with Tom Fulgieri. I did it on the phone, and I let Shauna Phillips listen in on another extension. And then, while he was still on the phone, she started to laugh. I knew it was mean, but I wanted to be cool more than I wanted to be nice. I hoped God forgave me for that one. I also hoped that God didn't put a whole lot of emphasis on underage drinking as a sin, because then I was really screwed. I didn't truly feel bad about doing it, and I had done it a lot. I prayed for God to know that I didn't want to die, that I didn't want to go to hell, that I didn't want to even go to heaven, for that matter. I just wanted out of this situation. But the fact that my legs weren't working, and I didn't have a flux capacitor to turn back time left me totally screwed. So I just made sure I didn't close my eyes.

The only thing I could control just then was my eyes. They were the only part of my body that wasn't hurting. I kept them open for my mother, for my father, for my sister, for my brothers, for my boyfriend, for my friends—I knew if I closed them I would be giving up on ever seeing those people again, on seeing anything else in my life again. I would never see a little kid with an ice cream cone or a leaf blowing like a confused butterfly in the wind. If I closed my eyes, I would never see the way someone looks right after you hug them. If I closed my eyes, there was the possibility that I would be in darkness forever. So I stared unblinking into the sunlight, fearfully gulping up as much light as I could. Plus, if God was going to take me, I wanted to see Him coming.

# CHAPTER TWO

# More

When the police arrived, I felt a wave of relief. *They are going to take care of me*, I thought. *This will be okay, the police are here.* After all, they did what I couldn't do—fight bad guys, save lives, kick bad peoples' asses. I always waved at the police. In high school I was polite when they found me doing things I shouldn't have been doing at the town docks. And then, after 9/11, out of nowhere, I found myself hugging a policeman just to say thank you. Two of my uncles were cops. They were strong and funny, and they made me feel safe and protected whenever they were around.

These policemen were not like my uncles—there was no warmth or kindness in their eyes. They made me feel like I wasn't even there. When they looked at me, it wasn't exactly disdain that crossed their faces, more like apathy. Of all of the emotions that I thought my situation would evoke, apathy was not one of them. I wanted them to like me, to care about me. I tried to fashion a joke about the fact that my ass was half exposed due to my lack of undergarments. When the officers didn't even crack a smile, I knew I was more injured than I had thought—because jokes about exposed bottoms are really funny, and if people aren't entertained by them, then something must be seriously wrong.

After my awesome joke went bust, a policeman with a mustache leaned over and told me I was going to be okay. I didn't believe him. I asked him if he had morphine; he said no. I asked him where the ambulance was; he said it was on its way. I asked if it could come any faster because I was hurting a lot. Big fat tears slid down my face. I tried not to sob, for fear that it would hurt my belly even more. Instead, I turned my head to the left and kept my arms stretched out and let the tears fall from my right eye over my nose to my left eye, then onto the pavement.

When I heard the ambulance sirens, I freaked out because I knew that when they came and picked me up I was going to go to the hospital, and then everything was going to get real, fast. The entire time I was plastered to the street, I was in limbo, suspended between reality and some sort of video-game dream. The ambulance sirens made it clear that I was not in a video game and that this was not a dream—I was going to leave this spot on the gravel, and I needed to do what I could to save myself from dying. My biggest fear was that the ambulance was going to take me to Kings County General Hospital. It was probably one of the closer hospitals in Brooklyn, but I didn't want close—I wanted good.

My best friend Maribeth was a nurse, and she had told me that when you are in an emergency situation you are still in control of what you want to happen. They can't make you go to a hospital that you don't want to go to. And I did not want to go to Kings County. A friend of mine had gone there after she broke her leg, and she didn't see a doctor for *eight* hours. I didn't know what was wrong with me, exactly, but I knew that my injuries couldn't wait that long.

It isn't clear to me how I got on the gurney, but I do remember them putting that neck brace thing on me, and me screaming. When I was finally secured in the ambulance, something came over me, and I started to speak in a voice that didn't sound like my own. "Excuse me, sir, I refuse to go to Kings County. I need to go to a hospital that has a good trauma center. Will you take me there?" It was as if my brain was on autopilot—it was doing what needed to be done to keep me alive.

The EMT said, "The best trauma hospital is Elmhurst, and yes, we can take you there because you requested it, but it will take us longer to get there than it would to get to Kings County." What I didn't know then was that Elmhurst wasn't just the best trauma hospital, it was the place where the city sent people who needed hospitalization while they were incarcerated.

I said, "Sir, I don't care, I need to go to a place where they can fix me."

I realized that I sounded like a snob, but I was being honest, and if there is ever a time to be a total bitch, I think being strapped to a gurney in an ambulance with tire tracks on your body is one of those times.

The driver and the other EMT argued about where was the best place to go for my injuries, while another guy kept asking me questions. Instead of answering, I just begged for morphine. I am not sure why I thought that every person in a uniform was carrying morphine with them, as though they had an IV drip right underneath their badge.

He looked at me and said, "We can't give you anything or else the medical staff won't know how much pain you are in—they need to know."

"Can't we just tell them that I am in a lot of pain? I mean, A LOT!"

He shook his head.

I was not liking him.

He continued to ask me questions and tried to give me oxygen, which did nothing except irritate me. Why would one put the equivalent of plastic wrap around my face and then ask me what my address was? Every time he asked me a question, I would take off the mask to answer it, and then he would put it back on me. It would have been comical if I hadn't felt like killing the man. I officially did not like this dude. He gave me no morphine, made me no promises of survival, and had cut off one of my favorite sorority T-shirts, the one that we made for our freshman formal. Didn't he know that I would have voluntarily taken it off if he had just asked nicely? Despite my protests, the bastard cut the T-shirt off, and then he cut off my shorts. I contemplated giving him a breakdown on my lack of panties but deemed him unworthy.

My sassiness dissipated once my clothes were cut off. I felt the cold air on my exposed body. I couldn't fathom that it would be possible to feel more vulnerable and scared than I had felt just a few minutes before, but my nakedness in front of a person who didn't love me left me as fragile as tracing paper. I didn't realize it then, but this was only the first of what would be many, many times I would be naked in front of a total stranger.

Mr. EMT continued to ask me questions: my address, my phone number, my parents' names, my parents' address, where I worked, my social security number, etc. . . . And the geniuses in the front of the ambulance not only hit every pothole in Brooklyn, but they got lost. And when I say lost, I don't mean like a wrong turn; I mean the driver got out of the car and asked someone which way the hospital was. If it wasn't so totally inappropriate in the moment, I am sure that I would have uttered something about wanting to kill myself.

Killing time while we drove around in a circle, Mr. EMT asked me all the same questions again. I realized that this was a ploy to keep me awake, but I was sick of repeating my social security number, and told him point-blank that there was no way in hell I was going to fall asleep or pass out. I was way too scared to do that. I had only blinked about forty times since the accident. I had been counting.

I remember there was a red awning over the door that led into the emergency room, which made it look more like the entrance to a catering hall than a hospital. The EMT from the front of the ambulance was the one talking to me now. He had a brown mustache. He told me I was going into the emergency room and that they were going to take care of me there. I wasn't convinced. I had no clue where I was. I was afraid of dying, and my body ached in ways that I never knew possible. And I was not going to trust anyone. My eyes were still open.

***

As soon as I was wheeled into the emergency room, there was a flurry of activity, everyone poking and prodding me and talking loudly. There had to have been at least twenty people in that room, including a nurse in what looked like themed scrubs. You know, the kind decorated with teddy bears getting their temperature taken. I felt pretty angry about it. I mean, we're in an EMERGENCY ROOM—shouldn't she be wearing something a little more serious? The blue scrubs would have been just fine. The kind that say, "You are in good hands. I am a professional," and not, "Do you have a tummyache?"

Everyone started asking me questions:

"Are you allergic to anything, hon?"

"No, no, I am not, ma'am."

"I am going to give you a shot in your arm."

"Okay, sir, may I have morphine?"

"You are going to be getting an IV now, okay?"

"Is my mom here?"

"What is your name, sweetheart?"

"Katharine McKenna, ma'am, but please call me Katie—what is your name?"

"Dr. Russell."

"Dr. Russell, I don't want to die, okay? Could you please check me to see if there is any internal bleeding?"

"We will, Katie. You don't even need to say please."

"Dr. Russell, can you promise that I won't die?"

"I can't do that, Katie, but we will do our very best to save you—okay?"

She couldn't even tell me that I was going to live. *Oh my God! I could really die, holy shit, I might die. She just told me this could be it. My parents, my family, my boyfriend, my friends—I don't get to say good-bye to them??? I can't keep my eyes open by myself forever.*

"We are going to put you under anesthesia and take you to surgery now, okay?"

"Okay, Dr. Russell. Tell my mom and dad that I love them, and tell my brothers and my sister too. My friends, please tell my friends that I love them, okay? Please. My boyfriend, please tell my boyfriend that I am sorry about the fight and that I love him, and I am sorry. Please don't let me die. I am so scared."

I felt her hand on my head. I looked at all the people around me and said thank you (at least I had my manners). There was another shot in my arm, and my mouth and nose were covered by something plastic as I said the Our Father again and begged God not to take me away. I lost my choice then. I struggled to keep my eyes open, but it wasn't up to me anymore. I stared into the halogen light above my gurney and let my eyes close.

\*\*\*

Now, I look back at all the times I've used the words *I may just die*. I remember uttering those words one morning in college after four too many shots of warm tequila the night before. Or after the first time I told a boy that I loved him, and he said nothing in return—I was sure I was going to die of embarrassment. This time I closed my eyes and thought I was going to die because my body had just been broken by a huge motor vehicle. Because it turns out that people are more likely to die from a wrong turn by a truck than from the misery of a hangover or the embarrassment of unrequited love. Until this moment I had thought the two were on an equal footing. Nothing made sense. The definitions of words I had used a million times now had a different meaning, a meaning that was deeper and darker and more permanent. This was when my heart broke. I was lost.

As the fog of anesthesia slowly enveloped me, my mind started racing, trying to think as much as it could before my consciousness vanished. Thoughts flew through my brain like a flood of words scrolling across the bottom of a screen. I was struggling to wrap my head around what had happened. My thoughts formed around a series of questions I asked myself and then attempted to answer: *There is no way this is happening, right? There is no way I can survive—there is just no way. But wait, how am I still awake? How come I was able to talk? I'm not brain damaged. How did that happen? I wasn't wearing a helmet, and I'm not brain damaged. I could live. No, no, there is no way—no one has eight truck wheels run over their body and live. It just doesn't happen.*

It was just so out of the realm of anything I would have imagined for myself. I should be dead, but I am not, at least not yet. *Does that mean I am going to live? Or am I one of those people who goes into the hospital and dies while everyone is in the waiting room? Fuck that, I'm NOT going to die. Holy shit, I'm going to die.*

I willed myself to live and tried to accept the fact that I wouldn't. There was no life-flashing-before-my-eyes reel playing in my head—all I could really think about was the fact that I wouldn't get to see any more of it. I didn't feel badly about the way I had lived. I just wanted more.

# CHAPTER THREE

# In Between

When my mother arrived home after dropping my dad off at the train station, the red light on the answering machine was blinking. An unknown voice screamed out of the speaker: "Hello! Hello! Your daughter has been in an accident! Are you there?! The ambulance driver needs to talk to you. Please, please call me back."

My mom stood in the kitchen, by herself, and began horror-movie screaming.

When she stopped screaming, she called back the woman who had left the message. Gisele said they had already taken me away in the ambulance, and the police wouldn't tell her anything. They told her they could only disclose information to the victim's family.

Trying to find the policemen who had been on the scene was not easy. My mom first called the general police department number in Brooklyn, and when she was asked what my current address was, she realized she didn't know. She only knew the address of my old apartment. The accident didn't happen in the precinct I used to live in, so she had to call another department. And when, after all her efforts, she finally got in touch with the right policeman, she was shocked that her personal tragedy was greeted with apathy and boredom on the other end of the line.

"What's your daughter's full name?"

"Katharine Clark McKenna."

"What's her address?"

"I don't know. She just moved."

"Are her roommates around so we can get her full address?"

And that did it. She snapped.

"I don't have time to call them—I need to know where my daughter is. I want to know where my daughter is now! WHERE IS SHE????" she screamed into the receiver.

"Okay, okay. She's at Elmhurst Hospital."

"Which hospital in Elmhurst?"

"Lady, there is only one in Elmhurst."

He asked my very frustrated mother a few more questions until she finally hung up on him. Exasperated and anxious, she dialed 411 and asked the operator for a hospital in Elmhurst, Queens. The operator told her that the only hospital in Elmhurst is a penal hospital.

"She can't be there!" she exclaimed.

"But that's the only one there is," the operator insisted.

She asked for the phone number, called the hospital, and asked the person who picked up the phone if I was there. I was. How I was being treated at a prisoners' hospital ceased being the most important question. It had been that kind of morning—she would take whatever was offered up. She just needed to get to me.

My mother drove out to Elmhurst on the Long Island Expressway, all the way remaining rational and responsible. She made sure that everyone was informed of what was going on. She did what all moms are supposed to do: she took care of everyone else.

When my mother arrived at the emergency room, she wasn't pushy; she didn't scream; she didn't make a scene. She waited patiently at the information desk until it was her turn. Cool, calm, collected, and still under the impression that her daughter had been hit by a car. She held on to the hope that if I was able to recollect her cell phone number and our home number, I couldn't be that bad off. When it was her turn, she told them she was there to see her daughter—Katharine McKenna. The woman at the front desk's face fell. She rushed over to the emergency room entry and announced, "The McKenna woman is here." A security guard came over and took my mom by the arm and ushered her into the ER. The color drained from my mother's face—something was very wrong.

A social worker, along with a doctor in his early thirties, with a sweet face, intense blue eyes, and a scruffy beard, came over to greet her.

"Mrs. McKenna?"

"Yes?"

"Your daughter is very, very, very, very sick."

The doctor, who my mother later learned was Dr. Khaitov, told her that my body had been crushed by eight truck wheels. They didn't yet know the full extent of the trauma, but it was substantial.

"I would recommend you come in and see her right now," he said. "We don't know what is going to happen."

The doctor led her to the room where I was being operated on; the only part of my body that was exposed was my toes, which were peeking out from the bottom of the sheet that was covering the rest of my body. My toenails were painted brown, in honor of autumn. She couldn't get close to me because there were ten doctors and nurses hovering over me. My momma approached the end of the hospital bed. She cupped my feet in her hands and kissed my toes, the way she had done when I was a baby. *How did this happen?* she asked herself. *How could this be good-bye?*

Every fear she had been holding at bay came rushing forward. Every hope that this was a minor accident had been decimated. Her daughter was dying. My mom's knees went out from under her, and she collapsed on the emergency room floor. Dr. Khaitov called the social worker in and asked her to take my mother out into the corridor.

There is a song by Death Cab for Cutie with the chorus "Love is watching someone die." That is what my mom did. She went in and watched me die. I have never questioned my mom's love for me—but I also have never been more aware of it than I was when I heard what she did in the emergency room that day.

My father was at seven-thirty mass when my mom first called him. He ignored the call—he'd phone her back later. He had just seen her forty-five minutes ago; what could she possibly need? It was probably an inquiry about what he'd like for dinner, or a question about the checking account. She called again, and again (in our family, more than one call in a row equals emergency), so he exited the church on Wall Street and rang her back. She told him I had been in an accident. They didn't know how severe it was. I was at Elmhurst Hospital, and she was on her way there.

This was not my dad's first dance with hospitals and car accidents. About forty years ago, when he was twenty-two, his sister, who was a year younger than him, had been sitting in the passenger seat of one of my dad's friend's cars. They were coming back from a party and had been drinking. Back then, drunk driving was viewed as more of a no-no than a reckless, horrible crime. The driver hit another car, and my aunt Marleen, who was not wearing her seat belt, flew forty feet in the air and landed in a ditch on the side of the road.

Aunt Marleen was in a coma for nine months. While my father was in his early twenties, he watched as his mother and father stopped their own lives and lived by their daughter's bedside. My nana prayed the rosary, knit afghans, and devoted every part of herself to her daughter. Everyone in his family lost those nine months. Amazingly, my aunt came out of the coma, but she was severely brain damaged, incapable of regular speech, and has been wheelchair-bound ever since.

My father's and my uncles' young adulthoods were spent helping their mother and father take care of their sister. They helped wash her and carry her up the stairs at night and down the stairs in the morning; they wiped her mouth when food fell out of it as she ate. My father is a man of faith, though, so when he spoke to my mother and she told him I had been in an accident, he told himself the accident couldn't be that bad. God would not let this happen to him again. There was a threshold for sadness and hurt, and he believed that he had already crossed his. He had to have.

He went into work and told his boss what happened, and they ordered a town car to drive him to Elmhurst. He soothed himself with the idea that all my injuries were fixable. If I was speaking and capable of remembering phone numbers and social security numbers, surely I would be okay. This would not be a life-and-death situation. I was a tough girl. Of course I'd be fine.

He got to the hospital and went straight to the ER. He found my mother sitting there in the waiting room, dazed but recovered from her fainting spell. They held each other and didn't speak for a bit. Then my mom told my dad everything the doctors had told her, but he had trouble processing it. It wasn't actually trouble, so much as straight-up refusal. He had it in his head that I was going to be fine. There was no way that God would take me from this world. It just couldn't happen. He had done all the right things: he went to church every day, he visited the sick and the old, he helped others when he could, he gave money to charity, and his life had already seen enough hurt. This could not, would not, happen. When a nurse asked him if he would like to see me, to say good-bye, just in case, he firmly told her no. "I'm not doing that. I don't need to see her. She is not going anywhere. There is no need to say good-bye."

I had always known my father was a stubborn man, one who believed what he believed and would not be swayed. He was not a person you wanted to argue with, because there was no debate involved. You would tell my dad that what he thought was wrong, and then he would tell you that you were allowed to have your own opinions, but he wasn't going to change his mind because of what you said. He said it had taken him a long time to become the man he was, and he wasn't changing now. But hearing later how he had puffed out his chest and jutted out his chin at the devil and said, "No, she is not going to die—I refuse to accept that," amazed even me.

The fact that my parents took exactly the same information and dealt with it in such completely different ways is what makes me love them both so much. My mother would never have forgiven herself if she hadn't said good-bye. She would have felt like she had let me go without letting me know how loved I was. My dad wouldn't have forgiven himself if he had gone in, said good-bye, and then I had died. For my father, good-bye was giving in; for my mother, good-bye was showing me that she loved me. And, shockingly, both choices were perfect and beautiful.

Conor, my older brother, arrived fifteen minutes after my dad. He had just moved back to New York after working for two years in Boston and was in his first month of business school at Columbia. When he told me that he was moving back to New York, I was thrilled to have him so close by. I began lists of all the fun things we would get to do together, tripping over my words in excitement. Conor eventually had to hang up on me because I wouldn't stop talking. (I have a tendency to overwhelm people with my enthusiasm.)

Spending time with my big brother had always felt like an escape. I could go out for drinks with him and feel no pressure to look good or to call other people so they weren't left out. I could get dirty drunk and not feel embarrassed when I accidentally vomited on his shoes. Also, he usually paid for stuff, which I was really into. We had been in the same city for about a month, but we hadn't done anything together yet. He was still settling into the routine of school, and I had just started a new job. But I wasn't worried. I figured we had all the time in the world.

Conor was in class when my mother called that morning. He hadn't picked up when she called the first time, but after that all-important second call, he stepped out of class. He heard the forced calm in my mother's voice as she let him know I had been in an accident and it would be a good idea if he came down to the hospital. He got a third call from my mom while he was in the cab. This time there was no forced calm. She told him he should get to the hospital AS SOON AS HE COULD—they didn't know what was going to happen.

In the backseat of the yellow cab, his frustration at not being with his family suddenly overcame him. He took all the money out of his wallet and threw it at the cab driver. "Please, get me to the hospital as fast as you can! You can have all this money—just get me there! HURRY!"

The cab driver said he didn't need to be paid more; he would drive as fast as he could.

By the time Conor arrived at the hospital, he was drained of all emotion. We stopped being his family and became small parts of the big picture that had been broken apart and now had to be put back together. He realized there were things he could do and things he couldn't. My parents were too distressed to handle the little things that needed attention, so that's where Conor stepped in. He parented my parents. He talked with the doctors. And he filled out paperwork. Conor handled the business of this emergency.

It probably would have seemed to someone else that he didn't love me, or that he was uncaring or cold. But in fact, nothing could be further from the truth. He loved me and my family so much that he gave up his right to grieve, to worry, and to be sad—he denied himself the luxury of showing his feelings so that everyone else could fall apart.

He had to see my mother in the fetal position on the hospital floor, and he had to watch my father as his body shook with sobs. Conor had to hear the worst of what was happening to me from the doctors and then relay the condensed, softer version to my parents.

None of the hospital staff would say what was happening exactly, but death was like a fine mist in the room. You couldn't exactly see it, but you felt it on your skin. It lived in the way the social workers and nurses talked to my family; they were quiet, subdued, and grave.

After two hours a team of doctors finally came to talk with my parents and Conor; two of them were bladder doctors, and one was a general surgeon. The bladder doctors got straight to the point: there was a large laceration in my bladder, and it was the cause of the internal bleeding. They were calm delivering their diagnosis, because they knew exactly what was wrong with my bladder. There weren't any questions my parents had about that specific part of my anatomy they couldn't answer. My parents took comfort in the doctors' confidence.

The general surgeon was a different story. Dr. Elizabeth was tough and matter-of-fact. She listed all the things that could potentially be wrong with me: there could be lacerations on my liver, there could be lacerations on my kidneys, and there could be damage to my large intestine. In fact, there were so many things that could be wrong that she scared the ever-living shit out of my parents.

At eleven a.m. on Tuesday, October 2, 2007, Dr. Khaitov came out to the waiting room and announced, "Mr. and Mrs. McKenna, we can't stop your daughter from bleeding—she keeps bleeding out."

What that meant was that the doctors and nurses were pumping blood into my body, trying to replace what had been leaking into the cavernous parts of my midsection. Later, when this was first explained to me, I imagined them pumping in blood from blood machines—and then all the blood just splashing out onto the floor. That was not exactly what was happening. In fact, the blood was transfused into my veins, but because there were so many wounds inside and outside my body, all the clotting agents had gone to clot other wounds. I stopped clotting, and all this donated blood they were pumping in was bleeding out into all the cavities in my body. They weren't able to stop the bleeding because, as Dr. Elizabeth had said, they couldn't tell what else besides my bladder was lacerated. All the blood was obscuring any wounds to my other organs, and I kept bleeding and bleeding. They had already transfused me with eight pints of blood, and the human body only holds sixteen pints. They continued to pump in the transfused blood and then, because I wasn't clotting, they would have to pump it back out again.

"Just keep giving her transfusions," my father, suddenly a professional medical expert, ordered. He now says, in hindsight, that he still hadn't realized the gravity of my injuries. I was broken. They would fix it. The idea of this being an unresolvable problem hadn't registered with him yet.

"No, if we can't stop the bleeding that's a big problem," Dr. Khaitov explained.

"What does that mean?" he asked, a little less sure of his medical prowess.

"If she doesn't start clotting in one hour, she is going to pass."

"What?"

The doctor looked to my mother and my brother for help. He didn't want to have to spell it out for my father.

My brother turned to my dad and said, "It means that Katie will die, Dad."

The three of them sat in the corner of the waiting room and cried. My father recommended they pray the rosary, but my mother protested. "I don't know how to pray the rosary. I'm not even Catholic—isn't that against the rules?"

"Margo, I think that today of all days we can be whatever we want."

They started to pray the rosary.

1) Sign of the Cross and say the Apostle's Creed,

2) Say the Our Father,

3) Say three Hail Marys,

4) Say the Glory Be to the Father,

5) Announce the First Mystery; then say the Our Father,

6) Say ten Hail Marys,

7) Say the Glory Be to the Father, and

8) Say the Our Father.

That's a lot of steps for one prayer. My brother and father, both veterans of the rosary, started speeding through each step. They were saying their Hail Marys as if the quicker they said them, the more effective they would be. My mom looked at my dad and my brother in disbelief—she said that all she heard coming out of their mouths was, "Blah blah blah Mary, blah blah blah Jesus, blah blah blah sins, blah blah blah God."

"Can you please slow down?!" she implored.

They slowed down for my mom, the newbie. The rosary done, they stared at the clock, counting down the minutes until the doctors would stop transfusing me—until the moment I would die.

At 11:45, fifteen minutes before they would know if I was going to live or die, my mom, always the planner, retreated into a corner and started to plan my funeral. What songs would be played (aside from "Solsbury Hill," of course)? What would I wear? Where would the service be? What readings would they do?

My older brother watched the door for my younger brother, James, and my sister, Callie. They were coming in from their respective colleges in Connecticut and upstate New York—if something bad was going to happen, he hoped they would get there in time.

My dad was in the hallway, on his knees praying—he says that he was begging God not to let me die—when he was suddenly struck with a feeling of total calm. It started at the top of his head and ended at his belly button. And at that moment he knew I would live. The worry just stopped.

At 11:50, Dr. Khaitov came in, and with an incredulous look on his face he announced, "She's clotting. She started to clot. She isn't bleeding out anymore."

***

I had clawed my way out of my first *the shit's going down* situation. I had a punctured lung and had broken all my ribs. The truck had ripped a hole in my bladder (that was the organ that was causing all the bleeding), and there was another gaping hole on my right side where the ten-speed lever had lodged itself into me as the truck had run me over. My pelvis was fractured in five places. The pelvic fracturing was the worst because I would be unable to walk until it healed, and there is no cast you can put around your middle. Instead of wraparound plaster, I was outfitted with a metal plate in my back to hold together the broken pieces of my pelvic bones.

Later that day, as the sun was setting and I had been moved to the ICU, my parents saw Dr. Khaitov as he was finishing up his shift. They went up to him and thanked him for saving me.

He looked at them with a confused expression on his face. "I have never in my career, ever seen someone with her kind of injuries survive. I have to be honest; I didn't think she was going to make it."

"I knew God wouldn't take her from us," my dad replied. "I knew He wouldn't let her go."

The good doctor sighed. "I didn't know whether we'd be able to save her, but I am really glad we did."

My father told me later that he got the feeling the doctor didn't believe in God. That didn't surprise me really. It must be difficult for a person who does what doctors do to have faith. When you work in an emergency room trauma center, where good people die and bad people live, having faith in a God that would let this happen must be almost impossible.

Personally, for one small, simple reason, I think that Dr. Khaitov had been cautiously optimistic about my chances. When he went to open me up, he cut me from the top of my rib cage to an inch or so above my lady parts, to see if I was internally bleeding and what the problem was. When he did this, he cut around my bellybutton. Now, if they thought I was going to die, wouldn't they have just cut right through it? What does a dead girl need with a bellybutton? They let me keep it. To me, that looked like hope.

***

There's one more character we can't forget in this little play of ours. Gisele. Whatever happened to Gisele? This is a question I used to get all the time. A few months after the accident, I wanted to write Gisele a thank-you letter. I wanted to tell her I was okay. I can't imagine how freaked out she must have been, and despite all the chaos around the accident, my parents were able to call her using the phone number they had in my mom's cell phone and tell her that I had survived. But after that they were so wrapped up in what was happening in the hospital that they never gave her any updates on how I was doing, and I never really got to thank her properly. All those months later when I wanted to reach out, my parents had lost her number. What she was faced with that October morning must have been an insanely scary and totally heartbreaking situation. Who wants to call someone's mom and tell her that her daughter has just been run over by a truck? Personally, I would be the first to shout out "No dibs!!!"

I've also wanted to ask her some important questions that many people have asked me over and over again: Was the pastor really there? Or was he a figment of my imagination? Maybe he was an angel? Gisele is the only person who can say for sure.

# CHAPTER FOUR

# I Get Knocked Down . . . and I Stay There

When I opened my eyes, everything was white. The afternoon sunlight was blindingly white, my sheets were white, and I was feeling white-hot pain. My whole body felt like the tip of a flame. What was happening was beyond anything I had ever felt before. I had heard people use *white-hot* as a descriptor, and it had never made sense to me until now. Before, when I thought of hot things, the color that came to mind was red. Now, when I closed my eyes I could see the color of my agony— and it was white. It was a reminder from my broken body that now everything had been flipped. I could no longer slip into the cool darkness behind my eyelids; even there, only bright, bright white lived.

A huge tube had been forced down my throat. It made a whistling sound as I breathed in and out and made me feel as though there were pieces of cardboard stuffed in my mouth all the way down to my stomach. I couldn't see how the tube had been inserted into my mouth, or how it got there, because you can't really see your own mouth all that well without a mirror, a fact I had been blissfully unaware of until that very moment. It's amazing the little lessons a near-death experience will teach you.

The fact of this tube scared me, and its presence prompted other questions: *Where was this cardboard tube coming from? Where was it going? Hadn't I gotten the morphine I had been begging for? If so, why was I hurting so much?* All these questions could only bounce around my aching head because I couldn't speak. I couldn't ask what was happening, and no one had any way of knowing what I was thinking. *What if I was going to have to live the rest of my life like this? Can I not breathe on my own? Am I paralyzed?* I needed answers, but I couldn't talk! What the fuck! All I really wanted, aside from the ability to speak, was two things: 1. To get this tube out of my mouth, and 2. Water . . . I wanted water really, really, really badly.

In fact, I came to discover tubes sticking out of every one of my orifices and wires extending from my fingers. I felt like a plastic octopus. The machines all around me, which these tubes were no doubt attached to, wouldn't stop beeping. *Was the stuff running in and out of the tubes causing the machines to beep?* If that was the case, then I would like for the tubes to tell the machines to tell the nurses I was thirsty! Exhausted from this thought exercise, I closed my eyes and fell back into the whiteness.

When I opened my eyes again, my mom and dad, Conor, and my boyfriend, Warren, were standing at the end of my hospital bed—the machines that surrounded me had blocked them from standing next to me. My father's face was bright red, and he had his fist up to his mouth. His shoulders shook as he sobbed. Tears slipped down my face as I waved at him and my mom, and then I pointed to myself and curled my fingers into the okay sign. I didn't actually feel okay, but I didn't think that a thumbs-down sign was appropriate—they looked worried enough as it was. In reality, having them there did make everything seem a little more okay.

"Hi, baby," my mom said as she pinched my toe. My tears didn't stop, but I felt soothed knowing that I wasn't alone anymore. That whatever the fuck was going on, I wasn't doing it by myself.

I stared hard at Conor, knowing he was my best chance at figuring out what my status really was. My weeping parents weren't the best barometers. They could be crying because they were scared or because they were happy—their tears were too ambiguous. Conor and I look alike in a way that you can only see when we are standing right next to each other. We both have brown eyes that reveal our true feelings. It doesn't matter what expression is on our faces, or what is coming out of our mouths—it's our eyes that tell the truth. I looked intently into his to see how he felt about this situation. He was scared, but I could also see that he was trying to be brave. I decided to try to be as brave as Conor.

Warren looked exhausted and concerned. It was weird seeing him standing there, in the midst of my family. We had been dating for two years, but the line between boyfriend and family was still pretty defined. Obviously the magnitude of the situation had blurred the line, so here he was, right there in the thick of things. Warren had achieved VIP status.

As happy as I was to see everyone, my need for water trumped any other thought I had. My thirst was so great that it created a miracle—I finally found a way to use something of what I had learned from 11th-grade chemistry class. I tried to make the chemical combination of $H2O$ with my fingers, but my hands and arms felt heavy. It was like they had fallen asleep and my attempt to wake them had promoted an attack by thousands of pins and needles. But my quest for water was worth the pain. The 2 and the O were not a problem, but the H was a serious challenge. I was having some trouble making a lowercase h with my double-jointed thumb. My efforts at an H were interpreted by my distraught parents as a possible seizure. God, why hadn't I studied those little blue papers I'd bought from the "deaf" people in Times Square. In retrospect, I wonder why I didn't just try to spell out the word water—that would have been a good bit more direct than the chemistry lesson I was trying to teach from my deathbed. My finger acrobatics left me exhausted, frustrated, and still thirsty. Defeated, I closed my eyes.

After I passed out, Conor walked out to the waiting room and asked if anyone knew the significance of the number 120. Was it my new address? Was it the cop car number? Maybe it was the license plate number of the truck? Did I want twenty dollars on the Giants with a one-point spread? Four hours later, they removed my breathing tube, and Warren and my family huddled around my bed, asking me the importance of 120. With oxygen tubes coming out of my nose, I breathed in deeply and said, "I was saying H-2-O! H-2-O! You know, water! Conor, Columbia Business School called—they want their acceptance letter back." I get a second chance at life, and it turns out that in my new life I'm a bitch.

With my mouth back in working order sans tube, I was now able to tell them what I wanted. It was such relief to be able to speak and to know that I wasn't paralyzed, but in that moment the best part was knowing they were going to bring me some water. They brought me ice chips instead. I was only allowed a small cup of those lovely little things, but they were magnificent. I know everyone always knocks hospital food, but I have to say that they do ice chips beautifully. That first glorious chip I chomped into had more give than a regular ice cube, and then it broke apart into hundreds of little melting snow-flakes in my cardboard mouth. I was elated.

Meanwhile my assembled loved ones had more pressing matters than ice cubes on their minds. They wanted to know where the accident had happened. I tried to remember, because I knew there was gravity behind what they were asking me. They were trying to find out if my brain was functioning, or if I had any gaps in my memory. I certainly felt out of it but couldn't tell if there was anything wrong with my brain. I wasn't even sure that was something I could deduce. Regardless, I wanted my head to be okay, but just like everything else that was happening, I wasn't in charge. I knew I hadn't been wearing a helmet when the accident happened, so it wasn't an unreasonable assumption that something might be wrong with my head. I should be brain damaged. *What in the hell was I doing not wearing a helmet?* Furrowing my brow, I got to work at thinking about stuff.

*If I am thinking like this then maybe I'm not brain damaged—my brain is pretty much working. I need to answer their question, though. They need to know that I have it together. I've got this—I'm okay, I'm okay, I'm okay.*

"I was riding my bike down Metropolitan Avenue (untrue). I made a right onto Meeker Avenue (false). That's where it happened," I recited.

Though I wasn't aware of it then, my family wasn't just asking me where the accident had happened because they wanted to know if the gerbil inside my head was still running; they actually had no idea where it had happened. The EMTs had left the hospital by the time they arrived, and the doctors didn't know either. Barring analysis of the gravel lodged in my skin by Williamsburg's CSI team, I was the only link to the scene of the crime. My family moved away from my bed, taking my boyfriend, who also lived in Williamsburg, aside and asked him if it was possible that the accident happened there.

He told them no. Meeker and Metropolitan don't cross, so there was no way I had made a right at that intersection. Katie was wrong.

They thought their voices were low enough and the pain-killers would have made me woozy enough not to notice what they were talking about. They wildly underestimated my ability to eavesdrop. I signaled for my mom to come close. She bent down, inches away from my mouth, and I whispered, "They think I'm crazy, but I'm not." Then I moved my head back and forth to indicate to her, "Not. Crazy."

***

Thinking about that corner, albeit the wrong one, ushered the memory of my accident back into my mind like a cockroach. I tried to step on it, to shoo it out, but it was too fast, too tricky. I saw myself at the stoplight, balancing on my feet on either side of the bicycle. I felt myself twist around at the waist and wave to the people in the black car behind me, my arm turning into a right angle at the elbow. I saw their indicator was off; they were going straight. Then I looked toward the truck in front of me. I stared at his taillight and saw his indicator was also off, but I waved into his mirrors anyway, letting him know where I was going.

I saw the light turn green and felt myself push off on the pedals. I made my right turn wide, gazing out at the rising sun in the deep blue sky. Then I heard the rumble of the truck. He wasn't going straight; he was turning right. I saw the chain-link fence on my right and the off-white body of the truck on my left, and in one horrible second I realized there was no place to go. The cab of the truck was right next to me. I had never been that close to a moving truck before. I started to bang on the side of the truck, but it was too late: he had already begun his turn, and I was trapped.

I lost my balance, and the truck knocked me down and broke me into pieces.

That was how I got here. It took twelve hours of emergency surgery to cobble me back together again. I was going to need some more ice chips.

# CHAPTER FIVE

# "Am I Naked?" and Other Important Questions

Later that afternoon, I was wheeled out of the ICU for another surgery. No one had asked me if I wanted this surgery. There was no mental preparation, no reassuring explanations. It was just what was going to happen, and that was that. I had no say over what was happening to my body.

I was still conscious as they took me past the waiting room, and I caught sight of my best friend Maribeth. We had met when I was four and she was five and her family had just moved into the house behind ours. I was hanging on to my mother's leg and Maribeth was clutching her mother's left hand. I remember that she looked like an angel. She had the cheeks of a cherub, straight hair—so blonde that it was white in some places—and a sunburnt nose. The little girl who had lived in that house before was Argentinian and had made my dark hair and olive skin look normal. This girl was different—or maybe I was different. . . . I wasn't sure at the time. I didn't care what she looked like; all that really mattered was that there was someone to play tag with.

As a child I couldn't say her name correctly, so I always called her Maribethes. Whenever I had anything new, or something that I thought was cool, I had to show it to her right away. I'd run through the back door toward her house, screaming, "Maribethes! Maribethes! I got something good! Come see! Come see!" She was a part of all my childhood memories and most of my adult ones too.

Maribeth was an oncology nurse at Sloan Kettering in Manhattan. She was phenomenal at her job, and I was so proud of her for becoming a nurse. I believed she understood what was happening to me more than anyone else. My gurney was being pushed by a tall man, and as he passed by Maribeth, she leaned in and said with a smile, "Kates, you have a male nurse. . . . That means he's going to see your hoo-ha." One would think that as a person is going in to have surgery, their dearest friend would tell them that they love them, or that everything is going to be okay. Not Maribeth and me; that just wasn't the way we operated. No, Maribeth decided that now was the appropriate time to make a joke about someone I didn't know seeing my naughty bits.

Now, I wasn't afraid of the nurse seeing me naked. He was a professional, and it was a part of his job. He had been trained in seeing naked bodies, plus I have been naked in front of strangers before—mostly by accident. I am generally irresponsible in the window blind department. But the idea that I could be naked in front of my family postsurgery was a totally different story. I knew that flew in some families, like my friend Whitney's, where going topless in front of her mom was no problem. Sisters sharing a changing room? Sure, whatever works for you guys. Brothers walking around in their boxers? That's fine for other people. . . . We just didn't roll that way. We each had our own rooms for a reason—that reason being never having to see each other naked.

We'd only had one slipup, when I was about nineteen, and I was home from college for summer break. I had just taken a shower after an early-morning run. I was in my room getting dressed and ready for my waitressing job, and I had turned on VH1 for the early morning segment of *Wake-Up Video*. These videos were my favorite, because they were always really upbeat hip-hop songs. This particular morning I had already dropped my towel in preparation for dressing when a new Beyoncé video came on, and my desire to be gorgeous, empowered, and a total badass made it impossible for me to tear myself away from the television screen. I was buck naked, my head tilted back, standing in the middle of my room when my father burst in to shut off the TV. I had no towel nearby for protection. I wasn't even in the midst of putting on clothes, so there was no buffer between my late-teenage nakedness and my poor father's eyes. It was doubly embarrassing because not only was I naked, but I was just hanging out, like a three-year-old with no shame.

"Oh Jesus! I'm sorry!" my father exclaimed.

Ten seconds later, through my closed bedroom door, there were mumbles of apology and an explanation about him coming in to turn off the television because he thought I was still out running. For the next few days we avoided eye contact, and then we silently agreed never to speak of it again.

This discomfort with familial nudity stuck with me. With all the other fears and vulnerabilities I was dealing with, I just couldn't handle any more awkwardness. As the anesthesia wore off, back in intensive care, my mind went back to Maribeth's words. I didn't say *hello*, or *good to see you*, or *I am okay* to the assembled family members. All I could say was, "AM I

NAKED? AM I NAKED?!" Only after my mother assured me that I was, in fact, *not* naked, did I breathe easily.

Making sure that there was something between my tube-punctured body and my relatives' eyes was about as much control as I had over my life right now. Although I was trying to crack jokes while I was conscious, what was happening when I was unconscious wasn't funny at all.

The second night in the hospital my mother and another one of my best friends, Annamaria, stayed over with me in the ICU. The truck had run over my diaphragm and made an enormous cavern in my body, and the immediate worry was that the space could very easily fill up with blood. If that happened, I would die. Annamaria, who was in her last year of medical school, felt better being there with me. It made her feel less helpless.

When I opened my eyes, my mother was resting in a chair across the room, and Annamaria was holding my hand. I understood what was happening. They weren't sure I was going to make it through the night. They had come to watch me; they were there to keep death away. I squeezed Annamaria's hand as many times as I could so she knew I was still there and that I wasn't going anywhere. She smiled at me with tears in her eyes and told me she loved me. I pointed to myself and raised two fingers—me too. I kept my face turned toward her as I closed my eyes. Not tonight, death, not tonight.

She told me later that I squeezed her hand every time I came to, and with each squeeze, she knew I was going to be okay. I didn't share her certainty then. I wasn't sure I going to make it through the night. I would open my eyes and for the first five seconds I didn't know if I was alive or dead. After all, I didn't know what the afterlife looked like, and who was I to say that the ICU wasn't heaven? I had never woken up in either before. I just kept squeezing her hand, holding on to something, trying not to let go.

The next morning, my third day in the hospital, my body felt as if it was buried in sand; a wet crumbly heaviness covered me. I didn't want to move my hands or feet, or any part of my body, for fear of seeing the cracks in the sand. A searing and continuous pain coursed through my body. I couldn't believe that the pain was actually worse than the day before. My eyes were open; the nurses had woken me up, for reasons I still don't understand. *Why were they waking me up? Didn't I need rest? Didn't I need to heal?* They took my blood and talked at me, but I couldn't comprehend what they were saying. I knew they were speaking English, but the way their words were being strung together was incomprehensible. They were speaking medicalese.

I tried to keep up, but all I heard was *wah wah wah wah wah wah wah*, like the teacher's voice in *Charlie Brown*. The doctors who surrounded my bed talked to me about what medications I was on, and why. I didn't know what the fuck they were talking about either. It was 6:00 am, and my parents weren't at the hospital yet, so I just nodded my head and said, "Yes, sir, I trust you." I was polite, not just because that was the way I was raised, but because I felt like they held my life in their hands. If I was nice, then they would care if I lived or died. I felt like having them like me was key to my survival.

The kind nurses flowed in and out of the ICU all morning. Their uniforms were sparkling white, and they had cool hands and soft voices. They were only responsible for a few patients at a time, as opposed to the ten or so patients nurses on the less dire floors had to cover at a time. What that meant was that they had much more time to devote to me. There was one nurse I was particularly fond of. Her name was Marie, and she had a pixie haircut and a huge smile, and she was in charge of me for the first few days.

I was confused about my surroundings most of the time, not sure of where I was or how I had ended up there. She patiently and gently reminded me of the why and where. She brought me ice chips and extra pillows, which was all I knew how to ask for at the time. She was the shit, though I didn't think it was appropriate for me to say so in those exact words at the time, so I told my parents that she was "the poo." My dad thought that it was funny enough to tell her about it, and luckily enough for me she laughed and wasn't so offended that she stopped bringing me ice chips or smiling at me. She was a little grandma angel sent to watch over me.

Most of the time, though, the conversations I had with the men and women in scrubs and white coats were about pain. They were deeply interested in my pain: How much or how little did I hurt? What was the severity on a scale of one to ten? Every time they asked me, my answer was ten. The pain did not come and go, it just lived in me. The shock of the trauma was overwhelming. Even though I was getting as much pain medication as a person my size could take without overdosing, I could feel the ache in every single muscle, the burning in my broken bones. Everything in my body felt like it had been ripped into shreds that could never be mended. I had never known pain like this, and it wasn't because I was a girl who hadn't taken a spill or two in her life.

I had been to the hospital numerous times before, all just day visits, but I wasn't a novice at injury. I had had three sets of stitches on my face, the most serious when I was seven years old, from a cut right underneath my eyebrow. I got that one for a good reason, dancing directly into a rocking chair. I hit myself so hard in the head that my parents could see my skull. My dad couldn't even look at it—he was too grossed out—but my mom calmly looked at the gash on my face, as blood dripped into my eye, and said, "I think that we should probably see the doctor, Katie."

She walked me to the kitchen, took ice from the ice cube trays, wrapped them up in one of our dish towels, and pressed it to my eye. Her intense calm pushed away my fear. We got to North Shore Hospital, the hospital where all of Arthur and Margo McKenna's children were born. I sat in a metal chair in the emergency room, my feet swinging above the floor. I clenched my dish-towel ice pack in my hand, the water from the melted ice dripping down my face. When I got in to see the doctor, I looked down as he stitched me up. I didn't move. I didn't cry. I didn't scream. I just stared at my feet.

My mother said the only times I would ever sit still were when I was in front of a doctor or getting my hair cut. Even at a young age I understood that for them to do their job well, I couldn't move. I made a few more visits to the hospital after that: a lacrosse stick to the face got me another set of stitches, a wrong move in a tree house gave me a concussion, a slip on some ice tore up my chin, and a nail file to my left eye and later a pencil to my right brought me straight back to those lino-leum halls. But I had never woken up there. This time it wasn't something that was behind me. I had just begun an uphill bat-tle, and I wasn't going anywhere.

***

When you spend your whole day in bed, going to sleep at night feels silly, like some ritual of a past life. The last three days in the ICU had been full of my slipping in and out of consciousness. The concerned faces of my loving friends filled my vision. Then people I didn't know asked me things and told me things, of pain increasing and then easing with the help of patches and pills. Going to sleep at night only signaled that another day exactly like the one I had just finished would follow. Hurt, sleep, concern, questions, white coats, blue pants, waiting, fear, vomit, thirst, hurt, tears, stares, hurt.

All these days lying on my back gave me ample time to critique the bedding. Hospital pillows feel as if they are made out of rain-poncho plastic wrapped around lumpy cotton. And the pillowcase feels like a recently starched shirt. Of course, the reason why my pillows, why all hospital pillows, are covered in plastic is to keep the cotton from getting stained with vomit, blood, or tears, which was practical, but it still made my heart hurt. Plus, these plastic covers made my face sweat, and I hated that. I liked to be cold when I slept. I kept the window a little bit open, all year long, even in winter. My college roommate, Kristin, said she could hear me in the night, flipping my pillow, searching for the cold side.

In the middle of that third night I woke up with my face damp from the nightmares that came with the painkillers. I couldn't flip or fluff my pillow. I couldn't move to make myself more comfortable. I just lay there, hot, sad, and helpless—desperately wanting to kick somebody's ass. *How did this happen to me?* I wondered. *Why wasn't I home?* I had passed the test. I had survived. Now, for my reward, I wanted my own bed. I wanted my own pillows. I wanted out of here.

On the fourth morning the doctors came in again, and they talked their medical talk again, but this time I didn't even try to listen. Anything that wasn't *Congratulations Champ! You survived, now you get yourself home and stay off those bicycles!* was completely worthless to me. They talked about overarching issues—about the next day's procedures and what would be happening in the next few weeks. They spoke in depth about my long-term care. I wanted this mess to be easily fixed, like everything else in my life had been. But now, for the first time, that was not the way things were going to happen. Those moments in my life that had been a "tragedy" had been resolved relatively quickly. If nothing else, there had been someone who said, *Don't worry we can fix this.* This time, no one was saying this was fixable. Everyone seemed scared. Because it was so different from the way I normally interacted with the world, I almost didn't understand it. I didn't get that this accident couldn't be taken back. That there was nothing else I could do except to suffer through it.

This was my first dance with mortality. I was human, I was fragile, and I was breakable, just like everyone else. No more brunching with the gods; from now on, someone else would be drinking my champagne and eating my ambrosia.

# CHAPTER SIX

# Visitors

As much as I loved brunch (with or without the gods), I loved entertaining even more. I like the way a friend looks when they are waiting right outside my front door. I like to peek at them through the eyehole, or out the window, and see them standing there with a look of excitement on their face. I love making people feel both comfortable and taken care of when they come to my house. I like taking their coat, making them a drink, and then force-feeding them appetizers.

My apartment is nothing spectacular. The coat closet is my bed, the drink was usually a glass of eight-dollar wine bought at the discount liquor store around the corner, and the hors d'oeuvres were usually something in the genre of Cracker Barrel cheddar cheese and Triscuits. But there was love in there.

Being around people has always made me joyful. I would tilt toward their love and attention like a flower to sunlight. I liked being loud, making people laugh, introducing them to other people—playing hostess was my jam.

As unspectacular as my apartment in Williamsburg was, my hospital room at Elmhurst was worse. The mood lighting was terrible. You couldn't find a decent drink in the place. (They only had Shasta cola—what's that about? I thought that soda had been retired with the mullet.) And there was no actual door for you to approach, just a curtain separating my bed from my roommate's. There was no expectation of a good time when you walked up to that hanging sheet. There was just the fear of seeing something really sad. And that sad thing was me.

During my first days there, I wasn't allowed to have visitors. The doctors were afraid my immune system was too weak to handle their germs. They were also worried that if I saw too many people I would get overwhelmed.

One afternoon during the first week, I was awoken by loud noises coming from just outside my room. There was laughing and talking, and I realized I recognized the voices. I called the nurse and asked her what was happening. She said, "It's your visitors in the waiting room."

Apparently the security guard, with startling accuracy, had started identifying my visitors as any person in either a peacoat or business suit and had expedited all of them to the ICU waiting room. At one point there were twenty people in there, and all of them were there for me. I know I should have been happy there were so many people who loved me, who wanted to see me, but I wasn't happy about it—I was jealous. I wanted to be out there, taking comfort in others, feeling less alone. I wanted to hug people, to be supported, to be loved on. I just kept thinking, *There should be no laughing! Everyone should be standing there moping, thinking about me! And there should be crying, lots and lots of crying. Don't they know that's what's supposed to happen in a hospital waiting room? What is wrong with these people?!*

My dad told me later that night all they needed was a keg in the corner and it would have been a pretty great party. I didn't like that sentiment, because I was afraid he was right. I was suddenly aware this could be my new life: I was going to be close enough to the party to hear it, to see it, but I wouldn't really be part of it anymore.

*** 

After a week I was allowed to leave the ICU. The doctors said I was stable, which should have reassured me. Instead I wondered how not being able to feel my legs and needing an oxygen tank to breathe was their definition of stable. The wonderful thing about leaving the ICU was that I was able to see visitors other than my family and my boyfriend. The first friends who came to see me were the girls I went to high school with. We had known each other since we were wearing retainers and training bras. Most of us had moved into the city after college, and a week didn't go by without seeing each other. They knew my family, they knew my dreams, they knew my insecurities, and they knew what I looked like when I was thirteen and wearing a jean vest and Teva sandals. They were my girls. The bravest of the group pulled back the curtain, and those seven girls stared at me in a way they hadn't looked at me in the twelve years we had known each other. I wasn't their pal who laughed loudly and told inappropriate jokes to their parents; I was something else. I was frail and pale, my body bruised and swollen. I wanted to tell them that it was me! I was still in here! I wanted them to know that they didn't need to be scared, but I didn't know how to. To be honest I wasn't even sure if I was still in there. I didn't feel like me, I didn't look like me, and I was scared shitless of me too.

I realized that I only knew how to be the fixer, not the fixee. Helping had always made me feel good. I was the person to call after you got drunk at your office Christmas party and accidentally told your boss he had a nice ass. If you tucked your skirt into your panty hose and didn't realize it until after you got off the subway, I was your girl. I'd make you laugh about it and then take you out for a drink. I prided myself on being the friend you could turn to when you needed to be soothed, to be loved, to be made to feel okay.

I was a fixer because I was sturdy. My feet were firmly planted on the ground. The world made sense to me. But suddenly this new life, with me in a hospital bed, with the excruciating pain, the being broken, and all of this hopelessness, made no sense to me at all.

My besties stood around the bed, all of us crying silent tears, with them very much alive and me mostly dead. No one was sure of what to say other than *I love you.*

That was until my friend Kerrin, this tiny slip of a girl, took my hand and said, with complete sincerity, "Katie, you look so good!"

"Kerr, do I look good good, or do I look just-got-run-over-by-a-truck good?"

Her tearstained face tilted in confusion, and I smiled. Then she laughed, and suddenly we all laughed. It hurt, but we laughed. Hearing them giggle at something I said made me feel right, like I was still a person. It didn't matter that I couldn't walk. It didn't matter that I couldn't lift my arms, or that I couldn't hug—I could still make someone laugh. That couldn't be stolen. It was still mine.

Talking to my visitors made me desperate for the life that had been mine only a few days ago. The little things that had seemed so insignificant, that had always been a given, now became my fantasies. I wanted sweet-smelling hair and a nose that was pink from the cold. I wanted to get up and eat a cookie when I was hungry. I wanted to *want* to eat a cookie. I wanted to get my ass grabbed on the subway. More than anything else, I wanted to be lifted out from under the weight of this crushing pain, out of this awful limbo land I had been thrust into. The world had continued to turn on its axis without me in it, and I was shocked. I couldn't believe it would insist on spinning when I couldn't really be a part of it, not the way I knew how to be.

After that first initial bestie visit, any new person who came into my room would get interrogated about the outside world. I would ask insanely intense questions like: What does the air feel like outside? Is it crisp or is there moisture in the air? Have the leaves started to change? What color are they? You saw a movie, what was it? Who was in it? What theater? What street and avenue? Did you get popcorn? How was the fountain soda there—flat or really bubbly? I felt like Frankenstein's monster, staring in at the life that real humans lived, my forehead pressed to the glass, my uneven breath fogging up the window.

Although I had no qualms about attacking my visitors with a litany of questions, I was nervous about them asking me any. I felt so boring. I had nothing to offer up to the conversation except the updates my doctors had given me. These were usually small things I felt like I had to make a big deal out of just so I'd have something to say, things like, "So, they think the numbness in my ass and legs is normal for my situation, which is really super great."

When I was a real girl, I used to love to talk to people about the way I felt about things and what was happening in my life. I liked to hear how other people saw the world. The interactions I had with people were fluid and spontaneous. Now, my interactions with the world were highly regimented. The world only interacted with me between the visiting hours of 12:00 and

8:00 p.m., and the topic was almost always the same: *How I was doing.* I took far less joy in answering that question now than I used to. During my first week in the hospital there was so little new to report that the fact that my favorite episode of *Friends* was on and that I could now lift a cup to my own mouth made it a HUGE, and very newsworthy, day. I was so tired of myself and this new life that talking about it with people from my past life made me feel pathetic.

It was three in the afternoon on my eighth day in the hospital. My mom and I were alone in the room, discussing the uncomfortable position of my catheter and how many bites of food I had eaten that day, when I turned to her and said, "Mom, do you remember when we used to really talk? When we would tell each other funny, happy stories about our lives? Instead of us having a full conversation about my peeing mechanisms and my slow death march toward starvation?"

She said yes, and then I started to cry, because I didn't, not really. That memory had been buried underneath layers of gauze and medical tape. My mind was always running so hard just to understand what was happening to me at the moment that it was too taxing to remember what my thought process had been before this hospital, this bed, this life.

*** 

I quickly realized having visitors wasn't always the most pleasant experience. Watching people walk away when you can't is awful. Knowing that they have the ability to go home when you can't is devastating. Wishing you were anyone in the world other than yourself is just plain sad. But the hardest thing about visitors was not letting my heart break when people I loved didn't come at all.

From a very young age I had been taught the importance of showing up. When something went wrong for someone you loved, you went to them, no matter what. When my accident happened, and some of the people I loved didn't come to see me, I was hurt. Didn't they know the rules? Didn't I matter to them? The more I thought about it, the angrier I got. I was mad that they were able to avoid me. That they never had to see the body I was trapped inside of. They said they were busy, they said there was never a good time, or—in those moments of supreme honesty—they said they were scared to see what I looked like, to see what had happened to me. It was all too real. Walking into a situation where you know you are going to get kicked in the face with that kind of vulnerability isn't only frightening, it's sickening. Of course I understood that. In truth, it made me sick too, and I was the one it was happening to. I got it. I understood it. But I couldn't forgive it.

From that moment forward, I separated my friends into two groups, those who had shown up at the hospital, and those who hadn't.

It is easy to love someone when they are pretty and perfect and fun and breezy, but it is a very different story when things are rough—when loving them means dealing with mood swings and tears, seeing them at their most helpless and needy. Those first weeks after the accident, loving me was hard as hell. I know this because in real life, I had had a pretty serious crush on me, and in that moment if I could, I would have run screaming away from myself. I felt as though I had nothing to offer anyone. I was all need, all the time. My family, friends, and boyfriend would pour their love, attention, and care into me and get nothing in return, except for access to as much Shasta cola as they could drink, my undying gratitude, and my aggressive, aggressive love.

In reality, no one wants to go into a place that is full of sick people. Full of people who are hurt, who are desperate, who are dying. And Elmhurst Hospital was an especially cheerless place to be. The walls and floors were vomit brown, and the only window in my room faced another brown concrete building. Plus there was always beeping and awkward lights blinking everywhere. You never knew what the beeping or the blinking meant, but you knew it was scary. And touching me was like a life-size game of Operation. My body was so tender, and everything ached. An innocent, loving squeeze could trip the sensors inside of me and like that X-rayed man in the game, my red nose would light up, and I would scream like a frightened four-year-old. Then there were the tubes; the tubes were everywhere. There were tubes removing pee, tubes cleaning out my wounds, tubes giving me morphine, and tubes giving me oxygen. I was like a cup full of straws with the face of a girl.

In spite of all this, the people who truly loved me came to see me; and they, astonishingly, came to see me often. I soon realized the reason why people came to visit was because their love for me overrode their fear of me. A visitor was a sliver of light. It was a crack in the darkness—a person who wasn't so afraid of me or of what my life looked like inside these linoleum walls. They had known me before all this, when I was a real girl. They still saw her in this new me. These friends and family with cold on their coats and love in their eyes helped me believe that one day I could be a real girl again.

How beautiful. How lucky.

# CHAPTER SEVEN

# You Must Be So Grateful

Every time my friends walked in the door and pulled back the curtain, they would get this look on their face that was not only sad, but completely bewildered. The fear of saying the wrong thing was enough to scare people into silence. When they finally found the words, I knew that I would hear one of these three questions:

**1. "How did this happen?"**

Now this is a tricky one. For me, the answer went one of two ways, depending on my mood. I would either get very factual and go into the entire story, beginning with, "On October 1, 2007, I got into a fight with my boyfriend . . ." and then tell them everything that had happened. I took every opportunity I could to tell the story, because I needed for it to be real to other people; I needed for it to be real to me. The memory of every step, every action that brought me closer to the moment I was run over hung on me like wet laundry.

Or I would decide to go the more dramatic route. I would put on a little play for the questioner, complete with props. Usually these props consisted of a pen and a piece of paper. The character playing Katie McKenna was the pen, and playing the part of the truck that ran me over was the piece of paper. (The scale may have been a little off, but in general I thought it was pretty dead-on. Plus the size of the paper truck increased the drama.) I would have Paper and Pen waiting at the stoplight, Paper on the left, Pen on the right. Then I would explain how Pen had signaled and Paper had not. I showed how Pen made a wide right, thinking she was safe, but then evil Paper came and also made the right turn. Then Paper would viciously roll over Pen's little pen waist. And Paper would keep rolling until it came to a stop a few inches later. Pen would lie there immobile. One of my friends looked away when Paper ran over Pen; office supplies just made it too real for her.

**2. "Why did this happen?"**

This was a toughie because I wasn't sure if the question was actually directed at me. Do I try to answer this one, or should I just tell them to direct their questions heavenward and let God take the reins? If this question was directed at me, the truth was I could think of a lot of reasons why this had happened. I was Catholic, and I was a sinner, thus I deserved this. I did a lot of bad things including, but not limited to, cursing, copying other people's homework, looking up celebrity gossip on the Internet during work hours, making out with boys, not going to church every Sunday, and wearing too much makeup. So I usually answered, "I don't know," and continued to hope the universe would explain it to me at some point.

**3. "How are you feeling?"**

This was the question I hated the most. It was the one I could bank on every time ANYONE entered my room. It used to be such an innocuous question, one people would ask when I was normal, but now it made me livid.

What I wanted to say was, "How do you think I feel? I WAS RUN OVER BY A TRUCK!!!! If your answer is anything other than 'fucking awful,' then I need for you to come over here and run into my fist as fast as you can." I didn't ever say that, but I wanted to—a lot.

What I had come to realize is that there are two reasons why people ask you how you are doing. One is because they care about you and really want to know what progress you're making. The other is that they want for the answer to be *better* or *okay* so they can feel a little less worried about you. It was easier for everyone if they didn't have to dwell on my problems for too long.

For the first time in my life, I couldn't lie and say I was okay or I was doing better, because it felt wrong to sugarcoat what was happening to me. I needed this feeling to be acknowledged, not buried under a layer of politeness. So I told my visitors the truth, the dirty, unattractive truth. I told them what hurt. I told them that I felt hopeless. I told them that I woke up every day scared of dying and worried about living.

***

Although I hated those three questions, I knew that all of them came from a place of love. On the other hand, some of the other things people would say to me, out loud, on purpose, apparently without thinking, were completely shocking.

Once I was moved from the ICU into a regular room, the general feeling was that I was mostly out of the woods. It was a time for hope, a time to look forward. One particular morning, a week into my stay in my "normal room," I met with a social worker the hospital had assigned to me. She described all the special services the hospital could offer me. It was all stuff I expected to hear again, so I didn't really listen. I tried to put on a good show; there was a lot of head-nodding and fake interest on my part. After she had gone through her checklist of things she was required to say, she stood up and said good-bye. She walked about five steps toward the door and then turned. "You must be so grateful that you aren't dead. You must feel so lucky."

It was as though she had strapped a metal glove on to her hand and slapped me across the face. I was seething with hurt, anger, and disbelief at her insensitivity. My thoughts raced around my immobile body like a tiger in a cage.

I cocked my head to the side and stared at her.

"Well, you've got me there, champ. I am the luckiest girl in the world! And, yes, I am so grateful that I am not dead. You are totally right. Being dead would be awful. But do you know what is worse? Lying here, immobile, watching you walk around anyplace your sweet ass desires, just spreading stupid everywhere you go.

"This is totally worse than being dead. Because if I was dead, I am pretty sure I would be in heaven. I know this, because I am sort of a sweetheart. I give money to charities, I volunteer. Fuck, I even worked in a homeless shelter. I recycle. I give up my seat for pregnant women on the subway.

"But instead of being dead, hanging out in heaven with the angels and Jesus and all the other nice kids who died too young, I am lying here, unable to move, listening to you explain how grateful I should be.

"What makes me want to punch you in the mouth is that I am sure you have never known real tragedy in your life. You have never been shattered by an event that has taken your vertical reality and turned it horizontal. You have never felt like the only reason why you keep on fighting to live isn't because you think your life is going to improve, but because you know that dying would just make the lives of people you love more difficult.

"Don't you understand that this is not how my life was supposed to be? I was going to grow up strong, funny, and able to stand upright. My life was to be full of innocence, joy, and love—buying flowers in spring, lying out on beaches in the summer, sledding in the winter, and walking the streets of New York City in the fall. That was what my life was supposed to look like.

"There was no fighting off death, no blood-splattered sheets, no loss of feeling in my legs in the grand plan I had for my life. Gratitude is reserved for a different time, a different me. It has no home here, not now.

"Oh and also, in case I wasn't clear earlier, I would love it if you could go fuck yourself. You're an asshole."

Okay. I didn't say any of that. But I am sure that if I hadn't been heavily sedated, and if I'd drunk all my sassy juice that morning, it would have totally happened. It was what I wanted to say.

Of course, I knew I was lucky to be alive. The entire sequence of my accident would play through my head at least eight times a day. So logically, I understood that there was no real, good reason why I was alive.

For the many weeks that I was in the hospital people would want to talk to me about gratitude. Every time they brought it up, it hurt more. I didn't want to think about the bright side. I didn't want to buck up. I'd been fighting to be positive since this accident happened. But I thought I deserved to feel sorry for myself once in a while. When someone said how grateful I must be for not dying, they took away my right to wade into the pity pool. It didn't make me feel better to think about cheating death; it made me feel exhausted. Then, on top of feeling exhausted, I felt bad about not being a better sport about all this.

The hits kept on coming from the mouths of the comment department. One of the more egregious statements was made by a gynecological nurse who came in to talk to me a couple weeks into my stay. After looking over some tests, and then checking the damage that had been done to my ovaries in the accident, she said, "Well, on the bright side, you won't have to pay for birth control pills anymore."

It took me a little while to process what this grown-ass woman had just said to me. *Was that a diagnosis?* I asked myself. *Did she just say that I wasn't going to be able to have children? If it was a diagnosis, I must have misheard her. No one could be that crass, that hurtful, that unfeeling. Maybe it was a joke? It couldn't be a joke, could it? If it was a joke, it was the worst joke in history.*

It turned out it was both. In her professional opinion, I wouldn't be able to have children, and her way of expressing that opinion was in the form of a joke. It was a double-decker sandwich of awful. By the time I realized that her intention was to devastate me and to make a funny all in one, she had left the room.

Not only did this woman decimate my dream of someday having children in one little phrase, but she thought that saving the forty-five dollars a month would make up for it. "Whoa, whoa, lady—I'd be saving forty-five whole American dollars!?!? We aren't talking pesos, are we, ma'am. Well, that just changes everything. I am turning this frown directly upside down."

Sweet Jesus, I live in New York City. I can barely go out for drinks for forty-five bucks. Not only could I not make any babies, but the trade wouldn't even equal a dinner and a movie.

There were also some other gems that I liked to call *complisults*. It seemed as though my nana was born to give me these. One day she came into the hospital and told me in a very matter-of-fact way that I should be happy I'd gotten so thin! I had finally lost all the weight I had gained in college.

And she wasn't the only one. *Now you can eat whatever you want* was something that fell out of the mouths of many of the women who came to visit me. They usually said this or some variation with a half laugh, as though it was a joke. As though being able to eat whatever I wanted was my consolation prize.

In fact, I was losing more and more weight every day because my muscles were starting to atrophy from not moving and because my body was burning a lot of calories. My doctors told me that when you are in pain you burn two hundred calories an hour, because your body is working so hard to make the pain stop. Katie Mac tip: If you want to fit into that swimsuit before Memorial Day, forget the gym; just crack a rib or something—you'll skinny up real fast.

I was so thin that I felt like a crippled supermodel, all heroin chic. I hadn't seen my face in a mirror since the accident, but I noticed my wrists were really small, like nine-year-old skinny; they were just missing the friendship bracelet made at summer camp. I knew I should try not to look so frightening. So when people asked me what I wanted or what they could bring me, I would ask for things like French fries, skirt steak, full-calorie cherry coke, pizza with any kind of salted meat on it, chicken nuggets, and doughnuts dipped in chocolate. I asked for anything I had ever wanted but had denied myself because I was watching my figure. *Bring it on, bitches. I am ready to fatten up.*

What happened when these loved ones came with armloads of tasty food broke my heart—I didn't want it. It was interesting that the pain would actually be able to steal hunger.

To lose touch with such a basic need made it clear that this hurt was serious. Now I looked at food and eating as an irritant, a chore. Maybe I had low blood sugar, but since I had come to expect all the awful thoughtless things that continued to come out of people's mouths, I invented a little game to save myself some heartbreak. It was called *How I Would Respond If I Wanted You to Hate Me Forever*. It went a little something like this: A friend would come to see me and would unknowingly place their foot in their mouth by saying, "Do you think you'll ever ride a bike again?" (Mind you, only two weeks after being run over by the truck.)

My real-life response would be, "No, I don't think so."

My game response would be, "Hey, dummy. Shockingly that hasn't been something I have been putting a lot of thought into. As of right now, I am concentrating on being able to sit up on my own, not about getting back on the death cycle that put me here. But I really appreciate the reminder. I had almost forgotten what happened to me for fifteen seconds. By the way, what you just said brought on a superserious flashback. I just heard my own bones cracking in my head. It was awesome! You're a peach!"

Another gem: "It's lucky this accident happened in the fall and not the summer. No one wants to be outside in the fall and winter. You'd be way more upset if you were missing the summer."

Real-life response: "Right, I know."

Game response: "Um, it's what? I don't care what time of year it is—I want to be able to be outside during the winter, spring, summer, and fall. I don't want to be forced to spend all my time inside. I have no fucking interest in spending my birthday, Thanksgiving, Christmas, Kwanzaa, New Year's, Martin Luther King Day, and Presidents' Day attached to a bed. On top of that, there's no promise that I will be able to be outside by the summer. So it looks like I'll be upset about missing every season this year."

"So, Katie, does this accident make you see life differently?"

Real-life answer: "Yes, it does."

Game answer: "Do you think the answer is going to be no? Nope, I see everything exactly the same. The only difference is that I now have a better understanding of the weight of eight truck wheels, which, in case you were wondering, are heavy. Are you hoping I'm going to drop some heavenly knowledge on you right now? Am I suddenly your own little prophet? Do you want to rub my belly for good luck or crack me open for your fortune?

"In truth, yes, this accident has made me see the world differently. It has made it really clear that you are an idiot and that you are developing a serious double chin. If it wasn't for the 135-degree tilt of my hospital bed, I would have never noticed that wattle. It's a whole new world."

"So, I know that you do stand-up. Are you, like, putting together a whole lot of material for your comedy routine from this experience?"

Real-life answer: silence and blank stare.

Game answer: "Yes. All I can think about all day is how unbelievably hilarious this is. Take it all in! Yuk it up, fucker."

# CHAPTER EIGHT

# Dr. Douchebag

On my fourth day in the hospital, a young doctor came to see me. He struck me as a kid who had gone straight from college to medical school. No fucking around, no late-night keggers, no Adderall-induced cram sessions, no postcollege tour of Europe for him. He was all biz. He had known he wanted to be a doctor since he was five years old. He knew it on the day he got that Playskool doctor's bag. This young man had strapped on his plastic stethoscope and was ready. He clutched his clipboard and pen, scanning his notes as he approached my bed.

"Hello. Who are you?" I asked.

"My name is Jonathan Goldberg. I am an intern with the surgery team, and I'm going to be working with you." Eyes still on the clipboard, skimming my medical history.

"So you're still in medical school?" I asked, trying to make conversation. "My best friend is in medical school. What year are you?"

This was me trying to make friends. I wanted a friend. And he was pretty cute, with his dark hair and dark eyes and wire-framed glasses. He looked close to my age, about twenty-five or so. Even though I couldn't do many things on my own—like walk, or move my toes, or you know, breathe in and out without a machine—I still thought I could make friends. I was good at friends. Unfortunately, Dr. Goldberg was like a vegetarian at a Brazilian BBQ; he was not interested.

"I . . . am . . . a . . . third year," he stammered, his eyes still glued to the clipboard.

Jesus, couldn't he have done that before he got in the room? It couldn't have been that interesting. Really, all that he needed to know was a couple sentences: "Run over by a truck. Play nice." And I, if he would just make eye contact, would have been happy to tell him that.

Jonathan put down his clipboard and started to take yet another inventory of me. There was poking and prodding and the usual doctor question: *What level is your pain, on a scale of one to ten?*

The answer was still ten. It was always ten. If there was a footnote to my medical notes, it should have said: *Do not bother asking patient what her pain level is. It is always going to be ten. . . . Don't waste your time.* I had been having issues with trying to verbalize what was happening in my body, how the pain just kept coming like a tidal wave. I never seemed to be able to really explain it to my doctors, and I was getting sick of talking about it. I had realized by now that what I was feeling was not going to get better any time soon, so talking about it just felt like complaining and that made me worse.

Jonathan Goldberg asked me his series of doctorly questions and then gave me a breakdown of what tests they were going to run. Then he moved to what medications they were going to try on me and what I should expect from said medications. Honestly, it didn't sound like anything interesting was really going on in the crippled life of Katie. All I wanted from my day was enough painkillers to make me forget where I was and more ice chips.

"So, any questions for me, Katharine?"

"Call me Katie. Katharine makes me feel like I'm in trouble," I replied, a little flirtatiously.

"Okay, Katie, any questions?"

"Can I drink Diet Coke yet?"

"No, you can't. You shouldn't have any carbonation for a while. It's really bad for your stomach, and the caffeine wouldn't be good for your heart, which has been through a lot of stress. Anything else?"

I thought for a moment, and somehow this came out of my mouth: "Do you think I'm going to be able to walk again?"

I'm not sure why I thought Jonathan Goldberg would be the right medical professional to answer this question. I hadn't asked any of the other doctors. I had been too afraid.

Maybe I asked him because he was my age, or maybe it was because my parents weren't in the room, but for whatever reason, the question had been posed, and I had committed to knowing the answer.

He took a deep breath, glanced at his clipboard for a moment, and then turned his gaze to me and said, "With the injuries you have sustained from this accident, it doesn't look good. The bones that you broke are integral to keeping your balance and holding up your entire body. If they don't heal correctly, you will not be able to walk. We also don't know what kind of nerve damage you have. If it is extensive, then your ability to walk would be severely limited. To be honest with you, my answer is no, you probably won't be able to walk again."

If I had had anything in my stomach, I would have thrown it up.

"That was harsh," I said, reeling from the honesty. I felt tears of shock well up in my eyes.

"I'm sorry that you feel what I said was harsh," he said, looking at me with unblinking eyes. "But the bottom line is, it's the truth."

I hated him.

\*\*\*

Like a fifteen-year-old dumped by a guy she thought she was better than, I started to talk shit about Dr. Goldberg in my head.

*What an asshole! He doesn't know anything. He'd spent like eight minutes with me, and he'd only looked at the chart and taken my blood pressure. I'll bet he barely passed his boards. He isn't even a real doctor yet! He isn't that cute. My boyfriend is way cuter. I'll bet he has no friends. I know I can drink a beer faster than him—that's for sure. I hate him. He's an idiot.*

His rotation in my wing of the hospital was three weeks, and any time my thoughts crept back to his prognosis, I allowed that angry fifteen-year-old to come back into my brain, and the conversation would go a little something like this:

*Does this mean that I won't be able to walk down the aisle when I get married?*

*Jonathan Goldberg is a huge dummy.*

*Who am I kidding? No one will want to marry a cripple.*

*Jonathan Goldberg loves to give rectal exams.*

*Will my parents have to take care of me for the rest of my life?*

*I'll bet he sleeps at the hospital because he likes it.*

*Is everyone going to give me* I'm sorry *looks forever?*

*I'll bet that the only way he can get girls to date him is to tell them he's a doctor.*

*Do wheelchairs work on the beach?*

*If my friends saw Jonathan Goldberg at a bar, I'm sure they wouldn't even let him buy them a drink.*

*What if he's right?*
*Jonathan Goldberg is a douchebag.*
Those conversations were a delicate balancing act. Some days I would tip toward hating him, other days I lived in despair. Personally, I preferred the hating; at least it was active. I couldn't believe he could have been so insensitive. It made me feel like just another body in a bed. What's worse, I was a body that was shattered and unfixable. It made it difficult for me to be hopeful about anything. Thinking about not being able to put my feet on the ground again made me want to just say, "Fuck it, somebody get me a Clorox cocktail." Ending my life seemed like a reasonable response at times like this. Part of me was dead anyway—why not go big and finish the job? Although I knew that I had been "saved," I couldn't help but feel as though I was dying. Fear hadn't left me. On the contrary, I knew what it was like to almost die, and now I couldn't shake the feeling that I was always on the precipice of losing my life. If I was always almost dying, why not just get after it and do it myself? I knew I would have to wait until I was out of the hospital. There was no bleach to be found in my room, and I couldn't leave my bed anyway. It wouldn't be much easier when I got home. I wasn't sure how I would reach the bleach on the top shelf of the laundry room.

But that was another worry for another day.

My grief was a private affair, though. For a whole month I didn't tell my parents what Dr. Douchebag had told me. I wanted this to be mine for a while; I needed to get to know it on my own terms. I needed to live in it, because whether or not I wanted it to, it was living in me.

Before the accident I had lived in a world full of yeses. I was young, athletic, educated, upper middle-class, cute, and nice. What was there in the world that I couldn't do? In the blink of an eye, that had all changed. Suddenly, I was hearing noes left and right. No, you can't go home. No, you can't eat that. No, you aren't in charge. No, you can't walk. Before my accident I had been told over and over that the world was my oyster, and I still believed that was true—it was just that now I didn't see a pearl, just a gooey mess of a mollusk who may or may not be in a wheelchair for life.

I would stare up at the tiles on the ceiling and try to work out what my future was going to look like. These tiles looked just like the tiles on the ceiling of my elementary school nurse's office. I remembered lying on the cot in her office in fourth grade, sick with the stomach flu. I had gone to school feeling fine, but then in the middle of the day it felt as though my organs were trying to exit my body via my mouth. I raised my hand and, with a wobble in my voice, told Mrs. Daly that I didn't feel so good. She sent me to the nurse.

The two flights of stairs I had to go down to get to the nurse's office seemed as arduous as descending Machu Picchu. At one point, I stopped in the middle of the staircase and put my forehead against the cool tile that lined the wall. Strengthened by the slight decrease in my body temperature, I soldiered on.

When the nurse saw my pale face and stooped-over shoulders in her doorway, she immediately showed the concern I felt my illness deserved. She laid me down on one of the cots in the back, put her cool hand on my hot forehead, and told me I was going to be okay. She turned out the light and then called my mom. The nurse's office felt safe; it was quiet, dark, and soft. I knew it was only the holding area until I could be in the protective embrace of my mother's arms, surrounded by love and saltine crackers. I looked up at those tiles then, waiting for my mother to arrive and make it all better.

Now, fourteen years later, here I was again, staring and waiting. Though I knew this wasn't anything my mom could fix, I waited for her nonetheless. What else could I do? I wasn't sure what it was going to be like to be a nonmobile person. I did what I could to focus on the bright side. I would get great parking spots; everyone would want to drive me places. I could use the disabled bathroom and not feel guilty about it. I would have superstrong arms. Ramps are fun. I could buy sexy uncomfortable high heels because it wouldn't matter if they hurt to walk in . . . because I wouldn't be walking. I could start a dance craze that was based on my wheelchair moves, like what Lisa did for the "Sprain" in *Saved by the Bell.*

The fucked-up thing was that all my energy was going to worrying and wondering—and it did nothing for me. I didn't get any closer to comfort or happiness by thinking about my situation. I only became more stressed and more freaked out. There was nothing I could do from this hospital bed. I wasn't even able to sit up yet. Maybe my feet would never touch the ground again, but there was no way for me to know that. Sure, Dr. Douchebag said things didn't look so good and I probably wouldn't walk again, but he couldn't know for sure. I decided I'd start choreographing the moves to my dance craze, "the Fall," after my tenth failed attempt at walking, but until then I needed to concentrate on something else.

I refocused the attention and energy I had been putting into worrying toward figuring out why Dr. Jonathan Goldberg didn't like me. I knew I couldn't walk, and that my conversational prowess was not as awesome as it had been when I was a real girl, but I was still pretty fun. Making friends was what I was good at. In high school I was voted "Friendliest." In college, during sorority rush, they would bring all the awkward girls to me because I would make them feel comfortable. When I was in Paris, my French cab driver liked me so much that after I got to my destination, he turned off the meter and took me on a tour of the city, and he didn't even try to rape or kill me. People liked me. If I had a superpower, it was my ability to make people be my friend just by looking at them. But Jonathan Goldberg was my Kryptonite.

Why I even wanted him to be my friend, I'm still not sure. He wasn't nice to me, he told me I wouldn't walk again, he didn't look me in the eye when he talked to me, and he didn't feel sorry enough for me. Under normal circumstances I would have said, "Fuck this guy, he's overrated," but these were not normal circumstances. Even though my family, friends, and boyfriend were spending every free moment they could with me, they still (selfishly) needed to sleep and go to work. There were gaps of time when it was just me and basic cable, and I wanted a full-time pal. I decided that Dr. Jonathan Goldberg was going to be that pal. When he didn't bend to all the things that made up my friend-making superpower—my kind voice, my interested questions, my attempts at humor—I got pissed. Suddenly that ticked off little fifteen-year-old snuck back in. *Who does this guy think he is? I know he (and about a million others) has seen what's under my hospital gown—and it isn't a pretty picture, but for fuck's sake, it used to be adorable.*

There were other contenders. I had begun to develop a nice relationship with the morning and evening janitors. I would ask them about the weather, and they would ask me about daytime TV. I usually forced them to take something from one of my gift baskets before they left. They were always very sweet, but they never stayed long—places to go, people to see, rooms to clean. I was a body in a bed. A smiling body, but still just a body nonetheless.

One Wednesday evening my girlfriends came to visit. Since their initial visit they had been coming at least once or twice a week to see me, their eyes full of tears, their hands full of presents.

In the midst of a round of noiseless giggles, Dr. Goldberg came into my room.

"Hi, Kathari . . . I mean, Katie. How are you?"

"Hi, Dr. Goldberg. I'm doing okay, thanks. These are my friends: Alysa, Linda, Erica, Colleen, Kerrin, Angela, and Annamaria."

"Please, call me Jonathan," he said.

(Ohhh, suddenly it's Jonathan. Interesting.)

The girls introduced themselves and were beautiful, charming, and sweet, the way they always were. I saw Jonathan Goldberg start to blush a little as he talked to them. I cocked my head and watched him behave like a real dude.

After ten minutes of conversation, he realized he had other patients to see and reluctantly made his good-byes.

Before he left I called out, "Dr. Goldberg, will I be seeing you later?"

"Yes, Katie, I'll see you in about two hours," he replied.

We had a friend date. It was going to be epic, I could tell.

"They're cute, right?" was the first thing out of my mouth when Dr. Goldberg returned to take my blood.

"Yes, very. It was nice to be able to talk to girls in New York City and not have them look over your head, or past you to see if there is someone better to talk to."

"They're awesome girls, really wonderful."

I paused.

"I used to be like them, you know?"

"I know."

"Good."

After that we understood each other a little better, and he started to see me as a person and not just a patient. In turn I started to hate him a little less. I saw him for what he was, just a twenty-five-year-old kid who was insecure, a little nerdy, and scared to death of the responsibility his new job entailed. He started coming into my room during his breaks, and we would eat candy from the gift baskets that my parents brought.

A day after he had met my friends, he was in my room when my parents came for their afternoon visit. They said hello and chatted for a bit at the foot of my bed.

"How's our girl doing?" my dad asked.

"She's doing well. I will tell you that she is one of the strongest people I have ever met. You should be very proud of her."

I blushed.

The next day, when Jonathan Goldberg came into my room to check on me, he asked me the usual questions about my pain and about how I was feeling. He let me know about my progress and what was happening with my body. He ran through everything that would happen that day, and then he asked me if I had any questions for him.

Today I did.

"Why were you so harsh with me when I asked you if I would ever walk again?"

He looked down at his shoes, as if he was a little embarrassed. "Katie, I'm a doctor. I've been trained only to deal in facts, and at the time the facts were exactly what I told you. I was harsh, but we were taught to provide worst-case scenarios. I didn't want to give you any false hope." He exhaled. "I realize it was unfair for me to have done that."

"It was fucked up, Jonathan."

"I know, I know—you're right. It was fucked up. I'm really sorry."

"Lucky for you, I'm a really nice girl, so you are forgiven. But my forgiveness comes with one condition—you have to promise me that you are going to try to be less of a douchebag when you're dealing with patients. Douchey is not a good look for you."

"Okay, I'll try," he said with a smile.

For the rest of his rotation he took incredibly good care of me. He even gave me his cell phone number in case I had any issues overnight or I needed anything. He saw me first thing every morning, and I was the last patient he checked on at night. By the end of the second week, he was rotated to another hospital to follow the doctors in the pediatric ward.

On his last night he came in to say good-bye to me and my parents. I thanked him for taking such good care of me that last week, and I apologized for being a pain in the ass.

He looked at me and laughed. "You weren't a pain in the ass," he said. "You are the reason why I became a doctor. I want to help people who want to get better, who want to live their life, and you are that person. You've made me a much better doctor than I have made you healthier. I have to thank you for that."

Then I started to cry.

"Well, when I get out of here, you can buy me a drink and we'll be even. How does that sound?" I replied.

"Sounds like a date."

"You wish."

I made him fall in friend-love with me! It felt so good to know that I was still able to achieve the goals I set for myself. Just because my body didn't work the way it used to, didn't mean that I was worthless. I was still capable of being a Friendship Superwoman, and no truck or douchey doctor was going to take that away from me.

# CHAPTER NINE

# Happy Hour Hunger Strike

By the second week in the hospital I had eaten less than a supermodel on a swimsuit shoot. My parents were worried of course, and they worked to find new ways to compel me to eat. These were different from the bribes and threats of my childhood. Those usually consisted of either the promise of dessert or, when they really got desperate, the threat of belting me into my seat until I finished dinner (I had a tendency to wander from the table if I thought no one would notice). Now my parents were using an innovative approach—a neighbor I had a crush on since I was seven, and the lure of adult beverages.

Handsome Doctor was the son of one of their friends who lived down the street from where we lived. He was an eye doctor and nothing short of a dreamboat. He walked into my hospital room, and I immediately straightened my wrinkled (but desperately attractive) hospital gown, redid my ponytail, and prayed to God that whatever the smell was, it wasn't me.

After we exchanged the normal pleasantries, he asked me a few doctorly questions in as friendly a way as possible.

"So you're not eating, huh?"

"No, I'm really hoping to get into that evening gown I got for New Year's. It was just a little too tight in the hips," I said with what I hoped looked like a smile.

"Well, you need to eat, Katie."

"I know, I know, and I wish I wanted to. It's just that the pain medications make me feel sick to my stomach and then all food just seems so yucky."

"And what about your bowel movements?"

*Oh fuck me, really?* I took a deep breath, and said, "No, no bowel movements yet, but I have my fingers crossed." *I officially hate myself.*

"Well, Katie, there is something you could do to kill two birds with one stone. How would you like a beer?"

"I would *love* a beer . . . I mean, I'm sorry, that would be great."

My dad looked at him and said, "Anthony, you can't be serious."

"I am. It's good empty calories for her. It will relax her a little bit and make her feel more like herself. It may even make her hungry, and it will definitely help to move her bowels."

*I hate my bowels. Why did it always have to come back to my bowels?*

That was the day my dad and mom and I started to host a daily happy hour around five in the evening. My dad would arrive with a six-pack in his book bag, like a sixteen-year-old sneaking bottles into his best friend's basement.

The beer still didn't make me want to eat, but it did make me smile more often. I was also more likely to stuff things in my face out of postdrinking habit. It made conversations a lot easier, and it made me take myself a little less seriously. Drinking made it okay to joke about my misfortune, and the alcohol actually made everything funnier. No one felt bad about laughing after a few drinks. I come from a family where drinking was a large part of how we socialized with one another. Having everyone around my bed with a beer in a Styrofoam cup, talking a little louder than they usually would, felt familiar. Honestly, anything that felt even halfway normal offered a glimmer of hope, a little cup of joy, and it tasted like happiness.

# CHAPTER TEN

# The Record

My dad took to carrying a black 11½ x 7 notebook with him after the accident. It had a red spine, and on the cover it said *Record* in faded gold letters. It was stuffed with bits of paper, and he'd wrapped it in two rubber bands to make sure nothing fell out. Others may have used a file folder or a binder, but this record book seemed to suit my dad just fine.

When any of my doctors entered, Dad would open up his book and take notes on anything he thought might be important. He would record my current diagnosis, the outcome of any tests, the name of the doctor on rounds that evening. My mom would also take notes on scraps of paper and give them to my dad who would then jot them down in the book. He was the one who was responsible for keeping everything together. I was very lucky to have him, because we were a family of losers. Not literal losers, but the rest of us—my brothers, my sister, my mother, and I—were people who misplaced things all the time. My father didn't.

I lost things pretty consistently, but I never talked about it. No one ever knew when I lost something. I tried never to get too attached to anything, so if I lost it I wouldn't feel too bad. If I had something that was important to me, I was so scared of losing it I wouldn't let it see the light of day. I believed that at some point in my future life I would be able to have nice things. In the meantime I tried never to love any one thing too much.

My mother understood her children's tendency to misplace things (*lose* is such a dirty word—it's so final). And she was the queen of finding them for us. She could find a lost contact lens in a swimming pool; it was incredible. She knew where all our things were, and she was so kind about not chastising us for being irresponsible. Of course, what I came to realize was this kindness sprang from a deep understanding of the condition. Once, when I was about nine years old, my mom took all four of us kids, plus two friends, to the Bronx Zoo. After we had seen the walruses and eaten Popsicles in the summer sun, my mom started to yell, "Wait! Wait! Where is James? Where's James?!?!?"

"Mom? Mom?! You got him," my four-year-old sister replied. He had been safe in her arms the whole time.

My dad didn't suffer from this condition, though. He knew where all his stuff was at all times. His keys went in the same place every night. He put his wallet on his bureau and his loose change in a cigar box. He knew where all his shirts were and how many ties he had. It's odd, because my father isn't anal retentive, he just knew where everything belonged and did what he could to make sure it went there. And for this reason he was the keeper of the Record.

I knew if the Record was there when the doctors came in, I didn't have to think, and I didn't have to remember because the Record would remember for me. After the doctors left, my dad would continue to pull words and facts and numbers out of the air and enter them into the Record with his ballpoint pen. And after all the information had been dutifully recorded, he would place the cap on the pen and place it in the front pocket of his button-down shirt in case he had to take notes again.

At about age five you usually start to have a few responsibilities: putting on your pajamas, brushing your teeth, bringing your dishes to the sink, kissing your great-aunt Sally even if she smells like mothballs. It's just what is expected of you as you become a more active part of the world around you. As exciting as it was for me as a child to feel grown up and to do what grown-ups did, the older I got the more wistful I felt for those days when everything was done for me. Those days when I didn't have to do my own laundry or make my own lunch, when I had an allowance and no credit card debt. Magically, I seemed to be there again; in the hospital my family alleviated all stressors. There were no mundane, real-life worries to contend with. My family and boyfriend took care of everything. My mom and dad fought with the insurance companies to get me coverage (because the insurance coverage from my new job had just kicked in the day before my accident). They dealt with the lawyers, and they got the names and phone numbers of all my doctors. They washed my hair, wiped my face, sat next to me, talked when I needed them to, and were silent when I asked.

My older brother acted as my personal filter, feeling out my moods, knowing when I could see people and when I couldn't. He took my phone and kept everyone apprised of what was happening so I didn't have to call. He protected me from doctors who tried to bully me or talk down to me. He made me feel safe and loved. My boyfriend, Warren, told me I was pretty, even though I hadn't showered in a month, and he only spoke in future tense, which made me feel so hopeful. My little sister let me cry when I was sad and then dried my tears so carefully, so gently, as if my cheeks were made of porcelain. She would entertain me with loud stories and silly jokes. My little brother didn't know how to care for me, exactly. He was only eighteen and very much the baby of the family. He'd always been referred to as the little one (even at 6'1") and, whether he liked it or not, he'd been the one we all wanted to take care of. James had just started college a month before—a time when you are supposed to be your most independent and selfish—and he had trouble wrapping his head around what was happening. But he towered over my hospital bed and spoke in a quiet voice and held my hand. He told me that everything was going to be okay. He wanted it to be true so badly that I wept at his earnestness.

The only thing *I* had to focus on was getting better. The same way a kindergartner only really has to focus on not peeing in her pants at school. All the things I would normally have had to think about were being put into the Record and then taken care of by various members of my family. One day I realized I hadn't thought about money, or about work, or about anything other than the hospital in weeks. It was a relief, but it was also confusing. I had hit the pause button on this part of my life, but who was I without these responsibilities?

Every day my dad's book got thicker and thicker, its virgin pages imprinted with different names and phone numbers and bills and papers stuffed into it. Every time I watched the Record come out of my dad's bag, I couldn't help but think it looked like my heart felt: worn out, full, and kept safe by someone who loved me.

# CHAPTER ELEVEN

# Roomies

One evening a friend of mine arrived at Elmhurst at around 6:30 p.m., bearing a bouquet of flowers and a fountain Diet Coke. He had just finished a full day of crunching numbers at his corporate finance job in Midtown. When he was being checked in at security, the guard let him know that there had been a little bit of excitement on the floor that afternoon. Apparently one of the patients, who was being treated for wounds he had acquired as a prisoner at Rikers Island, decided today would be the day he would make his grand escape. The only time any of the prisoners were allowed to be alone was when they were in the bathroom, and even then their wrists and ankles were shackled. This guy had some serious skills because somehow, while shackled, he was able to climb onto the toilet, remove one of the ceiling tiles, and then climb into the ceiling.

His plan was foolproof: he would get out of the building, unnoticed, above everyone's heads. He was four rooms into his escape when one of the ceiling tiles he was crawling over gave out under his weight. He landed in the hospital room of a fifty-four-year-old woman who just had her appendix taken out.

My friend walked into my room, the bouquet of flowers sagging in his hand, stealing sips out of the Diet Coke that was supposed to be for me, and said, "I can't believe you're living here." As if I had just leased an apartment in the roughest neighborhood in New York City. It wasn't on purpose, dummy. Every morning I would sing my favorite *Sesame Street* song to myself: "One of these things is not like the others, one of these things just doesn't belong."

That thing was me.

I'm sure no one feels like they belong in a hospital, but Elmhurst specifically made me feel like I was a pen at a pencil convention. This feeling was exacerbated by the women I lived with during my two-month stay at Château Elmhurst. During my time, I had four roommates rotate in and out; they were all completely different and equally fascinating. In the room's hierarchy, I had seniority, because I was long term. They thought their three-day stays made them hard-core. They didn't even know the meaning of *hard-core*. I laughed in their faces! Okay, not really. I was as jealous of their viral infections and broken jaws as I had once been of women with straight hair and twenty-six-inch waists. You may wonder what I got from my senior status: I was the proud recipient of the bed next to the window. The one with the view of a concrete wall. I love winning.

My first roommate was a twenty-four-year-old Chinese woman who was in the hospital because of complications with her second pregnancy. She only spoke Mandarin, and whenever she needed to talk to a doctor or a nurse, they would call in a translator. I listened to their conversations intently, as if I was watching a person speaking another language on the news. I tried to guess what she was saying before the translator translated. I was always wrong, but I enjoyed guessing. In general, I didn't get much chance to play this sad little game with myself, because the translator didn't come in that often. It seemed that my roommate never really needed anything— usually just someone to unhook her IV when she went to the bathroom. I wanted to be her for three reasons: 1. She could walk, 2. She never needed anything, and 3. She probably knew where to get *the* best soup dumplings in Chinatown.

By college standards she was a pretty good roomie. There were never any boys sleeping in my bed, she never made a mess on my side of the room, and she never tried to steal any of my hospital gowns. The only problem I had with her was her phone habit, which was a killer. Every night at around ten (ten in the morning in China) all her relatives in China would call. She would be on the phone, speaking Mandarin loudly, until about four a.m. I am not proud of this, but I am a champion eavesdropper. I swear it is not on purpose. I just like listening, and I find people I don't know infinitely fascinating. I hear people talking, and I want to know what they are talking about. It could be a friend, a coworker, a stranger on the train. I can't help myself. I can't stop eavesdropping; it's an addiction. I am not saying that hearing a person talk through the night is my idea of a good time, but I'm sure if I had understood what she was saying I wouldn't have been so frustrated. It was usually about one a.m. that the constant stream of unintelligible words would start to get on my nerves. Not because I wanted to go to sleep, but because I wanted to know what she was saying! Was she talking about the baby's father? The hospital food? Was she talking about me? INQUIRING KATIES WANT TO KNOW!

The morning after her marathon chat sessions, she was obviously exhausted and would sleep all day. One afternoon when she awoke from her daylong nap, I was crying in pain. I was on a morphine pump at the time, which allows you to control the amount of morphine you receive but only at six-minute intervals. This afternoon the pain was coming faster than those six minutes. As I stared at the clock on the wall, willing the minutes to go by, I heard the rings on the curtain that separated our two beds clink, and I saw my roommate for the first time. It was definitely weird to be living in the same room as another person and have absolutely no idea what they looked like. Being immobile takes things away from you that you didn't even realize could be taken away. She was standing there, hooked up to her mobile IV. She looked at me as if she was going to tell me a secret, and she shuffled toward me. Her right hand was clenched around something, and she held it out in front of me.

"Here, you take these."

Part of me was hoping she had a vial of ancient Chinese medicine that would heal all my broken bones and make the pain evaporate from my body like rain on hot asphalt. I watched hungrily as she opened up her hand. In her palm were two green Extra Strength Tylenol gel tablets.

"They better than the hospital, you take them."

I know it was a thoughtful sentiment, but all I could think was, *Fuck. Me. Is she serious with this shit?*

Instead, I simply said, "No, thank you," and pointed to the IV in my arm. "I'd probably better stick with this one."

She shrugged and gave me a look that said *You'll be sorry*. I never found out her name, and she left two days later.

I became a little better acquainted with Linda, my second roommate. For Linda, Elmhurst was a pit stop on her way to Rikers Island. Her boyfriend had broken her jaw with his fist (the reason she was in the hospital), and as a result she had stabbed him (the reason she was on her way to Rikers). Linda came with accessories: her own policeman to watch the door and chain handcuffs attached to her bed, her wrists, and her ankles.

Like a good roomie, I tried to learn a few things about Linda's likes and dislikes. Likes: *Tom and Jerry* cartoons, laughing, and pudding. Dislikes: getting her jaw broken. She was so nice that some of the people who came to visit me asked the guard if they could bring milkshakes or Jell-O or ice cream for her. The guard said no.

My nana came to visit the day after Linda moved in. Nana was born in Brooklyn and moved to Queens as a teenager. She spent her summers dating lifeguards and dancing to Frank Sinatra. She told me the reason she didn't get married until she was twenty-six was because she really liked dating lots of boys, and she didn't want it to end. Eileen McKenna isn't your typical grandmother. To be perfectly honest she isn't your typical anything. For example, she has introduced herself to all my boyfriends in this fashion: "I am Eileen McKenna, Katie's grandmother. She says that I'm hot—do you agree?"

She was eighty-seven now, sassy, and liked to wear a straw cowboy hat and an anklet when she went to the beach. One day, one of her friends told her that only sluts wore anklets. Nana cocked her head and said, "I'm a slut, then."

When Nana came to visit after Linda had moved in, she walked right up to the policeman and asked in her thick New York accent, "Oh, are you here to protect my granddaughter? That's very nice of you! She is very pretty, isn't she? It's very nice that you are here to watch her. I hear there are criminals in this hospital."

Watching her face as the policeman explained that he was not here to protect me but to watch over one of the said criminals who was living in my room was incredible. It was like watching an old building get blown up. You know it's devastating for the building, but you just can't look away. I could hear the shell necklace she was still wearing in October shake as she brought her hand to her chest. "Oh, oh, okay, then," she stammered to the guard. Her Aerosoles went as quickly as her sexy old-lady legs would take her past Linda's bed to mine. She took my hand and tried to soothe what didn't need to be soothed. Watching her try not to freak out was the most fun I had all week.

It was more difficult to feel sorry for myself when I was rooming with Linda, for all the obvious reasons. I was there because of an accident; she was attacked. I was pitied; she was scorned. I had my family and friends come to visit; she had a policeman at the door and wasn't allowed visitors. While I dreamed of being at home, she was happy to be here in the hospital, getting to watch cable and not eating prison food.

One night after visiting hours—both of our TVs at a low hum—Linda called out to me through clenched teeth, "Katie?"

"Yeah, Linda?"

"I have a daughter who's your age, and I want to tell you that what happened to you was fucked up. Real fucked up."

"Thank you, Linda. I really appreciate that."

"Your family, they're real nice. I'll be praying for you, Katie. Every night I'll be thinkin' of you."

"I'll be praying for you too."

After Linda left for Rikers, my next roommate was an old lady who seemed sweet. She didn't talk too much, and I never learned her name. Honestly, I was just looking forward to having a roommate who didn't talk on the phone all night, wasn't a felon, and who maybe also enjoyed some 7:30 bedtimes. Maybe we could both have *Wheel of Fortune* on at the same time, and it would be like the show was in surround sound. It would be awesome.

The day she moved in, her nephew came, and she and he talked about normal things. They talked about what he was having for dinner, how she was feeling, what the doctor's prognosis was, if everything was okay at her house, which plants needed water. It was all *I'm old and sweet blah blah blah.*

I need to preface the rest of this story with a small fact: one of the many machines that was hooked up to my body via tubes was a machine attached to the place where my tummy had been ripped up by the gearshift. It was one of my sexier machines. Its job was to help regrow the skin over the muscle that was left on my side. And it did this by constantly draining the wound. It felt as though a giant suckerfish was always at the right of my belly button sucking up fluid, regrowing skin, getting shit done. At this point there was no skin under there. There was only raw exposed muscle under this plastic wrap thing. It wasn't much of a bother except when I was getting a sponge bath. It was awkward to clean around, and it got itchy if any water got under the plastic wrap. But honestly, what *isn't* awkward when you are not only naked in front of someone you don't know, but they are cleaning you. I generally didn't notice it; it was just another tube doing another thing.

It was the second night with Old Lady Roomie, and things were going great! She went to bed at the glorious hour of 7:30, I was able to watch the *Wheel* in peace, and I even got to catch some of the very fascinating *Jon & Kate Plus 8*. For some reason, during my hospital incarceration I couldn't get enough of that show. Those kids were amazing. They were both completely annoying and totally cute. One moment I would want to kill them, and then the next moment I wanted sixteen of my own just like them.

I had fallen asleep wondering what I would name my fourteenth child, dreaming about my one-family soccer team, when I was awoken by Old Lady Roomie's face about an inch from mine.

"There is a fire! There is a fire in the wall, and you did it! You did it!" she screamed.

"What are you talking about? I didn't start the fire," I sputtered.

Please note that I didn't say, "What fire? There is no fire!" Instead, I inadvertently acknowledged a nonexistent fire. This empowered her. If I had chosen my words more carefully, I could have potentially slowed down the crazy that was about to unfold.

"You did! I can hear the beeping coming from your bed. You did it, and now the alarm is going off!"

That was when I realized that my wound suction thing was beeping—I guess it was low on batteries or something. The beeping had thrown her into such a state of panic that trying to explain the intricacies of my injuries and machinery was useless.

"You did it! You started the fire! I need to leave. I am not going to die here. You took my shoes! Give me my shoes! You took them!"

Apparently, not only was I a pyromaniac, but I was a thief as well. Keep in mind, her face was still just inches away from my face. She was so close I could smell the hospital toothpaste on her breath.

"I don't have your shoes. I didn't start any fire—go back to your bed. Go to sleep, please," I pleaded.

"Yes, you did. You did it, and you know what else? Your family doesn't love you. I heard them here today, and I know they don't love you. Did you hear how my family called me sweetheart and honey? Your family didn't say that to you! They don't love you! They hate you! And that's why you started this fire and why you stole my shoes, because your family hates you."

I know my family loves me. But when she accused me of not having a loving family and then had evidence to back it up, I actually started to second-guess myself. I frantically ran through the time my parents and I spent together that day. Had they called me honey or sweetie? Do they not love me? But then I remembered that my mom had said, "Do you need anything before we go, sweetie?" Me + My Parents = Love. Fuck that lady—she's a liar.

After that moment of clarity, I had another brilliant realization: I was a cripple. There was no way I could have done it! Hello, Get-out-of-jail-free card!

"Ma'am, I can't walk. There is no way I could have done this—do you understand? I was run over by a truck. I can't walk, so I couldn't have stolen your shoes, and I couldn't have started a fire. It's impossible!"

Saying out loud that I was incapable of doing anything made me feel so worthless. How did this happen? How did I go from being able to do anything at any time I wanted, to not being able to do anything except for lie in bed? I can't steal shoes, or start fires, and—most importantly—I can't get away from a really fucking insane person who is screaming in my face.

As she searched the room for her missing shoes, I pressed the nurses' call button and then began to cry the same way I did when I was a little girl and had a nightmare. I cried quietly, afraid the monsters might hear me if I was too loud, too scared to leave the island of my twin bed. I would lie there and hope my mom's radar would go off and she would be able to make it all better. This time I was twenty-four, and I wasn't too scared to leave my bed; I was too broken, and it was terrifying.

Reason didn't seem to do anything for Old Lady Roomie, but my sobs seemed to downgrade her from balls-to-the-wall crazy to still crazy but sympathetic.

"Honey, I'm sorry. Why don't you come over to my bed, and I will make you feel better. Don't cry. Then you can tell me where my shoes are, and I will get you out of here, and we'll be fine."

"I can't come over to your bed because I can't walk."

"Just come over here, sweetie," she said, the crazy creeping back into her voice.

This was when I pressed the call button a second time and did not stop pressing it. I decided I would give reason just one more shot.

"Ma'am, I . . . can't . . . walk."

Finally a nurse came in, and Little Old Lady Crazy Pants started to rant like a lunatic about the fire I had started and the fact that I had stolen her shoes. Suddenly, there was a shift in LOLCP's mind. It now looked like it was the nurse who stole the shoes. I was no longer the target. I couldn't have been more delighted.

Her new victim was better equipped to handle all the crazy this tiny person was throwing out, mostly because she was able to use her legs. She ran out of the room and got backup. Before I knew it, all the fluorescent lights were on in the room, and a nurse had come right up to my bed. Her name was Rosanna, and over my roomie's screams she tried to explain why Little Old Lady Crazy Pants was having a shit fit. Apparently when people are older and taken out of their natural environment, they get completely freaked out. This bugout is exacerbated by the amount of medication they are on in a hospital.

Rosanna also let me know that the nursing staff has to take away the older people's shoes and purses so they don't try to leave in the middle of the night just like LOLCP had been try-ing to do when she discovered her shoes missing to start with. As Rosanna continued to calm me and pat my arm on the sane side of the curtain, shit was getting serious on the crazy side of the room. As was her way, LOLCP was screaming her face off. Now her rant was directed at the six or seven nurses who were holding her down. She told them they were not real American citizens. She said she was the only real American in the room. She let them know she knew people, and the government would be coming after them for mistreating her.

I could hear them strapping her to her bed so her flailing arms and fists wouldn't hurt anyone.

Finally the doctor was called. His status seemed to garner her respect, and she calmed down some.

"Doctor, make them stop doing this!" she pleaded. "They stole my shoes, and this girl started a fire. Get me out of here please! What is that? I don't want that! Please no, no, no. No, no, no."

Rosanna told me they had just given her a sedative, and when she stopped thrashing around, I felt calmer. Fifteen minutes later they wheeled her out of the room. Never in my life would I have thought I would have preferred living with a woman who had stabbed someone to a little old lady from Queens.

It frightened me to think that this totally normal woman had lost her sense of reality after only two nights in the hospital. I was in for at least another three weeks. Was that what was going to happen to me? My fear of going crazy didn't worry me as much as the realization that if I was in danger, there was almost nothing I could do to protect myself. I was just this mess of bones, metal, tubes, and skin. I couldn't take care of myself, and the people whose job it was to take care of me were worryingly nonchalant about my safety. What if this chick had decided to hit me or move me or shake me? My body would have been rebroken, and there was nothing I could have done about it. I felt like even my heart was breaking.

I had gotten my fill of awful hospital roommates by now. What else could they throw at me? Didn't I deserve a single? No, the New York hospital system apparently thought there was another curveball I needed to take a swing at. The next pitch was a kind, but intensely religious, Latin American Catholic woman.

She moved in the day after LOLCP left. I was definitely not excited to see another old lady. Clearly, they were all loose cannons. And another little-known fact about old people in hospitals: they smell like stale corn chips. I'm not sure if it's because they haven't been submerged in water in a long time or if their sheets are washed in Frito crumbs. My daily fear was that I too smelled like corn chips. At a minimum once every three days I would pressure friends into leaning in and smelling me. I needed assurance that there was nothing about me that provoked a sudden craving for guacamole. . . . But I digress.

My new roomie's daughter actually worked in the hospital, which I thought was either a really, really wonderfully good thing or a completely terrible bad thing. (There was no room for gray in my new universe.) On the positive side, she would probably be closely monitored because her daughter worked there. So if she decided to go bat-shit crazy, the staff would be more aware of the warning signs. And if there was something wrong, like it was too hot, or there was water dripping in the bathroom, or if a convict trying to escape the hospital fell through the ceiling, the likelihood that someone would come and help would be greatly increased. And finally, maybe the nurses would be nicer to me if my roomie had family working there. Maybe I'd have an in.

On the flip side, maybe this tiny, frail old woman would bully me, and, like being coworkers with your boss's kid, even if she did something wrong, she wouldn't get in trouble. And what if she didn't like me and then told the nurses to terrorize me? Or what if she accused me of starting a fire in the wall and of stealing her shoes and her purse, and then told me that my family hates me? I didn't think I could handle that . . . again.

But I didn't have a choice. So once this new roomie settled in, I began eavesdropping, because as I've said before, it is what I am good at. I found out that she had just gotten a tracheotomy. That was a total gold star for her in my book because there was little chance of her yelling at me. And her daughter turned out to be extremely nice. She actually came over to my side of the room and told me that she had heard about me and my accident and that she and her family had been praying for me. Her mother included. I was touched. Praying for me is another gold star. This means she doesn't want bad things to happen to me. I am so into this lady.

Every night before she went to bed, Latin American Catholic Woman (I didn't ever catch *her* real name either) would pray her rosary in quiet, raspy Spanish. I could hear the clink of the beads as she went through each novena. My grandmother and great aunts would pray their novenas when we were on long car rides, or if there was a lull in conversation. It was always a damning indictment if the rosary beads came out during a family party. It was as if they were silently telling those gathered, *I am bored, I am old, and I am talking to Jesus because I am going to die soon so be nice to me.*

But LACW said her Hail Marys and her Our Fathers with such fervor that it terrified me. She was praying not to die, she was praying not to hurt, and she was praying to get better. It was as though I was hearing the echoes of my own prayers. I was in the same position. I didn't want to die, I didn't want to hurt, and I wanted to be healthy. I wasn't sure what my faith would bring me, but I didn't expect a miracle. I knew there was no way I was going to be able to just get up and start walking again. I knew that my life wasn't going to go back to the way it once was. But I had faith that things would get better and at some point the pain would subside. I believed that someday I would remember how to be happy. To hear someone else feeling the same way I did, desperate but hopeful, was good for me. It was company for my misery; it made me feel less lonely.

One night after the last of her beads had clicked, she said, in English, "I pray for you now." Just like when Linda the inmate told me she was praying for me, I felt unworthy of her generosity. I thought to myself, *Well done, New York City hospital system. . . . You have done good this time. I have a little old lady crush on this woman, and she is making me smile. I will send you a note of thanks.*

The next night, after my family and friends had left, I was settling into the sleeping section of my day. This was usually hard to differentiate from the rest of my day because every activity of the day involved me lying on my back on a bed. There were clues that it was time to sleep: they had emptied my catheter bag and given me my sleeping pills. This was also around the time I would put on *Nick at Night*. I absolutely loved the sitcom reruns. If I woke up in the middle of the night, it made me feel better to have something playing that was familiar, like the Huxtable family fighting.

As I shifted my body into the most comfortable of the uncomfortable positions, I heard conversation on the other side of the curtain. LACW's guests were allowed to stay a little bit later, due to her VIP status. I heard my roomie saying something to her daughters, and then the three of them came over to my bed and said in unison, "We have come to pray for you." I felt a little bugged out by this, but it was obviously a kind gesture, so how could I refuse?

These three women put their hands on my chest and began to pray in Spanish. I didn't catch everything. My C+ in college Spanish proved me less than proficient in the language. But what I did catch was that they were asking God to watch over me and to keep me safe. They prayed that if He thought I was no longer supposed to be living, that He should take me up to His heavenly home.

What was I supposed to make of that? While these strangers laid their hands on me, willing God to come and take my spirit (aka make me dead) if necessary, I bawled my eyes out. Now, I am not sure if they realized I was crying because they had just scared the crap out of me, or if they thought it was because I was so touched. I don't think I will ever know. Regardless, they stayed, very close to getting to second base with me, until their praying was over.

I understood that their intentions were good. But it was not the kindness I needed. I didn't want people to be keening over my hospital bed, praying that God would take me away. I just prayed my ass off to make sure I would be able to stay right here. My boyfriend's family had even called their people in Poland, who performed a two-day vigil to make sure I would not go to God's heavenly home. Don't take those points away from me, ladies. If that is what you're praying, keep it to yourselves. I don't want any. I'm twenty-five years old; I am not supposed to die. . . . Or is it just me and Jesus who got that memo? If God wanted me to go, He would have called my name weeks ago, not now. Right?

After weeks of people placating me, soothing me, calming me—telling me that I would not die, that I was going to be okay—hearing these women speak so frankly about this option was devastating. Maybe they were right. There was still a chance that something could go very wrong and I could come face-to-face with dying all over again. All it would take was a wrong move on my hospital bed, another wayward patient, a too-large bite of food and I would have no way of getting help

or even lifting myself up. I would die right where I was lying—
and this time I wouldn't see it coming.

I couldn't sleep that night. I asked for more pills. I wanted
to pray, but I didn't know if I could talk to God after those
ladies had had such an intense conversation with Him on my
behalf. So I decided that a quick note would have to do.

> *Hi God,*
> *It's me, Katie McKenna. Please don't listen to those*
> *ladies. I don't even know them. To be clear, I do not*
> *want to die. I want to stay here, please.*
> *I love you.*
> *Love,*
> *Katie*

He chose to listen to me. Which is nice.

# CHAPTER TWELVE

## How to Cure
## Nice White Girlitis

I have the mouth of a sailor but the manners of a Midwestern girl. I always say sir and ma'am, please and thank you. I remember to bring wine when I come to dinner. On the flip side, I also tell off-color jokes over after-dinner drinks. What I'd always found was that when I was kind, people were usually kind in return. If I said please and thank you to my cab driver, he would take me on a shortcut to my destination. When I said sir or ma'am to the cashier at the drugstore, I would get a smile. When I brought a present to dinner, I would get a heavier pour in my wine glass, or an extra-large slice of pie. (Who doesn't love either of those things?) I put out kindness and kindness was returned. It was a beautiful thing.

This kind of karmic give-and-take worked out pretty well for about twenty-three years, until the day I took a job at a nonprofit in the East Village, in an area called Alphabet City. Now, I am not talking about gentrified Alphabet City either; it wasn't near the brownstones next to Tompkins Square Park. That area was full of grown-up hipster moms who walked their ridiculously cool kids in designer strollers. Avenue A is now littered with coffee shops and dive bars full of more hipsters wearing three-hundred-dollar shoes and ten-dollar used suits. My office was only a few blocks away, but each step felt like you were going years into the past. On my way to work, I stepped over crack vials on the sidewalk and walked past prostitutes making offers in my ear. My boss demanded that my day end at four, so I would never leave the office after dark. My coworkers were convinced I would get jumped, no matter how many times I told them I had crazy ninja skills.

There were no women under thirty in my office, which made it difficult to make friends. Everyone had kids and families and all I had were hangovers and trouble committing to a long-term relationship. I was lonely at work, and I tried to make friends the way my parents had taught me to make friends: be nice, say please and thank you, and bring doughnuts. I thought it was pretty foolproof, but at this job it backfired. Instead of being a girl who would hold lovely watercooler conversations, I was an idiot kid who was trying to make everyone fat. I had accidentally made myself a perfect target for being walked all over. At this job, kindness was synonymous with weakness, and I was essentially a three-legged puppy with bad hearing. I wasn't very cute, no one was going to adopt me, and it almost made sense to kick me.

One day when I offered to help my coworker Yvonne with a project she had been working on, she turned to me in her swivel chair and said, "Katie, enough!"

"What? What am I doing wrong?" I replied.

"Every time you help someone here, how does that help you?" she asked. "Do people like you more? Do they help you in return? Are they nice to you?"

I looked at my hands and thought about each question. The answer to each one was no.

She looked me straight in the face and said, "That's what I thought. You got a bad case of nice white girlitis. You'd better cut that shit out, or else people will take advantage of you for the rest of your life. Do you understand?"

I nodded and turned to face the computer screen to hide the tears that had started to sting my eyes.

"And no fucking crying either!" she screamed at my turned back. "Shit, white girls just can't keep it together."

I can't say I stopped being a nice white girl. There had been too many dinners at the country club for that. I couldn't just flip a switch and unravel the please-and-thank-you scarf that had been knitted around my brain. To my credit, I did stop offering to help everyone, and I replaced my giant smile with a *don't-fuck-with-me* smirk. I became tougher. I was harder on people, and I stood my ground more. I wasn't as likely to just lie down and take it. I found that being demanding and unyielding made people at work more likely to respect me.

At my next job I was working with thirteen guys and one other girl for a financial firm on Park Avenue. In that environment my wit got sharper, my dirty jokes better, and my sports knowledge more extensive, but my "tough girl" bit disappeared. To be honest, it wasn't too hard to let go of. As soon as someone made eye contact with me and smiled, I was ready to hug them and offer to split the pudding snack I had packed for lunch.

Elmhurst Hospital was a lot of things, some that were good and some that were bad. It was an exceptional facility for trauma victims. It had a very special team of nurses working in the ICU. It had some phenomenal doctors who were the best and brightest in their fields. The men and women in the emergency room saved my life. And as I have said before, their ice chips were tops. Unfortunately, it was also where I encountered some of the most unfeeling human beings I have ever met in my life.

I had never really put a lot of thought into how I felt about hospitals before. In college, whenever a hospital experience was mentioned, it was usually in reference to someone getting their stomach pumped. As I got older, I had friends who were doctors and nurses, so I regarded hospitals as their offices. Mostly though, what came to mind were stitches, hot doctors, kind nurses, and babies. In general a hospital was a good place, a place where you went when you were broken and needed to get fixed, a kind of repair shop with very gifted mechanics.

During my time in the Elmhurst ICU, I was treated with kindness and care. In other words, I was tricked into thinking that was the way I would be looked after for the rest of my stay at the Hotel Elmhurst. I was wrong. Every preconceived notion I had about sickness, hospitals, doctors, nurses, and being a patient for that matter was decimated within my first two weeks on one of their regular floors.

The first thing that really shocked me was the nurses. I have always had wonderful interactions with nurses. I loved the school nurse, and every nurse who worked in the doctors' offices that I'd visited was always kind and smart. As I've mentioned, my best friend Maribeth was a nurse, and she was incredible. To me, nurses were this unbelievable doctor/parent/superperson hybrid. They had to deal with all the gross stuff—the cleaning of wounds, the bathroom business, the unruly patients. They took care of everything that had to do with healing that was anything but fun. And amazingly in my past experiences they knew everything—the school nurse could tell what was wrong just by looking at me.

Unfortunately, the nurses assigned to care for me at Elmhurst were not these kinds of people. Working in a penal hospital cannot be easy, and I am sure that it wears on a person's sensibility and their ability to be empathetic. I can imagine that having sick people scream at you, treat you unkindly, and generally be nasty to you makes being good to patients virtually impossible.

I was not, however, in as understanding a frame of mind at the time. I was not in a place to realize that their lives were difficult too. I couldn't fathom why these women who spent their whole day coming in and out of my room acted as though I wasn't a human being. It was as though they weren't aware that I had feelings and was in pain. I was treated like an itch—an irritant that if ignored would hopefully just go away. I didn't. I was still there, the whole time, in a fog of pain and confusion.

What really confounded me—what I would think about every time I asked for new bandages and was denied, or when the food that was brought for me was put on a table that was walking distance from my hospital bed, or when asking for a cup of water was greeted with an annoyed sigh and an eye roll—was why these people became nurses in the first place.

Isn't caring about people one of the prerequisites of being a nurse? If you don't like people, then become an accountant? That way you don't have to deal with other people; you can just crunch numbers and wear one of those visors. Or become a prison guard? Or an exterminator? Please be anything other than a caretaker of sick people. It is not your calling.

I recognize that there are parts of nursing that aren't exactly a walk in the park. If I'm going to be honest, there are many parts of nursing that suck. Most of the worst things were the very things I needed these nurses to do. Exhibit A: the sponge bath. I am very sensitive to the fact that it is probably not an awesome experience for most nurses (for some it may be super enjoyable, and if it is for you . . . I am not judging; I like picking lint out of belly buttons—we all have our things), but at the end of the day, it is a part of the job description. I am going to drop some knowledge on you all right now: Sponge baths aren't fun for the recipients either. Generally, being naked in front of strangers is not my idea of a great Tuesday morning. If I could, I would have washed my own body. Even under normal circumstances, being washed by someone I don't know sounds pretty awful, and if you add to that the new body deformities I was suddenly dealing with, it thrusts you into a new dimension of uncomfortable.

I hated seeing my own body the way it was. It was embarrassing to have the doctors come in groups and look at my body connected to machines I didn't understand and couldn't see. I hated the very idea of my stomach being stapled together like a term paper. Looking at myself was disgusting enough without having a complete stranger take it all in and give me the feeling of holyfuckingshitthissucks.

I had to brace myself every time a new nurse came to clean me up. I knew what would happen. I had a thick enough skin that I could deal with the sharp intake of breath and the disgusted look on her face as she removed my hospital gown. I would level my bed slowly, so as not to rip any of the stitches or staples and ease my body from its steady, reclined position to something a little flatter. Then the nurse would take the hospital soap and the basin of lukewarm water and mix them together to make my washing serum. None of the nurses ever looked me in the eye. I remember that distinctly—no eye contact.

What I didn't expect and couldn't deal with was the way they washed me. You know how you feel if someone is angry at you? That tension in the room when someone is very mad at you and you are just waiting for them to say what they're really feeling? Whenever the cloth touched my body, I could feel their anger. Because I am self-involved, I thought it was me. I felt like they hated me, hated me for being there, for being a bother, for being so hideous. I didn't know if that was why these people treated me the way they did; I just knew that was part of the reason I hated myself. As they washed me, they were rough around my wounds, and I would yell out in pain, but I never verbally complained. I never said, "I don't like this" or "Stop doing that" or "You're a whore," which were all things I thought. Instead, I tried to be good. I tried to be amenable. I even thanked them for helping me when I couldn't help myself. I still had nice white girlitis.

I felt particularly vulnerable with the nurses right after I had been moved out of the ICU and still had this apparatus screwed into my pelvis that was like a set of three monkey bars going up to my ribcage. I had to be careful with myself because the medical monkey bars were screwed into three different places on my stomach, and they stuck out about six inches. If I turned on my side, the bars would hit my hospital bed and then cause a lot of *ow Ow OW OW OW!* Now, I am aware that the back is a part of the body and that my body needed to be washed. I am not an irrational person. I knew it had to happen. I also knew that I didn't want it to happen. After my front had been washed, I would think to myself, *Maybe we'll just skip it today. No one even sees it—backs aren't smelly. It's just skin and bones. Yeah, I'm sure we'll skip it today. She looks really tired. Maybe I should tell her that she needs a nap and that if she skipped the back it would give her more time to rest. Wait, wait—maybe if I don't bring it up, she'll just forget it. I hope she forgets. I hope she forgets. I hope she forgets.* It was such an odd thing to wish for.

Inevitably, the nurse would say, "Okay, now we have to wash your back," and a chill would run down my spine. She'd place her hands on both of my shoulders and turn me onto my side. When she did this, the bars shifted and the medical steel cut through the skin and tissue on my stomach. Every second I spent being washed was worse than the one before. Not only was the whole process painful, but my embarrassment grew with every stroke of the washcloth. This particular nurse was an intimidating woman. She was tall and had very strong features. She scared the shit out of me. When my extremities were being washed, I could handle it—these were parts of my body that people saw all the time. It wasn't personal—it was like getting a manicure or a pedicure. I wasn't totally okay with someone touching my arms and legs, but it was in the vicinity of normal. The washing of my boobies was weird, though. I felt really vulnerable and exposed. I would ask the nurse to skip my stomach, because of the bandages and the metal biz, but she washed it anyway. The washing of my lady parts made me feel ashamed. I was ashamed that someone had to do it for me, ashamed that I couldn't clean the most intimate part of myself. I couldn't clean what was dirty. I couldn't fix what was broken. I was helpless. As I cried silently, she didn't say she was sorry for hurting me, or say it would get better, or even say good-bye. She just gathered the dirty cloths and threw them in the garbage as she walked out.

On top of all the rough treatment, hospital soap smells terrible. Because of that, I too smelled terrible, and I hated smelling bad. Smelling bad is at the top of my list of least favorite things, even above people not saying *God bless you* when you sneeze and the PT Cruiser.

At Elmhurst I came to feel like a prisoner in an action movie who is unnecessarily nice to her captors. If I were watching the movie of my life, I'd have my hand elbow-deep in a bucket of popcorn thinking, *What the fuck is wrong with this chick? Is she drugged? Or brain dead? Grow a pair and slap these bitches down, already. And why haven't you started making a rope out of human hair for your escape?* In that hospital bed, I had no fight in me, no escape plan. For some reason, I thought treating others as I would like to be treated would make them want to be nice to me. I blame Sunday school.

In most hospitals, when you need something, you ring a call bell right next to your bed. The bell is connected to a speakerphone at the nurses' station, which is usually right down the hall. They hear the call, and one of the nurses promptly responds via a little speaker next to the patient's bed, with maybe a *Hello* or a *Yes?* That way the patient knows they've been acknowledged, that someone is coming, that they'll be taken care of. This was not the way it worked for me at Elmhurst, at least outside the ICU.

Before I had the morphine pump, I would have to call the nurses if my pain medication started to wear off, or if my pee bag was full, or if I was really thirsty, but regardless of the reason, they wouldn't respond. For the first time in my conscious life I had no way of getting what I needed. Through their silence I was told, "You want something? Tough shit, kid, you don't matter. No one cares what you need." I think the real difficulty for me was in understanding where I was. This was an overcrowded New York City hospital that housed a large number of inmates—this was not the Four Seasons. These men and women were overworked and underpaid and not even a nice girl like me was going to be able to talk them into caring more.

Instead, I felt pathetic and stupid. I thought it was my fault that these people didn't want to take care of me. I believed it had to be me. Maybe if I had been nicer to the nurses or doctors? Maybe I had been bad, and that was why I was being ignored? I honestly came to believe after several weeks in this hospital that I was just not worth people's kindness.

In hindsight I know this sounds crazy. Of course I mattered; there were so many people who loved me, but they lived in the outside world. I was in a different world now. I was at the mercy of people who did not give a flying fuck about me and had no compunction about making me totally aware of that fact. They were in charge, and I was being kept alive by their grace. They held all the cards. They had the medication, the food, the water, and—most important—the ability to walk.

One day I had to be taken for X-rays. It was the first time I had left my hospital room in six days. The nurse who wheeled me out of my room and down to the X-ray area didn't think it was necessary to tell me where I was going or why. There was no talk—she just wheeled me down to what looked like a holding area for invalids, put the brake on the bed, and left me there.

Naively, I assumed I was next up. Why would they have brought me down here if it wasn't my turn? But then I looked down the hallway and there were about six other people just like me, all of us strapped to our beds, not moving, without any supervision. We were just left there like discarded socks. I was befuddled. Was this really happening? No, no, there was no way this was happening. It's not possible that a sane human being would just leave a person who is medically unstable in a hallway. That just would not happen.

It turns out, it would and it did. I was left in that hallway for two hours. Whenever anyone passed me, I called out, "Excuse me! Excuse me! When do I go in? What's happening?"

I was ignored. I didn't exist. It was as though I was a ghost and every real human was walking through me and I was silently screaming, "I'm not dead, I'm not dead!"

By the time I was finally rolled into the X-ray room, I was ready to lose my shit. "Is this seriously the way this hospital functions? You just leave people in hallways strapped to gurneys?" I yelled at the technicians.

They offered up a string of unembarrassed excuses: "Sometimes it's like this. We are just really busy today. It's not usually this bad."

"Well, I assume there is a way for you to talk to the nurses' station? If they tell you they have a person who needs to come down for X-rays, you can tell them you're backed up, right? Why would you have someone wait in a hallway for two hours? It is irresponsible!"

Jesus Christ, was I a tough bitch. "It's just irresponsible!"

Good one, Katie. You told them! The me watching this action movie would be proud of the heroine now. *She's finally taking a stand,* I'd think to myself while going for more Jujyfruits.

The technicians were shockingly unaffected by my tirade. After they shot radiation at me, I was rolled back out into the hallway, and the bed was locked again. It became very clear I would not be going anywhere soon. I waited in that same hallway for another hour and a half. Not one hospital staff member made eye contact with me. But it did seem that they shivered each time they walked by.

Now, it's not like I don't know a thing or two about being ignored. During middle school I went mostly unnoticed by my peers, unless you count the times I was shoved or told that I couldn't sit with the cool kids at lunch. I felt weak and impotent then, but this was much worse. Now there was no safe place, like my home, to escape to. This horrible hospital was my home.

\*\*\*

You would think that being abandoned in the hallway would have been the straw that broke the camel's back. Maybe the little prisoner inside of me would have started to look for a nail file to slowly cut the rope tied around my wrists. Nope. It turns out that I am a sucker for punishment.

I had been in Elmhurst for two weeks when I was scheduled for surgery to remove the monkey bars and insert my external fixator (soon to be known as Roberto) as well as a plate in my back to hold together the pieces of my pelvic bone that had shattered under the weight of those eight wheels. The operation was scheduled for the day after my twenty-fifth birthday. My parents came into the hospital at five a.m. and waited with me in the prep room, which was the size of a junior high school gymnasium. Green sheets separated me from the other patients who were waiting to go under the knife. There was just enough room for my hospital bed and one chair, which my parents took turns sitting on.

I was nervous. I had seriously thought I'd had my fill of being nervous. I mean, the worst had already happened, right? What else did I have to fear? It turned out I still had a lot of fear left in my little body. My brain was going bat-shit crazy thinking about all the things that could go wrong.

*What if they hit a weird nerve and I develop a facial tic?*

*What if my body rejects the plate and I spend the rest of my life getting it removed and then put back in?*

*What if this makes me hurt more?*

*What if I die?*

Because this was not an emergency situation, there was more time to think, to worry, to drive myself insane.

I got to tell my parents I loved them that morning. I had called everyone I knew on my cell phone the night before and told them I loved them too. I didn't want to go into the operating room; I didn't want the surgery; and I didn't want to get knocked out again. What if I didn't wake up this time? I kept holding my breath and then releasing it, slowly—feeling what it felt like to breathe on my own. My parents kissed me and I was rolled into the operating room. As I breathed in the sleepy air, I prayed the Hail Mary.

When I opened my eyes again, I was back in the junior high gym of a waiting room—my parents sitting at the end of the bed. Everything felt foggy, but I wasn't in pain. There was a tube down my throat helping me breathe, and my arms were incredibly heavy. I wanted my parents to know that I was okay—that they didn't need to look so worried. I laboriously lifted my index finger to my eye, let my hand drop down to my heart, and then, with my last burst of energy, I pointed at both my mom and dad. They looked at me and then copied my motion but pointed with their middle fingers and their index fingers at the end—show-offs. They loved me too.

A tiny, old Asian nurse in the post-op room rushed my parents away after they saw I was awake and basically okay. Half an hour later, she carefully removed the tube from my mouth and took the IV from my arm. She gave me an oral painkiller that she promised me would last until they rehooked me up to the morphine pump.

My parents were able to stay with me until visiting hours were over. I felt safe when they were there. I knew that when they were with me they would take care of me. They were actually happy to get me ice chips when I asked. They didn't ring the buzzer when I needed something—they went straight to the nurses' station and made it happen. God, walking is so awesome. You could do anything!

After they had made sure I had a full pitcher of water, a huge cup of ice chips, and the McDonald's fries they had brought close by, they kissed me good-bye and told me to call if I needed anything.

About an hour after they left, the trauma of the surgery started to kick in. I felt sharp pains in my back and belly. An allover burning ache ran through my body. It had obviously come from the doctors moving my body in ways it hadn't been moved in weeks. They had to turn me over on my side to insert the back plate, and that had in turn disrupted the broken bones in the front of my pelvis and rebruised my broken ribs. I felt like it was the morning after a bar fight where I had lost . . . badly.

I reached up and pressed the call button and asked the nurse on the other end if I could get the morphine pump back in my room now.

"It's coming. It will take another twenty minutes."

I was so confused. "Why is it going to take so long? I think it was ordered for me this morning."

"The hospital is very busy, and they haven't gotten to you yet."

It had been so many days of these people treating me like I didn't matter that I'd started to believe them. I thought I was insignificant, that I was not worth their time or effort. I believed I was supposed to be in pain. It was just the way things were; this was the way hospitals worked.

I counted down the minutes by the clock on the wall. As each moment passed, I became more panic-stricken, more frightened. I was worried they wouldn't give me any medication. I was terrified this pain wouldn't stop. I was scared I would never be better. I tried to be hopeful, and I tried to be optimistic. I told myself they wouldn't leave me without medication. After twenty minutes of gritting my teeth and wishing and hoping the next set of sneakers padding down the hall would be for me, I gave up and pressed the call button again.

"Ma'am, is my morphine pump here yet? I really need it. I'm in a lot of pain."

"No, it's not here."

"Please, can I have another pain pill? I can't handle this. Please."

"No, you only have a prescription for the morphine pump. You get that or nothing."

"Can you call the doctor and get a new prescription? I need something, please, please. Ma'am, I need it."

"We will see what we can do."

I started to cry . . . hard. I started to pray to God, out loud.

"God, I can't do this, please help me. I can't I can't I can't— help me."

Linda the inmate was my roommate at the time, and she had overheard my whimpers. The next thing I know, Linda is yelling into her call button, "Come here! Somebody get in here now! Katie is in pain! You'd better get in here and get her some pain medication. This is fucked up."

She started to talk to me softly. "Don't worry, Katie. Don't cry, don't cry. I'll take care of you. It's going to be all right, okay? Don't cry, baby girl, don't cry. I'll take care of you."

"Thank you, Linda," I whispered to the sheet that separated us.

For the next fifteen minutes, she called every minute. She yelled into the intercom, saying I needed medication, that this was against the law, that this was fucked up. I guess the nurses were so sick of her screaming into the intercom that they fetched the on-call doctor and got me a new prescription for painkillers.

When they brought me those pills in the little plastic cup, I was so happy I could have done a little bed dance. In that cup was my salvation. It was freedom from this pain prison. I wasn't going to have to hurt anymore; those little purple pills would take it away. I wanted to kiss the pills, to hug them, but, more than that, I wanted them inside my belly, breaking down into compounds that would end my torture. My panic eased as I swallowed those forty milligrams of magic.

"Linda, Linda, are you still awake?" I whispered.

"Yes, baby girl, I'm here."

"Thank you so much for doing that for me. I don't know what I would have done without you."

"That was messed up, but from here on you have to take care of you. Next time they ignore you, you keep pressing on that call button. You throw water, books, cups, whatever you have near you. You scream your fucking lungs out! Don't let them pull that shit again—okay?"

"Okay, I promise."

Hearing that the way I was being treated was, in the opinion of a woman who had spent time in prison, fucked up was exactly what I needed to cure my nice-girl disease.

I knew I was never going to be as tough as Linda. It just wasn't in my makeup. I am not that awesome at tantrums, or screaming, or breaking things—but like many of my peers I am awesome at phone calls. I called my parents and finally told them what had been happening in the hospital with the nursing staff. I told them about the mornings they didn't give me breakfast, the time I had been left in the hallway, the calls that had been ignored. They were appalled, and heartbroken I hadn't told them sooner. I wasn't sure how to explain to them why I hadn't realized I deserved better.

My dad immediately called the patient rights advocate—I didn't even realize there was a job like that. My dad doesn't really do small, so he also called the president of the hospital, wrote a letter to the mayor of New York City, and called our lawyer.

The next morning I woke up, and my dad was there by my bed. He looked at me and said, "Katie, there has already been enough pain in your life. You do not have to go through any more."

"I know, Dad. I know."

"You don't, though. Being nice is wonderful, and I am glad that you're a good person, but this kind of behavior is unacceptable. It's not right. You could get seriously hurt. When I deal with people, I have a set of rules for how I treat them and how I expect to be treated. I give them three chances to treat me with respect. And when they are unkind, I'm nice, I'm nice, I'm nice—then I'm not nice anymore. And when I'm not nice, I'm really, really not nice. You are tougher than you think—and after all you've been through, you are not to be messed with. Do you understand me, Katie?"

I did. And, finally, I was cured.

# CHAPTER THIRTEEN

# Roberto

I have a knack for creating nicknames for people, animals, and inanimate objects alike. The car that I drove during college was a 1994 Jeep, and I named him Jake. No one ever called this car anything other than Jake. We even referred to it as *he*. My parents would ask how Jake was, my friends would ask, "Can Jake give us a ride?", and my mechanic would write *JAKE* on the receipt.

When I got the external fixator implanted in my lower stomach, I couldn't stand to call it an external fixator—so I named him Roberto because he was implanted south of my belly button border. Not only did my family and friends call it Roberto, but after a while so did all the doctors. They would catch themselves referring to the external fixator as Roberto and look sheepish. It was awesome having the doctors use a made-up name for a piece of medical equipment that was designed to stabilize my pelvic bone and the soft tissues at a distance from my body. It was working to fuse my pelvic bones back together, and it was the only thing I liked about Roberto.

Honestly, he was a dick. He was hurtful, made me look like Frankenstein's monster/RoboCop, and I hated him. But he was going to be in there for a while so I thought I'd be better off treating him like a rude houseguest than the metal apparatus that was sticking out of my flesh. I needed to laugh about him so I would start off conversations with "You'll never believe what Roberto did today . . . ," and I would ask my friends to bring nachos for him, hoping that the food of his native country would make him less of a jerk. Sometimes, when Roberto would hurt me, I would curse at him in Spanglish—"Dios Mio, Roberto! Tu eres un asshole!"

# CHAPTER FOURTEEN

# Pain Management

In my first few days in the ICU they gave me a pain patch that went over my heart. It was called fentanyl and it looked like a square piece of Scotch tape. The doctors told me I was getting the same dosage in that little patch as those with terminal cancer. Well, maybe terminal cancer hurts less (which seems crazy), because this patch was not cutting it. I still felt lightning flashes of pain in every part of my body. (I found out later that the medication on that patch was so strong, people had overdosed just by touching it.)

A week after the accident I was moved out of the ICU. The doctors felt I was stable and ready to be in the regular part of the hospital. I didn't want to leave. The ICU was so bright, and people talked quietly and treated me delicately, as if I was special. But I guess I didn't need their intensive care anymore, so I was kicked out. There wouldn't be people watching over me at all times. No one would be checking in on me, making sure I felt okay, asking if I was thirsty, or pushing the hair away from my face. When I moved into my new room, the first thing

I noticed was how much darker it was. The window faced a cement wall so almost no light could squeak in. I stared out the window anyway, searching for a sliver of sky. I lay in my bed struggling to imagine what was happening in the real world, thinking about what I would be doing if I were out there too.

I felt more frightened in this new room, even though there was no reason to be. From my waist down I couldn't feel anything, and the thought that something terrible could happen in my legs and I would have no pain to warn me filled me with dread. I didn't like the new room, and I didn't like the new nurses. No one in this wing of the hospital wanted to know how I felt. Instead, they wanted to rush through, changing my sheets and taking my blood pressure. I became what I truly was in this place: a female patient in room 403B, bed number 1. No one other than the doctors even bothered to learn my name during the three weeks I was there.

On this floor the doctors did rounds about three times a day, with the morning rounds being the longest and most important. In that meeting they would tell me about what was going to happen during the day and do a once-over of me and all my medical biz. The rounds lasted about five minutes or so and, in that time, they threw as much information at me as possible. Their hastily delivered medical jargon would leave me confused, full of questions, and wishing that my parents were there to take notes. I never asked questions myself; I was too intimidated. My new body was like a little baby that had been thrust at me suddenly and for whom I was solely responsible. It needed so much, and I had absolutely no clue how to take care of it. So, I put all my faith into the doctors, believing they had a better idea of how to take care of me than I did.

One morning a group of three doctors came in looking more serious than usual. There was a lot to brief me on— first and foremost that was the day we were covering pain management. The phrase *pain management* always made me laugh a little. It sounded as though it was a department in the company of my body: "And on your left is where Katie manages her pain, sets up schedules, hires and fires, and sets standards and goals for her pain."

If there really was a pain management department, I was a crappy manager. My pain was all over the place. No one showed up on time, no one followed the dress code, and not one person filled out their W-2 correctly. It was a shit show.

Every morning they checked in to see how good a manager I was by asking me my pain level, and every morning, I told them it was a ten. Every time. It was always ten—that is, unless I was feeling like a smartass and felt like dropping an eleven on them. Those were usually the really slow mornings.

"Katie, do you feel like your pain comes in waves?" one of the doctors asked that morning.

"Yeah, it gets worse sometimes. Like when I move, or breathe too hard, or do anything with my body. But, if I am completely still and barely breathe, it is a steady pain." I was really good at explaining how I felt to doctors—when I breathe, it hurts. When I don't, I feel much better. According to my synopsis, all I had to do was barely breathe, and I'd be just fine.

"Okay, so what we think will be best for your pain management would be if you got a morphine drip that would be attached to a pump, so you can use more medicine when you're in a lot of pain and less when the pain is not as intense."

The idea of a morphine pump made sense to me; this way I could get the meds I needed, when I needed them. I could try to manage what was happening to me better. No one understood my pain like I did, so having this pump as a weapon in my managerial arsenal seemed like a good idea. The doctors left me feeling confident that this would be the answer to my problems.

Later that day the nurses brought in this huge hulking machine, offering startling little instruction. They inserted the IV in the vein on the inside of my elbow and attached it to the pump. This machine would allow morphine to be pumped directly into my veins every six minutes. They were giving me the maximum amount of morphine my body could take without overdosing. If I got any more, I could unintentionally kill myself like an '80s punk rocker. I figured I'd be floating on a cloud of feeling better.

I was mistaken.

The nurses took off the fentanyl pain patch that had been excreting medicine into my bloodstream slowly, carefully, and without me having to work for it. They put the clicker that was attached to the pump into my hand. It was cylindrical and had a button at the top that fit my thumb perfectly. Left with this huge machine, and the instruction to press the button when I felt pain, I assumed my pain would somehow oblige by making an appearance every six minutes or so.

My body knew the patch had been removed about a half hour after the doctors and the nurses left. The lightning bolts were brighter, stronger, more frightening than anything I had felt thus far. I simply couldn't comprehend that my body could feel this bad without me actually dying. In my first act as official pain manager, I forcefully pressed the button down with my thumb until I heard the click of the pump. A second later there was a rush of cold that spread down my left forearm into my fingers and all over my body, dulling the pain.

Relief and release: this pump was a manager's dream. The pain was still there, but it felt controlled. It felt like it could be handled. It felt amazing.

But then five minutes after pressing the pump, something changed. The morphine and its numbing fingers wore off, and when I pushed the button again, there was no click, no rush of cold, no relief. The pain was still very much there, and it was pissed. I kept pushing down the button with my thumb over and over again, waiting, hoping enough time had passed. *It has to have been one minute already. Sixty little seconds. They must have passed. THIS IS THE LONGEST SIXTY SECONDS IN HISTORY!* When I was about to lose my mind and rip the pump out and beg for the patch back, I heard the click, and then the cold rush, and finally the relief. It became crystal clear to me how people could become addicted to morphine. I felt the craving and the desperation.

Those last sixty seconds became the worst moments of my day. Wanting it to be six minutes, needing for it to be six minutes. I stared up at that clock, feeling the pain invade my body and fearing that it would never go away.

I made up excuses for why this wasn't working: Maybe the doctors messed up the dosage? Maybe they just didn't realize how tough I am? I know my chart says I can't take more morphine than this and not have my heart explode, but I know I can.

I begged for more medication, for a little higher dosage to get through that sixth minute. They told me they were sorry I was having this pain, but they couldn't give me any more morphine because there could be serious complications . . . like me dying. I knew the truth though: my doctors were a bunch of unfeeling pansies—*Okay, Katie might die—gotta be careful.* Bullshit. At this point I didn't care if I died. I just wanted to stop hurting.

This whole situation was complicated by the fact that I was never very good at math. All the adding up of minutes confused me. Luckily, I had been pretty decent at my multiplication tables up to the tens, and miracle of miracles, six was within that realm! So, one day I began my pumping at 6:00 a.m. exactly, and from then on I knew at what position the big hand on the clock would need to be at when I could get my medicine again.

I wrote out the numbers on a napkin: six, twelve, eighteen, twenty-four, thirty, thirty-six, forty-two, forty-eight, fifty-four, sixty. Those were the good numbers. Every other number was a bad one. I stared at that clock, wishing for multiples of six, worshipping them, dreaming of them . . . which, on top of being sad, was a little creepy.

I would click the button and hope for a glitch. I would pray for the machine to break and give me a little more, just a little more to keep the pain away. When my six minutes were up, I would hear the click that made the pump go, and I would stare at my forearm and watch my veins take in the painkiller. I believed I could see the pain actually being killed, everything easing, my muscles and bones healing, all that was wrong becoming right again, at least for the next five minutes.

As time went on, the space between the electric shocks of pain lengthened. And as I became a better pain manager, I tried to stretch out the periods of time between pumps. It was a game I played with myself, trying to stave off pressing the pump. I would try for twelve minutes instead of six, and if I made it, I would feel excessively proud of myself. If I got to fifteen, I would call a managers meeting with myself and offer me a raise, an award, the promise of a promotion.

One day I set a goal for myself—a serious I-am-not-messing-around goal. I was going to wait thirty minutes between pumps. The lightning bolts of pain came at around fifteen minutes, but I breathed in and out, concentrating on what was happening on *The Golden Girls*. From what I could tell, Rose was dumb, Blanche was slutty, Dorothy was sarcastic, and Sophia was just sassy. As diverting as this show can be, I willed the ladies to be dumb, slutty, sarcastic, and sassy faster. I wasn't sure I could hold out without pushing the trigger, but time crept by at its own stubborn pace with no interest in how I wanted it to roll.

When the last joke was uttered and the canned applause began, I felt an incredible sense of pride and accomplishment. I had fought it. I had fought the pain! I had fought and won! I felt flushed with my victory. That afternoon, I threw myself a little party in my body's conference room. There was a sheet cake with *World's Best Manager* written on it in blue frosting. And I don't know much about much, but if something is written in blue frosting, you have a moral obligation to believe it.

So I did.

# CHAPTER FIFTEEN

# Breaking Out

After three weeks at Elmhurst Hospital, I stopped dreaming about home or walking or being well. Instead, I began to dream about leaving Elmhurst and going to a different hospital. That was how desperate I was to leave this place. I believed things would get so much better if I could just get to Glen Cove Hospital.

Glen Cove Hospital became the answer to my prayers from the moment my parents brought up the idea of going to rehab there. It was a pretty hospital, located only twenty minutes from where I grew up and where my parents still lived. We actually knew one or two of the doctors there. And the best turkey club I had ever eaten was made only about one mile from the hospital at the Barefoot Peddler. If a good sandwich doesn't give you hope, then what does?

The doctors said I was only two days away from being cleared to move. I was ecstatic. All I could think about was getting out—it was the light I squinted at from the bottom of the sewer I was living in. With every hour that passed, I felt my heart lightening just a little.

I wasn't the only one who thought Glen Cove was the answer to all our problems. My family, my boyfriend, my friends, everyone would say, "When you get out of here things will . . . (insert something awesome)." I needed for Elmhurst to be in my past, something I never had to speak of again. I wanted to dig a hole in the desert and bury it, like a secret that was too toxic to live inside of me but was too terrible to tell anyone.

The day before I was supposed to be sprung from the hospital, one of the doctors came by to give me a final checkup, and what I assumed would be my one-way ticket out of Dodge. It was my favorite checkup so far—I was actually happy about it. *Sure, poke me, prod me, whatever you want. Go ahead, lift up this medical gown, check it all out, take my blood. Want a urine sample? It's in the bag on the right. Sure, check my skin— swab it up, brother! No problem at all! Do whatever you want, my scrub-suited friend, just as long as you let me get the fuck outta here.* He left after running through all the tests and said he'd be back.

He returned about two hours later, and I greeted him with a huge smile.

"Katharine . . ." (Jesus, I hate it when people call me Katharine. My name is Katie. Just because it's on the chart as Katharine doesn't make it my name. Wait, that sounds weird. Anyway, I had told him my name was Katie. Ah fuck it, let him tell you what he needs to tell you.) "You have a staph infection."

"A staph infection? Like the kind people have on the news?"

"Yes, you have that same kind."

"What does that mean? I can still leave, right?"

"No. You can't leave; we need to keep you here."

"Wait, what? How long will you have to keep me here?"

"It may be a couple of days until we can control the infection. Or your doctors may want to keep you here until you're
not contagious anymore."

After everything I had been through, this was it. This was
the thing that made me lose it. I threw the kind of temper tan-
trum I didn't know I was capable of.

"What? What? What? Why? I want to leave! I have to leave!
Let me leave. I don't want to be here. No, no—don't make me
stay, don't make me stay," I screamed.

I called my mother even though I was so upset that I could
barely breathe. I was gulping for air, sobbing my fixator out of
position. She was teaching but picked up the phone anyway. I
wailed into the receiver. I told her they weren't letting me leave;
they were quarantining me. I was never going to leave. I tried
to express to her that I thought I would die without actually
saying that I was going to die. My mom told her class that she
had an emergency . . . again, and had to leave.

She told me later she had never heard me so upset in my
entire life.

I knew my mom would call my dad, so I called Warren and
told him what was going on, still in complete hysterics. By the
time I had sobbed out what had just happened, he was shocked
into silence. He literally had no words for me. Internally, I raged
at him for not being able to soothe me, for having no way to
make it better. But, honestly, what could he say to me? It was an
awful situation, to be sure, but he had no experience with anything like this. He was twenty-five years old, in love with a girl
whose problems were bigger than he could ever comprehend.
What did I want him to say, that he was going to bust me out of
the hospital? I didn't know what I wanted. I just knew I wanted
him to say the right thing. In all honesty, there was no right
thing. I put so much pressure on him to make it better, and he
crumbled under my unfair expectations. I hated that I did this

to him. All he wanted was to fix it, and all I could do was feel frustrated with him for not having the tools. We were in a lose-lose situation. After he whispered, "I'm sorry, I love you" into the phone, I said, "I know you do, I know" and hung up.

My thoughts raced in circles of despair and fear. *What am I going to do? I can't stay here, but they won't let me leave because I am diseased. I can't go anywhere. I will make everyone sick; no one will touch me again ever. I will never get to leave here. I am going to die here. I know I'm going to die here. I will never get better. They will never let me get better. I will never get better. They will never let me get better.*

Two young medical students who had been checking in on me as a part of their regular rotation found me lying there, weeping and raging. They were both about my age; one was a girl, the other a guy. They had laughed at my attempted jokes during their rounds, and they knew how desperate I was to leave. The girl was very pretty even without makeup on. She had alabaster skin, light brown freckles, and straight glossy brown hair pulled into a ponytail. She had a sweet face, and she looked me in the eye as I cried. She made me feel like the fact that my world just got fucked up was important to her.

"I know," she said. "I wouldn't want to stay here either."

I was still full-on flipping out, but suddenly I felt a little less alone.

As fate would have it, staph was all the rage in New York City at the time. People all over the city had been dying from it. Schools were closed, students and teachers quarantined. It was a full-blown epidemic. In the midst of all this hysterical bull-shit my broken ass decided that in my last week at Elmhurst Hospital I should pick it up too.

I got to leave my room for the first time in ten days, only to be rolled fifteen feet down the hall to a single room for people who had to be quarantined. After only a few hours in my new room, I realized this wasn't an upgrade. The room was completely bare and stank of disinfectant. It felt really eerie to be in this hospital room by myself. I had gotten so used to having freaks and weirdos to distract me from myself that lying there with just me and my thoughts was a new kind of hell.

In reality, I hadn't thought too much about the actual infection. All I had been thinking about was how I could fashion a gurney out of bedsheets and dinner trays to lower myself out of there. When the doctor had said staph infection, I had a flash of the local news reports I had seen. I remembered a woman on the news, with blonde hair, too much blush, and a smart suit jacket, saying the staph was really only dangerous if you were young, sick, or old. In my past life that would have made me dismiss its dangers entirely, but suddenly I fit into one of those categories—I was the sick. I changed the channel to *Wheel of Fortune* not long after seeing that news report. My life bummed me out enough—hearing about the shitty things that were happening to other people just made me sadder.

Elmhurst wasn't going to let me forget what was happening to me, though. Halfway through another mindless television show, the head of infectious diseases at the hospital and his eager brood of medical students had decided to take a field trip to see me in my new solitary confines. There were about twelve of them in a circle around my bed. They were all wearing protective gowns and caps and plastic gloves, and no one was coming too close to me. It was as though they thought my infection could jump out and bite them. They were almost all men in their midtwenties. I wondered who they really were, how they acted when they were at home, if they had any friends who looked like me. Did they wonder who I used to be? Would I even know what to tell them if they asked? Did they feel sorry for me? Did any of them even care?

The head of infectious diseases was in his midforties and had a comb-over. He started to explain to the premeds what a staph infection was. All the eager beavers standing around my single bed had studied my chart, and he questioned them about me as if I was a cadaver they had to dissect and understand. He asked them what had put me in the hospital in the first place.

A girl with a ponytail braid shot up her hand. "The patient was in a high-impact trauma accident where her pelvis was broken in five places. She had internal bleeding coming from her bladder, broke all her ribs, and punctured her lung. She has a plate in her back and also an external fixator in her, from hip bone to hip bone, to fuse her front pelvic bones back together."

"Very good," replied Dr. Comb-Over.

All these kids looked so serious. It was so weird that I was the subject they were being quizzed on. Suddenly I was the War of 1812, the process of photosynthesis, long division. Their knowledge of me was a part of what they were being graded on. It was like I was something that had happened in the past. I lay very still and tried to pretend I wasn't there. I was still pretty hysterical, but I attempted to keep it under the covers until the strangers left and my mom got there. I was saving all the hysterics for her, lucky lady.

Dr. Comb-Over then asked how I had gotten my staph infection, and a cute Indian guy raised his hand. He proceeded to explain that the metal in my stomach had attracted the infection, which I could have gotten from a number of places. He said it was most likely from a medical professional who may have been infected or had recently touched another infected person. He said that because of poor cleaning practices the infection had stayed on my skin.

Dr. Comb-Over seemed impressed and happy that his future MDs had taken the assignment seriously, but now it was his turn to show these premeds what real doctoring was all about.

"Although the infection is now only on the patient's skin, it could get into her bloodstream through the open wounds she has on the left and the right sides of her abdomen at the site of the fixator. If this disease does get into her bloodstream, the staph bacteria will produce a specific protein that loosens the 'cement' holding the various layers of the skin together. This creates blister formation and sloughing of the top layer of skin. If it occurs over large body regions, it can be deadly, similar to a large surface area of the body having been burned. It is necessary to treat scalded skin syndrome with intravenous antibiotics and to protect the patient from the dehydration that can occur if large areas of skin peel off."

WHAT. THE. FUCK.

Did he really just say that large pieces of my skin were going to fall off? Is he serious? Is this really happening? Why didn't anyone tell me this? There had been talk of pills and ointments, but there had been NO talk of blistering and peeling like a burn victim. Jesus Christ, these doctors just drop knowledge, don't they? No warning, no "We are going to freak the fuck out of you in about five minutes—brace yourself. Here's a swatch of leather. I'd recommend you bite down."

I looked at the faces of these strangers surrounding me, learning things about me at exactly the same time as I was learning them. I stared at these premeds and thought about how I used to look just like them. I had seen pictures of my face looking happy and bright and alive. I used to be one of them, but now I wasn't. I was something different, something that no one—not even Dr. Comb-Over—could explain. I was a motionless jumble of veins and bones and muscles in the shape of a girl. A girl who now might or might not have to watch her skin peel away until the world could see what was left of her, leaving her the way they were making her feel—vulnerable, totally raw, like a freak of nature.

I had visions of myself as a live *Bodies* exhibit, my face without skin, every muscle and bone laid bare on the giant billboards over the Brooklyn-Queens Expressway. The South Street Seaport Museum would become my final resting place.

I should have asked this team of professionals hovering around my bed some questions. I should have said something, but I couldn't say anything. I was too scared. Knowledge was not power; knowledge was debilitating. I wanted to be ignorant. This was much too real for me. I needed the sugarcoated information my parents doled out, the wishful thinking of my boyfriend, the false positives of my friends. This truth burned itself into my mind and heart, and I didn't want any part of it.

My mom was almost at the hospital when I called her again to cry into her ear after the swarm of premeds filed out of my room. I couldn't even wait until she got to the hospital. Nope, I had to freak her out before she even walked through the door.

"What do you mean your skin is going burn off?" my mom said on the phone. "The doctors have never said anything about that. Who told you this? Who is this person? What are they saying? I don't understand why they would say that to you. I am coming. I'll be there, Katie. It's going to be okay. I am almost there, Katie. I am almost there."

This was her way—when my heart was breaking and I was scared, she rushed to me. She came to fix me because she loved me. She wouldn't let my skin burn off. My mom won't let it burn off. She would put on cold compresses, and she would get aloe and make my skin stay on my body. I was going to be okay.

On her way to the hospital she called my dad. He said he was calling the head of the hospital, because the doctor shouldn't have done that to me without my family there. My dad called and told me I was going to be fine, that he was sure the doctor was just trying to show off his knowledge by describing a worst-case scenario to the students. The reason why my doctors hadn't told me this could happen was because it was unnecessary to scare me with that kind of information. The chances of that happening were slim to none.

*As slim as getting run over by a truck?* I thought but didn't say aloud. Instead, I said I understood and I was sure I was going to be okay. Attempting to keep the cry out of my voice, I told my dad I was glad I would get to see him in the hospital gown that he would have to wear over his clothes.

"Wait, Dad?"

"Yeah, Katie?"

"Daddy, they aren't going to let me leave. They said so. They won't let me leave. I don't want my skin to fall off, but I have to get out of here. Please."

"We are going to get you out of there, Katie. I swear to you. As soon as we can move you, we're getting you out of there. It's going to be soon, I promise."

I was sick of promises.

***

Through the window to the left of the closed metal door to my room, I watched my mom put on a disposable gown over her clothes and a cap over her hair. I watched her sanitize her hands and then put on gloves. I watched everything she had to do to separate her aliveness from my deadness. Then she entered my new sterile room, pulled a chair up to my bed, and smoothed my hair with her plastic-covered hand. My momma, my momma—she was here.

A few hours later my dad rushed into the room at an almost-run. He took out the book—his Record that was full of all my medical information, all the names and phone numbers of the people he could call. He took out his cell phone and he started to dial. I got the feeling he would call every person he had ever met who had a *Dr.* in front of their name, any person who had ever gone to a hospital charity ball. Anyone who could do anything was going to get a call from my dad, and then they would do something.

I watched him tear through that book. It now made sense to me why he had been keeping such meticulous notes this whole time. He had been saving the numbers and names of every doctor who had seen me. He had figured out the hierarchy of Elmhurst Hospital, and he went from the top down.

Every three minutes, I heard, "Hello, this is Art McKenna. My daughter Katharine McKenna is a patient here at Elmhurst. She is supposed to leave to go to Glen Cove tomorrow—we need for that to happen."

(Pause)

"Really? I don't accept that answer. Who is your superior? I need their name and number."

Then there was the click of his pen and the turning of a page. "Okay, thank you."

He called and he called and he called until he got in touch with someone who gave him an answer that provided him a foothold. They told him what paperwork needed to be filled out, who needed to sign what, and when it needed to happen.

While my dad was calling, clicking, and writing, one of the doctors from my ICU days came in. He had mistakenly given my father his cell phone number, and my dad had badgered him until he agreed to come to my room.

My dad asked him the questions about the staph infection I had been too freaked out to ask. I listened with my eyes squinted, hiding from the truth as if it was the boogeyman. What Dr. Comb-Over had not told me—or the entire room of premeds—was that it's common for anyone who is in the hospital for any period of time to get a staph infection. Staph lives on our skin all the time, without manifesting into an infection. The issue with me was twofold: 1. There was a staph epidemic right now, so everyone was supersensitive and totally freaked out (if I am going to go I should go big—why not get a staph infection when there is an epidemic?); and 2. Not too many people leave a hospital to go to another hospital; usually they just leave, so this kind of testing wasn't necessary.

"So what you are saying is this is a relatively common infection and that she doesn't have to stay at Elmhurst. Is that what you are saying?" my dad asked.

"Provided the other hospital will take her even though she has the infection, yes, she can leave."

"Will you write that down somewhere official and make it possible for her to leave?"

"Sure I will."

"Can I walk with you until you do it?"

"I am sorry, what?"

"Can I walk with you to make sure this happens? It isn't that I don't trust you; it's just that things get lost in this hospital," my dad said, looking at me.

I looked at the doctor and nodded. Things do get lost in this hospital. My humanity had gotten lost in this hospital. My joy had gotten lost in this hospital. My hope had gotten lost in this hospital. Surely he could see that I couldn't let anything else get lost.

So my dad and the doctor took off their protective clothing and sanitized themselves. My dad trailed that MD like a shadow until pen hit paper saying it was okay for me to leave, and he had been given instructions about what needed to happen so he could bust me out of my cell.

As my dad fought for my freedom, my mother took on the more difficult job of dealing with me. I was so far from being fun or understanding or willing to see this as something that could end in anything other than total disaster. She worked hard, though. She entertained me with stories of her first grade class. My mother told the best stories in the world. No detail was ever too small, no smell, no color too insignificant, no emotion left out. She would even go so far as to do impersonations of the little kids in her class, and it always made me giggle. Lying there, watching my mom stand in the middle of my hospital room acting like a six-year-old to make me happy was pretty beautiful.

Before my parents left on Thursday night, my father had spoken to about thirty people. He had gotten written okays from doctors and administrators at Elmhurst. He had called in favors at Glen Cove, and he had gotten verbal agreements from them that they would take me in. I felt like the deviant child from a wealthy family whose dad had pulled every string to get her into Princeton. All that was left to do was to get the signature of Mary the social worker at Elmhurst, and I was free.

My dad bought beers from the bodega around the corner from the hospital. He took Styrofoam cups from the nurses' station and poured all three of us drinks. We drank quickly and quietly so as not to disturb any of the careful plans we had laid out for the day ahead.

*** 

The next morning my father arrived at the hospital at 8:00 a.m. to get the last signature, from the social worker. She wasn't due in until 9:00 a.m., but he was as anxious to get me out of there as I was, and he thought he was better off being early. My parents hated having me there. It literally hurt them to see me in a place where I was being ignored and was so unhappy. They hated that they couldn't control what was happening to me.

There had been nothing they could do for me until now, but today they were using every weapon in their arsenal to get me out.

Dad sat tensely next to my bed as he drank his coffee. He had brought me a doughnut with chocolate frosting and a Diet Coke for breakfast. There were few things that made me more joyful than seeing my health-conscious parents come into a room bringing junk food and soda for my little emaciated self to eat. Oddly enough, the fact that my mom and dad were willing to go outside the norm of responsible breakfast food made me feel particularly loved. I drank my Diet Coke and licked the frosting off the doughnut, chewing the fall-themed sprinkles. They were orange, crimson, and brown, and a few of them were in the shape of leaves.

We didn't put on the TV that morning. We needed to have our wits about us for my escape. At 8:55 a.m., my dad left my room and went searching for Mary. Alone in my room, I lay in my single bed and thought about how my life was going to change when my dad walked back in. In all my excitement, though, there was another emotion that found its way into my consciousness: fear. I didn't *know* that this next hospital was going to be any better than Elmhurst. I knew that my family had told me it was going to be better, but how did they know? What if it was worse? I was pretty sure nothing could be worse, but I didn't really trust anything anymore. I used to speak in such definitive terms. I was so sure about so much—but now I had trouble having faith in the idea of a better hospital. I had trouble having faith in anything. After all, hope had landed me in quarantine.

I believed in God, in angels, and, for far too long, the tooth fairy. I used to believe in the goodness of people, and that everything happened for a reason. Now I couldn't find it in myself to think like that; I must have lost the ability somewhere within these linoleum walls.

My dad came back to the room at 9:45 with all the paper-work in hand but no signature. He couldn't find Mary. She was in the hospital, but he couldn't find her. He gave me this update and then went to search some more. Tears welled up in my eyes. It wasn't going to happen. I was never going to leave. I felt like they were torturing me. It was the entire hospital against me. Suddenly, I was in a thriller, watching my chances for safety and freedom dance and flutter in my hand, and then as I went to close my hand around them, they would jump out of my fist. Had I been too cocky? Too hopeful? Did it serve me right for thinking this would work out? Was God punishing me, or was He just testing my faith?

I gave my dad a tight smile and said it was going to be fine. My heart filled with bruised hope. My eyes filled with tears. I believed in him. He was strong, smart, savvy, and charming. I had faith in him and what he could do. My belief in my father was stronger than my fear of this hospital prison. He could do this.

I just had to have faith, so I prayed. I prayed to God and angels and dead relatives. I whispered every prayer I had ever heard. I begged Jesus to let me leave, for this to somehow be okay. *Please let me leave here. I need to leave. I need to live, please.* I prayed and prayed and prayed.

\*\*\*

In the weeks since I had been admitted to the hospital, many people wanted to talk to me about my faith. They wanted to know if I felt stronger about God now that I had been "saved." For their sake I said that I did—that I couldn't believe how lucky I was that God had spared me. I didn't want them to know what was actually going on in my head. I thought that God had forgotten me. The accident made me lose faith, not gain it. The pain that I was in was unbearable, and it never stopped. It was like living in a pain hurricane—it hit me from all angles. I used to be able to run a mile in five minutes and eighteen seconds. Now I couldn't even lift my legs. What kind of God would let that happen to a nice girl like me?

I tried to go on a break from God for a few days. I decided to give him the silent treatment. I got through the day just fine, but, like a needy girlfriend, I was still praying to him every night. He was the only person I knew would be up, and even though I was mad at any God who would let this happen to me, I was grateful to have someone to talk to (even if it was just in my head) about the things I didn't want to say out loud. God offered me comfort even when I felt let down by him. I couldn't stop myself from praying.

***

Two hours later my dad came back into the room, victorious. He had found her. He had combed every floor, asked anyone who worked at the hospital where she could potentially be, and gone there. Finally he found her and coerced her into signing my release papers. She later came into my room and asked me, "Do you really want to leave us?" I said, "Yes, yes, I would really like to." "Why?" I shrugged, not being bold enough to say, "Because this place is a hellhole."

By the time the paper was signed, there were new nurses and doctors on duty, so the people who had been scheduled to check me out were already gone for the day. My dad had to find an entirely new group of people to be made aware that I needed to be checked out. I don't know why I had a hope that these people would care. That somehow, everything would change and I would become a priority.

It didn't happen.

As the hours crawled by and I stared down the barrel of another weekend in this hospital of horrors, helplessness became a different feeling altogether. It was no longer something I could understand as the product of a wrong turn or of broken bones and mushed-up insides. It became a life I was now doomed to. I was never going to be able to break out of this awful place. I had the feeling I was trapped, and no matter how hard my family fought for me, we were powerless, helpless, and broken. I felt like a seahorse that had died and been washed onto shore. I was a shrunken shell of myself, light as air and still looking the same as if I was alive.

My mother arrived at the hospital at three o'clock, joyfully ready to help with my transfer, but instead she walked into a scene where I was hysterically crying and my dad was in the hallway screaming at the nursing staff. I needed to get into the ambulance before six that evening, or else Glen Cove would not take me. There wouldn't be anyone in the hospital to admit me. Finally, at four o'clock, one kind woman took the time to bring over the paperwork and sign everything that needed signing.

I was too scared to think about what would happen if I didn't make it to the other hospital on time. I was terrified that things would either get worse once they knew I really wanted to leave, or that we would just have to go through the entire process again with the same results. I didn't truly believe I was actually going to get out of there until my parents and the nurses began to cover me in blankets and coats. They wrapped me up like the baby Jesus in swaddling clothes, until only my eyes were showing. My mom and dad held the bags of everything I had with me in the hospital. The cards and gifts, the little blanket I couldn't sleep without. They looked as scared as I felt. We didn't know what to expect. I picked up a card I had been given by a friend that played a song when you opened it. As we went down the hall, I looked at both of my parents and smiled, then opened the card. Gloria Gaynor's voice belted out "I Will Survive," and I kept the card open as I said good-bye to every person I saw in the hallway. We laughed in spite of ourselves.

The doors slammed open as my gurney was pushed through. I couldn't believe how crisp and beautiful the air was. It felt and smelled incredible. I had forgotten that a season had passed without me. I didn't ever want to close a door again. I just wanted to breathe and breathe and breathe and have the air land on my skin and clothes and make me feel new and fresh and perfect. Had I always breathed this air this time of year? How had I not known how delicious it was? How was that possible?

With every step the EMTs took out of Elmhurst, I felt lighter. That place was so toxic; it was like I had been deep-breathing sludge—a sludge composed of insignificance and self-hatred, of fear and agony. But now the people who had tried to poison me had lost. I'd gotten out. The worst had to be over. I was leaving, moving toward a new experience, toward being a real girl again, and it made me feel like I had been reborn. It felt good.

The EMT who had to lift my gurney into the back of the ambulance was capable of doing it himself, but my dad insisted on helping. He also had had enough of other people doing the wrong thing. It was time for all of us to take matters into our own hands.

Once in the ambulance, the EMT locked the wheels into the floor and made sure I was tightly strapped onto the gurney. I rode alone because there was no room for my mom and dad in the back, plus it just wasn't safe. I needed the time to myself anyway. I lay there quietly and thanked God and my dead relatives and the angels and Mary and Jesus for letting me leave that penal hospital. I promised to be a better girl, to be happier and sweeter. I would be a girl who had hope and love, and I would try harder. My prayers had been answered, so now I owed the world the person I promised I would be.

# PART II

# Putting Your Pieces Back Together

# CHAPTER SIXTEEN

# Indulged

The first order of business when they wheeled me into Glen Cove Hospital on the gurney was to weigh me. I thought they were joking. How would they weigh me if I couldn't stand on a scale? The answer: they were going to put me in a huge tarp that was connected to a rope that was connected to a scale standing to the left of my hospital bed. In other words, in the same way they weigh whales. I knew they had to do it. I just wished it could have been the next morning, or—I don't know—never. Couldn't they just say thinner than normal? That seemed scientific enough.

Conor had met my parents at Glen Cove to help me get settled in. They all stood by my bed and held my hand for as long as they could. The orderly lifted up my left side first and slipped the tarp under my body. The cloth was bunched up and wedged underneath me until the orderly came to the right side of the bed and lifted me up to pull it through. I started to cry. I wasn't only crying because I was in pain and because I was exhausted, but because I was beginning to realize that I would be coming in contact with an entirely new group of people who would have to see that I was completely incapable of taking care of myself. I couldn't even lift my shoulders up to help.

The orderly linked a carabiner to the rope that was slowly lifting me up from my bed. He called out my weight: one hundred ten pounds. What? I hadn't been one hundred ten pounds since the ninth grade. I teetered between disgusted that I had lost so much weight and kinda happy I was so thin. I knew it was a fucked-up way to think, but five years of being on the chubby side had clearly warped my perspective.

After the orderly left, I looked at my parents' faces, and for the first time I saw everything they had been through. They looked so tired, so sad, so disillusioned. They just wanted the nightmare to be over, for things to be all right. I could see that they were aching for normalcy—maybe even more than I was.

They sat in chairs on either side of my bed, and we told each other how much better this hospital was than Elmhurst. How we just knew it was going to be a completely different experience. I said how happy I was to be here, and we all commented on how nice the place was. There were Thanksgiving decorations on the hospital walls! There was greenery outside the window! Things were going to be wonderful here, we knew it, we just knew it. As good as I felt about this change of scenery, though, I broke down in tears after they left. I just didn't want to be alone again.

Loneliness had been an occasional side trip for me before the truck ran me over. Now it was the place where I lived. It was empty and bottomless. I think it sprang from knowing that every time someone came to see me, they would have to leave by 8:30 p.m. I hated the way the sound of white sneakers on linoleum floors was the universal soundtrack of evenings at the hospital, the gentle reminder that visitors' hours were ending. It didn't matter which hospital. It got harder and harder to be left. Every visit was tainted with that knowledge. Every hello made me more and more aware of the impending good-bye.

I felt like no one would ever understand what I was talking about, and I didn't think I could ever express it to them. I wasn't mad at them for leaving; I understood. I really did. They needed to take care of themselves. They needed to sleep, and they needed to eat, and they needed to sit in chairs that were not composed of squeaky plastic. They needed to go home and live their own lives.

And now my life consisted of staying here and getting well. They couldn't take me with them. This was where I belonged for now. This was my home, and that fact, more than anything else, devastated me. I didn't want to belong here. I didn't want for this to be the better version of awful. I didn't want to be strong. I didn't want to be made into a better person. What I wanted to do was jump out of my bed and run out the front door into the night that had been so cold and delicious on my skin only hours before. I wanted to wipe my mind clean of this hurt and of this life. I wanted to be the one to leave the room.

***

The first morning at Glen Cove I was awoken at six a.m., by a beautiful Jamaican woman.

"Give me your finger, sweetheart," she said gently.

I obliged, not speaking, not questioning. I had given up trying to understand why anyone was doing what they were doing. I was just one of the morning chores, like checking e-mail.

She pricked my finger, and I watched my blood turn into a ruby-red bead on my fingertip. She placed a tiny plastic tube on my finger and it sucked my blood up like a mosquito. I winced, and tears welled in my eyes. Anything could start the waterworks in the mornings. The process of remembering where I was, why I was there, and why I couldn't walk was exhausting and made me feel even more sensitive.

Yet when this nurse saw the tears filling my eyes, she touched my face with her latex-gloved hand and said, "It's okay. It's going to be all right. No need to cry. You don't have to cry."

Which, of course, made me cry more. I mumbled through my tears that I was sorry.

"You don't have to be sorry, sweetheart," she said as she put a cotton swab on my finger and wrapped it in medical tape to stop the little trickle of blood. "I just don't want to be the reason why you're crying first thing in the morning," she said through a smile.

I smiled back at her and said, "Thank you. I'll try not to cry next time, but I can't make any promises."

This was the nicest interaction I had had with a hospital person who was not a doctor in the last four weeks. I felt a warmth spread all over me even before I pulled my sheets up to try to go back to sleep.

I woke up an hour later, my body screaming at me for putting it through so much movement the day before. It was pissed, and it was letting me know all about it. "Could you not have jostled so much? Why did you need to twist your body then? Couldn't you have just said no to the weird weighing machine?"

I had no good answer or reason for why I had let all these awful things happen, so my body decided that I needed to be taught a lesson with its favorite punishment—absolutely outrageous pain. I pressed my call button and was shocked when a nurse appeared at my door just a couple minutes later, kindly asking what she could do for me.

"Do you think that I could please have some pain medication?"

I braced myself for her reply. Maybe because I had just been checked in, because I had gotten medication last night, it wasn't time, they needed to call the doctors at Elmhurst to get the okay to give it to me. But there was no pushback. There was no fighting. There was no dismissive tone. There was only "I will go get that for you, just give me a minute."

"Thank you so much. I really, really appreciate it," I called out to her back as she walked out of the room.

When she returned three minutes later with a plastic cup containing two little pills and a small cup full of water just for me, I felt such deep love for this woman I thought my heart would explode.

"That was so fast. Thank you for getting that so quickly. Thank you so much."

"No problem. Is there anything else you need?"

"Do you think that if you have a minute, you know, either now or later, if it isn't too much of a bother, could I please have a cup of ice chips?"

"Of course, I'll go and get that for you right now. Do you want some fresh water too?"

"That . . . that would be great," I stammered. "Thank you so much."

I was as effusive in my gratitude when she came back into the room with the ice chips and water. She cocked her head at me and said, "You know, you don't have to thank me like that, right? This is my job. It really is no problem, I promise. This is absolutely no trouble. Okay?"

"Okay." I smiled as I drank my water and crunched on my ice chips.

When she walked out I felt myself exhale for what seemed like the first time in four weeks. Even through my broken ribs, it felt really, really good.

\*\*\*

My mom and dad had been on edge for the entire time I was in Elmhurst. They hadn't felt safe while I was there, and they were like watchdogs every minute. When I arrived at Glen Cove, they could finally breathe too. They knew I would be protected and they could take a bit of a break.

"Katie, how would you feel about us going up to Vermont for two days?" my mom asked a couple of days after I had been transferred to Elmhurst. "It would be a really short trip, and we would only be four hours away. A hop-skip away from here, honestly," she reassured me, pausing awkwardly, before continuing, "If it's not okay with you, then we don't need to go. But we would really like to. . . ."

I couldn't believe they were asking for permission from me to go away without supervision.

"Of course you can go!" I said. "You don't need to ask me—you're the grown-ups! It will be so nice for you guys to get away. Will you do me a favor, though?"

"Yes, Katie, anything!" my dad replied.

"Would you mind bringing me back some colored leaves? Red and orange are my favorite."

They nodded and promised me some maple syrup too.

"I hope you guys have a lot of fun together. I'm sure it's going to be a great weekend."

I was terrified.

They set up a rotation of family members to visit and take care of me in their absence. I was happy for them to get a break, but the idea of them being far away from me kicked my anxiety into high gear. Even though I felt comfortable in this new place, it was still a hospital full of strangers. I was afraid they would turn on me at any moment. My ability to trust anyone had been stripped away by Elmhurst, and I was unnecessarily wary of every person in scrubs or a white coat.

Mom and Dad were headed for Vermont on Saturday morning. They called before they left and told me the rotation of people who were coming in to see me. My brother would be here on Saturday morning, my boyfriend on Saturday afternoon and evening, my aunt on Sunday morning, and my boyfriend again that afternoon. They would be back on Sunday evening and would be calling periodically to check in on me. On Friday evening they had looked so excited, as well as a little bit guilty. It was the way I had felt the night before I left for college for the first time, when I chose going out with my friends instead of hanging out with my family. I was so happy to be with my friends and live in that moment in between being a child and an adult, but I felt guilty I wasn't spending my last childhood evening with my parents. Now, lying in my hospital bed, I felt like my parents must have felt then: I was thrilled for them to have that time together, to be able to take care of themselves, and to make themselves happy, but sad I wasn't going to have them near me. I felt more like a child than I had in sixteen years. A little nine-year-old girl worried about missing her mommy and daddy, caught in the body of a twenty-five-year-old. I didn't dare cry until I knew they were down the hallway, though.

After my parents left, I started to freak out about what could possibly happen. I calmed myself with the idea that by now I had a pretty good handle on what was wrong with my own body, which was true. What I didn't have a handle on was how much my body liked to constantly keep me guessing. Just as I thought I understood it, there would be a new surprise ailment that messed my whole world up. One where I would need my parents to save me, but for the first time since the accident they wouldn't be able to.

At Elmhurst there had been no focus on what was happening day to day. No questions about how I was going to become a functioning person. There, they were more focused on the first act of triage: take care of what needs to be done for this person to stay alive. Do your best not to let this person die, and then, when they are well enough, move them out.

Glen Cove was not concerned about whether I would live or die. They knew I would live. Their responsibility was to reintroduce me to the world. By the time I arrived at Glen Cove, I had lost interest in eating. My stomach always hurt, and I felt full all the time.

That Saturday, I tried to eat some of the Frosted Flakes the orderly had so nicely brought me. I ate four bites and drank a little bit of orange juice, and immediately I felt as if I was going to be sick. I tried to fight it. I clenched my teeth and I stared at the ceiling, telling myself the same thing I had told myself every time I'd ever felt sick in my life: "You will not throw up. You will not throw up. You will not throw up. You will not throw up. You will not throw up."

It was my sick-girl mantra.

In hindsight, it was kind of adorable that I still thought I had any control over my body. Everything that had happened in the last month should have made it abundantly clear there was nothing in this situation that was mind over matter. The bod is saying, "I am going to throw up." Fuck it, sister, all the chanting in the world is not going to stop your stomach from lurching and you from vomiting all over your hospital gown. Get over yourself.

What made throwing up so much worse in this new life was that I had no stomach muscles left; they had all atrophied. The usual way one would throw up would be to clench your stomach muscles and allow your organs to reject what you had put in your body. I still felt the lurch and then the vomit creeping up my throat, but I wasn't able to get it to go anywhere. Instead I just made a series of strange noises:

Hueh. (Only midway up the esophagus.)

Hueh, hueh. (This time about three-fifths of the way there.)

Huuu-eeehhh, hueh. (Still at that three-fifths mark.)

Huuuuuu-eeeeeeeehhhhhhh, huuuuuuu-eeeeeeeeeeeeeeh, hueh, hueh. (Got it done.)

And then I just had to lie there with my breakfast and bits of my dinner dripping down the front of my hospital gown.

I pressed the call button and cried in the same amazed and confused kind of way I had when I was little and had thrown up. It wasn't as though I hadn't known it was coming. I knew what was going to happen, but the process of watching food that you had just put into your mouth suddenly be rejected threw me for a loop. It was like reality had been turned inside out. I felt a horrible awkwardness, layered with the pain from exhausted muscles that had not been used in a very, very long time. On top of that, the pushing I had done on my stomach had shifted Roberto and made him very unhappy.

I tried to control my tears as the vomit cooled on my hospital gown. A nurse's aide walked into the room in brightly colored scrubs.

"What happened, sweetheart?"

"I got sick. I don't know why. I'm sorry for making a mess, I'm really sorry."

"No, no, it's fine. Let's get you cleaned up."

She fetched warm paper cloths and helped me wash off my face and neck and changed me into a new hospital gown. She was gentle and kind and looked sympathetic as I peeled off the filthy gown and winced at the sight of myself. I felt better in clean clothes and new sheets. She brought me a ginger ale and some pain medication and told me a nurse would be in to see me soon.

When the head nurse came in a few minutes later, she sat down in the chair next to me with a pad of paper and a smile.

She asked me questions about what I had eaten and whether any of the medications I had taken that morning were new. Had I ever had a reaction where I felt as though I was going to throw up before? I told her no, this was the first time I had thrown up, but I had been feeling sick to my stomach a lot. Then she started to ask me when was the last time that I voided. (Weird medical speak for pooped.)

"Um . . . maybe October 1, the day before the accident."

Shock crept over her face.

"That's a month! They weren't worried about this at the last hospital?"

"No, they never really brought it up. I guess they were more focused on other stuff. Resetting my bones—things like that."

"Katie, this needs to be taken care of immediately. It is awful for you and for your digestive tract. The reason you're throwing up is because your body can't process any of the food you're putting into it. The food just has no place to go. You need to get nourishment, and if you aren't keeping down anything you eat—we will have a real problem."

"So what do we have to do?"

"We are going to give you an enema, and hopefully after that you will be able to void."

"But I can't sit on a toilet. How will I do that. . . ."

"We'll get you a bedpan and you will just be able to take care of it in your bed."

WHAT?!?!?!??!?!?!?!?!

"I'm sorry, what?"

"It's fine, Katie. This is just something that happens in the hospital all the time. It's nothing to be embarrassed about. Everyone understands."

Sure, everyone here understands, but I don't. I don't want to understand.

There have been certain things I have had to tell myself are acceptable. I have had to say that it is okay for strangers to see every part of my body. I have had to say that it is normal for me to have staples from my rib cage down to my lady parts like fucking Frankenstein's monster. I have had to say that I can deal with having a bag of my urine next to me at all times—but to have to poop in a room where people are coming in and out without warning? That is just something I am not okay with.

My mind reeled at the entire process. I am going to have to turn on my side and expose my backside to another group of people who I don't know, and be aware of the fact that they are sticking something up my ass to make me shit out one month's worth of poop. Then I am going to have to sit on a bedpan, which will be filled by my moved bowels and then be taken away by another person.

I want to fucking die.

I used to be a cute girl. I used to be funny and fun. I used to have my whole life ahead of me. Does everyone know that? I can't understand this. I can't stand that this is my life.

"Do I have to do this? Sincerely. Is there any way we could put this off?"

"No, I am sorry, Katie, this needs to happen as soon as possible. There will be a few nurses coming in and taking care of the enema for you in about a half an hour."

I felt myself clench up every time I heard the sound of white sneakers on the floor. I called my parents, and their phones went straight to voice mail. I was horrified. How could they not be available when I needed them? What could they be doing? Don't they know that I am their priority? That I am the thing that matters? They shouldn't be on any road where there is the possibility they could not have phone service. I was in the middle of a bathroom emergency, and they weren't here. How selfish could they be?

I left a message with as much calm as I could muster. I laid everything out in technical terms, hoping that by me saying it all out loud like a doctor, I would be able to understand and accept this terrible turn of events.

I called my brother and begged him to stay away today. He pressed me for a reason.

"Conor, it has to do with bathroom stuff, and I just think I'll be way better off if you're not here. I will just be too embarrassed. I can't handle it. I'm sorry," I said by way of explanation.

He didn't understand, but he was kind enough to respect my wishes. He continued to call and check in with me every hour just to make sure the "bathroom stuff" was okay, though.

Warren was a tougher sell. There were some things going on that I really did not want for him to see / be around. There are some people who are cool with going to the bathroom with the door open in front of their significant other, farting in front of each other, talking about poop. I am just not one of those people. I knew there was very little in this new life that was sacred between us. He knew everything about my daily hospital life; he knew what my new body looked like; he had seen the bag of pee on the right-hand side of my bed. He had seen the gook that had been pumped out of my lungs. But, if at all possible, I would like to be able to keep poop out of our relationship. I knew I would be completely incapable of looking at him in a romantic way if he witnessed what I was going to have to do on this specific Saturday. I still had control over this one, so I begged him not to come.

"I need to be there, Katie. I told your parents I'd be there. I can't let you be by yourself all day. You'll be so sad."

"Seriously, Warren, please don't come here. Please, please, please don't come."

"Why? Why can't I come?"

"It's bathroom stuff. I would prefer not to elaborate."

"Katie, you know I don't care about any of that."

"I realize that. I know you don't care, but I do. You have already seen me at my worst, and I know in my heart that there will be no way you will ever be able to kiss me again if you come here this afternoon. Please, if you love me, you will not come to this hospital."

He was understandably angry and confused. He didn't know why I would try to keep him from being there for me. Plus, I wasn't telling him what was going on, which also seemed to freak him out a little. I just couldn't tell him. It was as if the process of having to tell him I would be spending the day trying to clean out my bowels would have stripped away the very idea that I could be attractive to him ever again. I asked him to understand and, thankfully, he eventually did.

An hour later the nurses entered my room, ready for business. I was not. I would have preferred to throw up for the rest of my life than to have this happen. I wasn't in charge, though, so I didn't really get a say in the matter. This was something that was going to happen whether I liked it or not, like having to eat green vegetables or paying a ridiculous amount of rent for a small apartment in Brooklyn. It was just the way the world was working for me now. If I wanted to get better, I had to follow the rules. I just really fucking hated the rules.

Everyone was very kind; they had warm hands and understood my discomfort, and they were sympathetic. I was told to turn on my side after I was violated by the enema and wait for something to happen. Nothing did. I was given three more enemas. The nurses said they hadn't seen something like this in a long time. My bowel was completely impacted. From what the nurses told me, three enemas in one day was pretty aggressive treatment, and all for no result.

The doctor was called, only to inform me that we couldn't do any more enemas. Now they had no choice but to disimpact me. I didn't know what that meant, but I was pretty sure I didn't want to find out. *Disimpact* sounds pretty harmless from the outset, right? It sounds kind of clinical, sure, but nothing one couldn't handle. Well, when I asked for details, things changed a bit.

One of the nurses would have to actually go up into my lower intestine and pull out my cement-like feces, with her fingers.

Kill. Me. Now.

I really started to dislike Glen Cove. Why all this attention on my bowels? I am sure there are bigger things to be concerned about, like, I don't know, blood clots, or, um, bladder infections. Maybe something about my legs? Let's deal with my legs; I can't even feel them. Why couldn't they ignore me the way they had at Elmhurst? Couldn't they just bring me food at seven a.m., twelve p.m., and five p.m., and other than that just forget about me?

God, the maxim "Be careful what you wish for" had never rung so true. Clearly I only wanted attention and care when it was convenient for me. When there was something the medical staff wanted to do to me that I didn't like, I had no interest in being attended to. It was the same sort of rationale I used when I was a little girl.

The fact that people I did not know were, once again, going to be getting up close and personal with parts I couldn't even see in a mirror was unnerving to say the least. This compounded with the knowledge that nothing in this vein had happened to me since I had potty-trained. On top of that, there was the wild and unrelenting embarrassment that there would be people who would have to do this for me. I had been able to do everything on my own. I drove long distances by myself.

I killed bugs myself. I could make the best grilled cheese in America—and now I didn't have the muscles in my body to go take a shit without assistance.

"So if I don't want this to happen I am shit out of luck?" I asked the group of doctors and nurses who had assembled in my room.

And to my surprise they actually laughed at my joke, which made me feel proud and happy. I tried to focus on that good feeling as they turned me on my side and got to work.

I didn't die, but I did scream a lot. I little-kid screamed. I screamed the way children do when they are angry and hurt and confused. When it was over, I apologized to the doctors for screaming and fell asleep, exhausted from all the worrying and the pain.

I woke up when my phone started to ring. It was my parents. They were frantic, saying they shouldn't have ever left me, that they were so sorry. I told them it was all right, that I understood, but I was shocked that I didn't really feel that way at all. I didn't understand. I had become so selfish I couldn't feel good about them not being here when I needed them. For all my talk about wanting to do everything on my own, I wasn't trying to do that at all. I had no interest in handling problems head-on. I wanted to be carried and taken care of and protected. I made no moves to shoulder this unforeseen event. I wanted them to fix it, to calm me. I refused to do it by myself. Not only that, but I began to think about different ways I could punish my parents for leaving me alone. But then I realized I had been indulging myself and behaving like a spoiled child because no one had told me not to. Everyone kept telling me I was entitled to feel what I felt, even though my feelings were selfish and shitty. I understood that I didn't want to feel those feelings anymore. I didn't like the way I was behaving, and that was a big moment for me. If I hadn't figured it out on my own,

I am sure no one else would have had the heart to explain it to me. There are very few people who would have the balls to tell a person who may not walk again to stop being such a bitch. Not having my parents around to save me reminded me that the world was bigger than my hospital room.

# CHAPTER SEVENTEEN

## Katie's First Steps

About ten days after the accident, when I was at Elmhurst, I dreamt I was running. The morning was chilly, and my face was pink and stinging from the cold morning air. The dew from the grass had seeped through the mesh of my sneakers, and I could feel the dampness on my socks. Grass clippings were stuck to my ankles. I wanted to take the blades of grass and touch them to my lips, but the dream ended too soon for me to bring them up to my mouth. My hand was in the gray zone between waist and face, blades of grass pinched between my fingers.

I woke up happy, still thinking that I was well, that I was back to being me, that someone or something had returned me to my real life. I desperately wanted to stay in that moment between dreaming and waking.

But that wasn't where I lived anymore.

I lived in between white sheets that made me itchy in places I couldn't scratch. They felt like sheets of duct tape, stiff and sweaty. I lived in a hospital room, where I had no clue what the floor looked like. Where I had already forgotten what it was like to have feeling in my legs. I had to strain to remember how it had felt to walk. Before I went to bed every night I prayed I would not dream of pretty things. I didn't want to dream at all.

Every morning when I woke up disoriented and confused about where I was, I would have to remind myself about my situation. My conversations with myself went a little something like this:

"Good Morning, Katie. You are still in the hospital. You can't walk yet. They think that you might be able to at some point, but you might not. Don't cry, don't cry, not yet, wait wait wait—it will be okay. Let's think about something good—maybe you'll get Frosted Flakes for breakfast. You love Frosted Flakes. I think Mom is coming at ten. You have about three hours until she comes. That means you can watch six sitcoms—*Saved By the Bell* is on at seven. That's in nine minutes, and it's on TBS. You can watch some CNN in the meantime; it will be good for conversations later. Visitors will think you're very smart and world-savvy with your nine minutes of news.

"Katie, *Saved by the Bell* is great. Remember when it was on every Saturday morning after the cartoons, and you felt like such a grown-up because you were watching a show about teenagers?

"See, you just got through one half hour. You can do this. The orderly is coming in with your breakfast and—YES! It is Frosted Flakes. Smile at the orderly, Katie, smile at him. It's not his fault you're here. Ask him about his daughter. It will make you feel better. See? Thinking about other people is good. It's good. You don't have to eat all the cereal, but drink the milk . . . please, just drink it. I know you want to throw it up, but you need it. Your bones, you need it for your bones.

"Ow ow ow ow ow ow ow ow ow ow ow ow ow. Breathe. Breathe. The drugs are wearing off. Press the pump. It's every six minutes, press the pump. Don't worry, I know that it's early, press it until it's time. You don't have anything else to do. Press it—it will make you feel in control.

"You can do this. Your mom will be here in two hours. It will be better then. Maybe she'll bring doughnuts, and even if you don't eat the whole doughnut you can lick the chocolate frosting off. You can do whatever you want. It's only two more hours—you can do this. Just wait a little bit longer. Things will get better."

***

I spent a lot of time waiting—waiting for something to break up the monotony that had become my life. I would search for anything to look forward to. When I woke up, even though I wasn't ever hungry, I would look forward to breakfast. After breakfast I would think about lunch. After lunch I would think about dinner. After dinner I would think about *Jeopardy*. Then I would wait for the sleeping pills, and then I'd lie awake staring at the ceiling, waiting for fuzzy sleep to come. It made me feel as though I was a sad, old person. It made me want to call my nana and tell her I loved her, that I was sorry I didn't spend more time with her. That I was sorry I didn't do more to make her life a little more interesting. But I didn't call her. I wanted to, but I didn't. This was because when I wasn't with people who were visiting me, or thinking about my next meal, I was pretty busy feeling sorry for myself. I didn't have the energy to do anything for anyone else.

***

In the beginning, the main thing I was waiting for was my move to Glen Cove, to getting out of the awful place I was stuck in. I was thinking about it, praying for it, wanting it with my entire body.

When I finally got to Glen Cove, I felt like I was staying in a five-star hotel. There were nurses there who cared about me, who worried whether I was in pain. They wanted me to be well. They touched my face gently and were sorry for me. It was heaven.

It was still definitely a hospital, with the same white sheets, the same plastic-covered pillows. But they didn't make me sweat as much, and every day the sheets felt less stiff and uncomfortable. My elderly roommates still smelled like stale corn chips, but I didn't mind the smell as much as I had at Elmhurst.

I knew that Glen Cove was not just a healing hospital where I could simply lie there and get better—they were going to make me start physical therapy. I wanted to look forward to it—I desperately wanted to want it, to be excited, but I wasn't.

Instead, I wanted to throw up.

I hated that I couldn't walk. I hated that I was helpless and listless and had no control of my body; but I hated the idea of leaving my bed way more. I had become well acquainted with the pain I was in when I was in bed. I knew what it looked like. I knew what it felt like. I knew what was hurting and why. In my bed I knew where the remote control was. I knew how far I could tilt my bed before the shock waves of pain would start, but I didn't know anything else. It had taken me weeks to get accustomed to this hurt, and I wasn't sure I could handle a new kind.

The idea of the pain was terrifying, but more than the pain I feared the doctors would be right, and maybe I wouldn't be able to walk again. I kept the hope I would be normal again tucked away in my heart. *Maybe I will be able to sit up on my own. Maybe someday I can stand. Maybe someday I will be able to walk.* That *maybe* was what I clung to. With physical therapy there was no maybe—it was either sink or swim. I wanted to crawl under the cardboard sheets and never come out again. I wanted to live in the hope, let it surround me, untested. If I had my way, I would never have to try; it would just happen. I would wake up one day, and I would be able to walk, and everything would be normal again. I would be just like Pollyanna.

In the past, failure and I had stared at each other from across the room a few times, but we did not know each other intimately. I had gotten a D+ on a test once but had never failed a class. I had never lost a huge sum of money or gotten fired from a job. I wasn't much of a gambler; I usually wouldn't do things unless I felt prepared for them. I didn't want to know what it felt like to be a failure, especially at something that used to be so basic, like walking. In my heart of hearts, I had hoped that just surviving this whole mess would get me on the fast track to recovery town, and that I could skip all the hard work that would go into being a normal person again. I wanted what I had been through to be enough, but the world wanted more from me. I was going to have to play another game, and this time it was a game I could lose.

It turned out there was no need for me to be as scared of my first physical therapy session as I had been. My therapist's name was Lou. He had an Italian last name that I don't remember now, and in my opinion no concept of the gravity of this situation. This was a big deal for me. Not just a big deal, a HUGE deal. If I did this physical therapy business correctly, it would bring me to another level of my recovery. If I didn't, I would sink into a deep, dark abyss that I wasn't sure I would be able to climb out of.

The thing that made it superclear to me that he didn't "get" what a big deal this was for me was that he was whistling. Whistling? This is not a happy occasion, friend. This is not the bridge in a country song. Are you not aware of how desperate my situation is? Don't you feel sorry for me? Aren't you worried I won't be able to do this? Get with the program: Katie + Trying to Sit + Right Now = Potential Heartbreak.

Both my parents were in the hospital room with me at the time, covered head to toe in protective garments because the staph infection wasn't completely healed yet. Everything around me was yellow—all their protective gear, the head caps, the apron-gown things. The walls and the lights in the room were all different shades of yellow. It was like being inside a box of Lemonheads. They were expectant, they were nervous, they were hopeful. I hadn't told them I was scared. I was so sick of telling them I was scared or incapable or sad—I had decided this time I would keep it to myself. I hoped somehow I would be able to pull myself up by my own bootstraps, even though I wasn't wearing boots at this exact moment, and just get it done. If the whole bootstrap thing didn't work, I had a plan B that included chickening out and then crying like a huge baby.

"Okay, Katie, you are going to sit up on your own now," Lou said to me breezily. He started to tilt the bed slowly upward, the mechanical hum lifting me closer and closer to change. With each inch toward sitting upright I became more and more aware of my rapidly beating heart and my sweating palms. It felt like I was about to go on a first date, but I couldn't text my bestie saying, *OMG—So nervy! I hope that my legs still work!!!! Xoxo Katie.*

I was almost upright when I suddenly became very aware of how my fixator looked attached to my body. When I sat upright it stuck out like a twelve-inch-wide boner coming from my belly, but there was no time for embarrassment— Lou was a man of action. He took his huge bear paw of a left hand and put it behind my shoulder blade, and then looped his right hand underneath my knees. His face was about a foot away from mine when he said, "Now we are going to sit you up." More out of habit than pain, tears sprang to my eyes as I moved. As I leaned forward, I felt a wisp of cold air on my back, and I realized that my gown was completely open in the back and that everyone in the room was going to see my ass. Before I could move my arm to at least attempt to close my gown, Lou had rotated my fragile body ninety degrees to the right. I was sitting up on the side of the bed with my feet dangling off the edge!

The room was different. I could see two corners of the ceiling at once, and I could see people walking by the open door. I was so excited! It was a new world! Then I started to feel as though I was falling to the right. "I'm falling, I'm falling," I screamed. In actuality, I had only tilted about two inches, but my equilibrium was off after a month horizontal. I had no sense of myself or my place in the world. My body couldn't process what was happening. After Lou steadied me, I waved at my parents. "Hi, I'm sitting up."

Now that I had been successful in step one, there was no going back. If I had failed, I would have been allowed to temper-tantrum my way out of this day of PT. But I hadn't failed; I had succeeded. Fuck. Me. I stared at the walker that had been placed at the right of my bed and decided it was time for us to have a chat—time for me to lay down the law with the walker, if you will.

"You are my Everest walker, did you know that? I'll bet you never thought that one day you would be the biggest challenge in a twenty-five-year-old woman's life. I'll bet you thought your whole life was just going to be assisting old people, or serving as a prop for kids to use when they are pretending to be someone's grandma. I know, I know, I didn't think we would be here either—but there you are, and here I am . . . and I think that we should just kind of go with it. I only have one rule in this new relationship—'Your front wheel brake has to be on.' I know I should have complete faith in the fact that you are not going anywhere, but I have been fooled by seemingly benign wheeled vehicles before. I feel it is necessary to tell you, if you make a move, literally one move, I will stab you with a welding iron and feel no remorse about it. . . . None."

After my little mental chat with the inanimate object, I listened carefully to Lou's instructions. I leaned over my bed and took hold of the top of the walker with my bony hands. They looked so small and fragile on the gray plastic handles. The last time I had gripped something metal this tightly was my first time on the monkey bars when I was five. My knuckles were just as white.

I gripped the walker in my hands and straightened my arms. I willed my forearms to lift my body, and with Lou's help, I touched the ground with my feet, which felt like plaster of Paris. It was as though my feet would sink into it, and then the floor would mold around them. Lou circled around, spotting me as I lowered myself into a real big-girl chair. Its back was stiff, and it was totally uncomfortable. I wondered how I had ever sat in something that didn't recline. The blood started to return to my legs, and it felt like they were waking up after I had crossed them for too long. I loved it. I loved the feeling of ANYTHING in my legs. They felt like they were a part of me again. They weren't just lifeless rag dolls attached to my torso. They had worth; they had feeling.

In that instant I stopped being so frightened of my future. Living a seminormal life became something I could wrap my arms around, something I was actually capable of achieving. I had willed myself to sit up, to stand, and then to sit again. I did that. No more waiting and hoping for wellness or happiness or mobility. I had been able to go and get it on my own. I wanted it, and I made it happen.

# CHAPTER EIGHTEEN

# Pennies and Ring Rosaries

I feel the need to take a moment here in the story—between grueling PT challenges and thrilling accomplishments—to recognize my parents in this whole ordeal. My parents are spectacular humans. You might already have guessed this. They are hilarious, kind, and energetic, and they sometimes make me want to punch myself because of the ridiculous things they say out loud. I love them with every ounce of my being. While other people felt sorry for me, I felt sorry for my parents. They got totally screwed in this situation—they were scared to death about what was going to happen to me, but they couldn't ever show it. They had to be strong and funny and positive even when there wasn't too much to be hopeful about. But even though they had gotten the shaft, they somehow found a way to be sincerely grateful, even to the point of wanting to give back to the world that had hurt them so badly.

My father kept about twenty ring rosaries in his pocket at all times. Whenever he spoke about me, he would offer one to the person he was talking to, with the caveat that they had to include me in their prayers. After I had healed and would go anywhere with my dad, people would come up to me and take ring rosaries out of their pockets or purses and say, "I've been praying for you, Katie. I'm so glad that you're well."

If Dad's lucky charms were those rosaries, my mom's were pennies. My mom and I have always loved finding heads-up pennies. They were the ultimate good luck charms. I would collect them in a jar next to my bed—trying to keep the luck as close as possible. While I was in the hospital, she felt so lucky that I was still alive, that God had saved me, that she left heads-up pennies everywhere she went—like the luck fairy. She wanted other people to feel as lucky as she did.

It isn't possible for there to be better role models on how to see things positively and the importance of giving back. Every time I see a heads-up penny, or meet someone who has my dad's ring rosary in her purse, I feel humbled by how loved I am and how I want to spend the rest of my life being the ring rosary in their pockets and the heads-up penny on their sidewalks.

# CHAPTER NINETEEN

## Physical Therapy

Just like those heads-up pennies, all my life I had wanted to feel as though someone would be able to put me into their pocket. I wanted them to keep me safe and warm and make me feel completely protected. It was what I wanted love to look like. I knew it was a lofty goal, not just literally but also conceptually. (I'm only 5'4", but I've always known that I'm not really small enough to fit in anyone's pocket.) I also knew love lived in the space where the person who loved you was at least trying to make you feel protected, warm, and cared for.

Being in Glen Cove gave me that feeling. It may have been because they were trying to make me feel all those things, or it may have been a result of previously being in a place that was so harsh that anywhere I wasn't ignored felt like heaven. But I think it was more than that. In everything the staff did for me, there was real, genuine care, even when they did things I hated. I knew in my heart this was the nasty medicine I needed to swallow to get better.

In another little Glen Cove miracle, I was given my own room only a few days after arriving. That nasty and persistent staph infection actually had an upside: because of it, I was not allowed to share a room with anyone who wasn't infected. My first roommate, a lovely Irish woman who also had staph, was moved into intensive care. So there I was in this huge room by myself, waiting for my next bestie to move in. When they told me I would be getting my own room, I was floored. I couldn't believe it—my own room just for me. I never thought I'd be this grateful for having staph. The room they rolled me into was even bigger than my bedroom in my apartment in Brooklyn. The bed was tucked into the back left corner so I had a good view of the TV and the door. It was the ideal position, in this perfect penthouse suite.

The Sunday night before my first full day of physical therapy at Glen Cove, I lay in my perfectly positioned bed, in my killer penthouse suite, hot tears dripping out of the far corners of my eyes and slipping into my ears. There was no light in the room except for a sliver peeking through the crack at the bottom of the door. Another luxury: they let me close the door here. They would ask me before they left at night if I wanted the door closed. I always did. I felt like the fanciest person in the world. I had a closed door instead of a flimsy hanging sheet. And the ultimate luxury—I was able to cry in peace. No one asking me what was wrong, no need to stifle my minisobs.

The reason for the waterworks on this night was that, while I was ready to start making progress, I was not completely ready to stare my disability in the face. And that was what PT meant. I was not ready to see that I was not the person I had been before. I wasn't ready to see that I was no longer the girl who could run a mile in five minutes and eighteen seconds. I lay in bed with the full and certain knowledge that I was going to go into this session tomorrow, and I was going to be bad at it. I had won my first battle against gravity, but getting out of bed that time was so much harder than I had anticipated. I was sure this next step in the direction of better was going to be even uglier.

Everyone hates being bad at things, after all. There is no person who meets up on game night and says, "You know what? I'm really shitty at Jenga. Let's play that!" People want to play to win, and I was no exception. I strove to be perfect, and so far in the aftermath of my accident, I'd been doing a pretty awesome job. I hadn't died. (SUCCESS!) I could still laugh at myself, and I was trying my best to keep a good attitude about my future. I was talking positively about therapy. I would say how pumped I was about being stronger. I would jibber-jabber about how I couldn't wait to get started—but suddenly all the talking ended, and the future was staring me in the face. What if I messed this up? What if everyone was disappointed in me? What if I could not do this? Then what?

I focused my blurry sights on the light under the door. When I was a little girl I hated having the light on in the hallway when my room was dark. After putting me to bed, my parents would turn off the hall light. As soon as they thought I had fallen asleep, they would turn the hall lights back on so they wouldn't have to bump around in the dark while they did all the exciting things adults did after kids fell asleep: make lunches, fold laundry, pick up toys. I would wake up when I saw the light go back on and, in a huff, stomp out into the hallway and shut it off.

Things were different now. I didn't like the dark anymore; I was grateful for the light in the hallway. It reminded me I wasn't the only person who was awake, thinking and not dreaming. I stared at the light under the door until the anti-anxiety pills kicked in and I finally fell asleep.

When I awoke the next morning, it felt like the first day of school. There was so much to do that there wasn't time to be worried. The same beautiful Jamaican woman who pricked my fingers and took my blood greeted me with a smile and asked me questions about myself and my family and about what had happened the day before. I bit my lip hard and was able to hold back my tears until she left the room.

Breakfast arrived as I watched *Saved by the Bell* reruns, and afterward the nurses' aides came in to ready me for my day. They gave me warm water and cloths to sponge-bathe my body and kindly allowed me some privacy as I washed up. After eight minutes one of them knocked on the door (oh the novelty!) and helped me get into my clothes. Another day, another stranger getting to see me naked. After I had put on my day jammies (pajama pants and one of my dad's old polo shirts that was large enough to cover Roberto), I was ready for what lay ahead. It was the first time in the hospital that I had actually prepared for Something. It felt almost like real life. Though there is nothing like fitting a travel catheter to shatter that illusion. The aide who had been helping me to dress unscrewed the bag that hung on my bed and attached a bag to my leg. Even though I couldn't move my legs, I could still feel what was happening around them. The first time that I peed with it on, I felt the same panic I did when I had accidents as a three-year-old. Now, instead of ending up in a puddle on the floor it was being held in a bag next to my ankle. Sexy! Then they took the goo-sucking machine that was still sucking all the gross stuff from the side of my body and attached it to the back of my wheelchair. Even sexier!

I was dressed, fed, and urine-bagged. What more could an invalid on the go need? An orderly helped transfer me from my bed into my wheelchair. This move—which just the other day had been my whole day's workout—was now only a warm-up.

Then she wheeled me to the physical therapy room. It strangely felt like I was being walked to school. She asked me if I was excited, if I was ready for my day, and what I had for breakfast. It was a weird exchange, but it was better than silence.

The PT room was absolutely beautiful. It had floor-to-ceiling windows, and the fall light streaming in was brilliant and golden. Outside there was a patch of oak trees whose leaves were in various stages of changing—from gold to red to brown. Every single one of them was gorgeous. I couldn't stop looking at them and thinking how lucky I was to be there. *I get to see this every day! I will know what the weather is . . . I CAN TALK ABOUT THE WEATHER AND KNOW WHAT IS HAPPENING! This is amazing.* My bedside conversation just jumped up like thirty-five percentage points. I am going to be totally knowledgeable about the outside world. This is so completely awesome. I felt the conversations running through my head: "It was pretty overcast today, wasn't it? Can you believe that sunshine? Did you get caught in that storm? Looked pretty windy!" This is going to be great.

Finally, pulling my attention away from the marvels of the outside world, I noticed the room was filled with men and women who were all much older than me. I was definitely the outlier in the room. As I was rolled in, no one talked to me, but they did talk *about* me; I could hear the whispers of the older woman: ". . . Truck . . . twenty-five . . . not sure of what will happen . . ." It was like *Mean Girls* for seniors.

My physical therapist, Lynn, was only about six years older than me, and she was still tan from a summer spent at the beach. She was a Long Islander too—sweet but tough. She reminded me of my slightly intimidating high school soccer coach. I always wanted to impress her with my skills and effort, yearning to be the perfect middle halfback for her. When I messed up, I would chastise myself on the field and apologize to her on the sidelines. I got the same tough-as-nails vibe from Lynn, but I am pretty sure that is part and parcel of being in her profession. I don't think you can be soft when you're trying to push people to relearn how to move their broken bodies. I am sure almost everyone in the room felt like I did. They were scared and unsure and worried about not being able to do what was asked of them.

When Lynn asked what had happened to me, I took on my medical tone and told her in detail what had happened and what injuries I had sustained. Her jaw dropped, and she said, "Wow, I can't believe how well you are doing. You must have been in incredible shape before this."

I beamed with pride. "I was working out a good amount. I was biking and running and just being an active New Yorker; I walked all over the place." I felt my eyes prick with involuntary tears, and I did my best to blink them back.

"And your age is really a huge benefit. What do you say today we just get you onto this mat and just try to stretch you a little bit?"

Getting out of my wheelchair and onto the mat was difficult. Anytime something new was introduced into my altered universe, I became unnerved. It had taken me so long to get used to my present reality that, when a new element came into play, my anxiety skyrocketed. I worried that anything new would be the thing that would break me. But Lynn wasn't having any of it. She hooked her arms under my armpits and guided me onto the mat. I had flashbacks of being a child and seeing my dad and uncle lifting my poor aunt Marlene in the same way, moving her from her chair into bed. I remembered not understanding why she couldn't do it herself. While this young woman was helping me to do something I used to do without thinking, I imagined what I looked like to other people. In my head I saw myself as a sack of potatoes in plaid pajama pants and a high brown ponytail.

Lying down on the mat, I looked up at Lynn expectantly. I watched as she lifted up my leg and moved my foot around. It felt as though steel ropes were being whipped against my legs. I bit my lip, hard, but I didn't scream. I didn't want to scream in front of all these old people. God, what if I gave one of them a heart attack on top of their broken hips? That would certainly not endear me to any of these mean girls.

After the "stretching" had loosened me up and made me want to kill myself, Lynn told me our goal was to rebuild the muscles in my legs. Apparently, in only one month of being stationary, a person loses five years' worth of muscle mass. Geez, why does it always work that way? So hard to get in shape, so easy to fall out of shape. So we started small: I only had to clench my quads, hold it for fifteen seconds, and then release the muscles. The first five times I tried, nothing happened. I did everything I could to make the muscles work, but they had no interest. I stared at my legs underneath my pants as I worked to make them move. It had never occurred to me to wonder about whether it would happen or not. It was as basic as eat a cookie, want another one, eat another cookie, feel full and a little guilty. Tell muscle to move, watch leg make that movement. But this time . . . nothing. My brow furrowed. I gritted my teeth. I focused all my mental energy on that one part of my anatomy—still nothing.

I looked up at Lynn with tears in my eyes. I had failed. The first thing that was asked of me, I couldn't do. I was never going to be okay. I hated myself.

"I'm sorry."

She cocked her head at me and asked me why.

"Because I couldn't do it, because I couldn't do what you asked me. I'm sorry. I'm sorry for wasting your time and for being a mess. I feel embarrassed. I'm sorry."

"Katie, I didn't expect you to be able to do it yet. You have nothing to be embarrassed about, and you have absolutely nothing to be sorry about. As long as you try then I am so happy with you. Reconnecting with your body and just reminding your muscles of the way they used to behave is a good thing. Don't be so hard on yourself! For right now, just trying is all that we expect from you."

After my aunt's accident, she was severely brain damaged. She didn't talk like herself, she didn't look like herself, and her new life didn't make sense to her either. She did not have the mental ability to comprehend everything that had happened. It had been her will to live that had pushed her through the initial trauma, and her sheer determination to recover that pulled her out of a nine-month coma. When she gained consciousness, she didn't have the mental acuity to handle the physical therapy that she desperately needed to relearn how to walk. When she came home, her family worked with her, and she made the most progress. She was even able to walk around the house on her own. She was still unstable, but she could walk. It was very hard work, though, and sitting in the chair was so much easier. My dad believed at some point she just quit on herself. She stopped trying, and from then on she didn't get up out of her chair without help from another person. My aunt Marleen lost her chance to live a life with some freedom, because she wasn't able to try anymore.

As Lynn and another therapist helped me sit up, I looked around the room and took the time to notice I was sitting up. I was almost fully sitting up, not on my own, but I was up nonetheless. It was something I hadn't been able to do a week ago. I felt like a tadpole watching its tail shrink.

As a different orderly wheeled me back to my room, he asked me about therapy—how it went, what I thought about my therapist, if I was in any pain. I answered all his first-day-of-school questions with enthusiasm, really enjoying the feeling of my upright body whizzing (okay it just felt like whizzing, I am sure it was at a very safe and careful pace) down the halls. I took everything in. My previous trips down hospital corridors were from a horizontal position, which made staring into other people's rooms pretty difficult. Now that I was able to move my neck a full 180 degrees, I was looking in every door that had foolishly been left open.

I saw rooms filled with flowers and rooms with no indication that a living soul knew that the patient was there. There were soap-opera romances unfolding on television screens in every other room. I saw patients lying down. I saw some with walkers, some in wheelchairs. I got a glimpse into other people's lives. Lives that looked a little like mine, except with more wrinkles and decidedly cuter therapy clothes.

Back in my bed, I felt an old familiar pain, like the pain I used to feel after a long-distance run. Back then I liked it because even though it hurt, that pain let me know that I had pushed myself as far as I could go. It felt like I had done something good for my body and for my mind. I had the same feeling that day. In this new reality, moving from my bed to a chair three times and then attempting to move my leg muscles five times was the equivalent of a five-mile run in the past. Still, I felt a little more like the person I used to know.

I couldn't worry about what was going to happen next or if it was going to hurt or if I was making progress fast enough. I was in uncharted waters. There were no maps except for those that had been drawn up when I was a baby. From now on, I would have to draw a new map about how I moved around. It was going to be shitty. The results weren't going to be as dramatic and as instantaneous as I would want them to be, but I knew that no matter what, I wasn't going to quit on myself. That fact alone made me feel safe and comfortable and loved.

# CHAPTER TWENTY

## *Jeopardy*

Alex Trebek became a large part of my life during the month of November. I had never really been interested in the game show he hosts. I found Alex pompous. He always acted like he knew the answers; of course, it didn't hurt that he was holding the answer cards. He was unlike the other game show hosts—there was nothing about him that was innately likeable. I didn't want to hang out with him the way I did with Pat Sajak or Bob Barker, but man, while I was lying in that hospital bed at Glen Cove, did I love *Jeopardy.*

My parents would come every evening at about 6:45 with a bottle of wine and plastic wineglasses they had sneaked into the hospital. It was our own little happy hour. Sometimes other people would come too. My boyfriend or my brother Conor would stop by. Sometimes friends who were on Long Island for the weekend would come in for a visit. We would kiss and hug hello, and they would pull up their chairs and pour the wine into their glasses and mine into a plastic cup so you couldn't tell that I was drinking alcohol. (Even though we knew it wasn't bad for me, it was still an awkward conversation with the nurses when I got caught.) We would chat as the six o'clock evening news was wrapping up (usually with a heartwarming story to finish off the hour so that the viewer wouldn't leave thinking the world was a heartbreaking and awful place . . . because look, there were puppies and butterflies and things that made the world beautiful). I appreciated that about the evening news, tying everything up in a "life isn't so bad" bow.

But all talking ceased when those melodic *Jeopardy* tones rang out, followed by "This iiiiiiiiiis *Jeopardy,* with your host Alllllllllllllllllllex Trebek"—only hospital-visiting virgins would continue to talk after that point. I had made the rules pretty clear: discussion was saved for commercials, and everyone complied, because I was a cripple. To be honest, the Katie-imposed silence game was not appreciated by some of my guests. They had made a lengthy trek to this hospital, probably in traffic, after a long day at work, and they wanted to talk—unfortunately it didn't happen that way between 7:00 and 7:30. They were in my world now. I wasn't a total tyrant; if they wanted to say something to each other, notes were allowed, or they could go into the hallway, which was festively decorated with turkeys, Indians, and pilgrims, and continue their conversation. Nothing was going to get in between me and hearing questions in the form of answers and answers in the form of questions.

I watched intently as the announcer revealed the names of the contestants, where they hailed from, and what they did. Then I would decide who I was going to root for, based on very objective criteria like, did I like their outfit? Where did they live? Did I know someone I liked from there? Were they nerdy and adorable, or were they a little too stuck-up? Were they the underdog? Did it seem like they'd need my support that evening? Once my contestant was chosen, I put my game face on.

I was ready to yell incorrect answers to every question that Alex was going to throw out during the next thirty minutes.

I am not what one would call "smart," per se. I got pretty good grades in school because I worked really hard at it. My brothers were the smarties; my sister worked even harder than I did, and her grades were proof of that. I was better than average in school, but I never dazzled anyone with my brilliance—other than the summer I taught my five-year-old campers how to make their own Play-Doh. I wasn't too interested in school or facts. I was far more fascinated by the way people interacted with one another. I couldn't tell you who the ninth president of the United States was, but I would be able to remember the story you told me about the time your red-headed cousin, Erin, got a marble stuck up her nose and the method your aunt used to get it out (olive oil and prayer). For this and many other reasons, *Jeopardy* should not have been my game. *The Price is Right* was more my intellectual speed. But for some reason, while I was in those four walls of Glen Cove Hospital with Roberto as my only constant companion, I absolutely loved that show.

Everyone in the room played along—I don't blame them, it was either play or not talk at all (unless they wanted another of my death stares). As soon as Alex began to ask the easy questions at the beginning, we were all at the ready, hearing the answer and thinking of the question. It made me feel good to use my brain, even if the question I confidently told my friends and family was wildly wrong. It felt like brain exercise. After a day of working on rebuilding my muscles, it was my little brain workout. This was as close to educational therapy as I was going to get. The pain was still so bad that I couldn't concentrate on reading. The words on the page were not as distracting as the flashing lights in the television. I had really hoped I would be able to read while I was in the hospital and become a smarter person. I had imagined myself reading all the books that people had ever recommended to me. I would devour the classics, from Shakespeare to Dickens to Proust. I would be brilliant. I would be able to drop literary allusions into my everyday speech. Unfortunately, anytime I picked up a book in my hospital bed, the effort of making the words turn into images and stories proved to be more than I was capable of. Instead I would flip on the television and watch another rerun of *Designing Women*.

And the best thing about my choice of educational therapy was there was no punishment for a wrong answer. No points were deducted, and there were no disappointed looks, just a cheer of "Oohhhh man, so close!" no matter how off base your answer was.

But, of course, being right rocked. The rush of pride, the accolades, the respect. . . . It was delicious, and it happened for everyone. There were congratulations and *wows* and impressed high fives. The correct answer would then be discussed during the commercial break. *How did you know that? Where did you learn that?*

*Jeopardy* erased the awkwardness that could sometimes come with these visits, because it gave all of us access to easy conversation. We didn't have to talk about me or about what was happening in real life or what surgery or step would be next. We could just talk about how my mom knew the capital of New Zealand. We were all very present in that half hour, and we were all the same. It didn't matter that I couldn't walk; it didn't matter that I was hurting; it didn't matter that my mom was tired from work or that my brother had a group project for business school. We were all just right there—waiting for the next answer, struggling to figure out the question. We were all even. I could play the same way they did. And I could forget about myself, and so could everyone else, for that blissful thirty minutes every day.

# CHAPTER TWENTY-ONE

## Mackers

Some areas of a hospital are always a flurry of activity. People are running around, doors are opening and shutting, gurneys are rolling up and down hallways. It had certainly been like that at Elmhurst. At Glen Cove everything was so quiet. It was like I had suddenly moved from Times Square to Cooperstown, where all they had to offer was the Baseball Hall of Fame, and even that wasn't too exciting.

In a way the hush was nice; when you're trying to heal, it isn't really necessary to hear people crying, or machines beeping, or medical staff yelling in five different languages about what the others had done wrong. In another way it bored the crap out of me. I knew there wasn't a need, but there was a want. Now that I was feeling better, I missed the excitement, though. I wanted something interesting to happen, something that was real—not just something I saw on TV.

One afternoon, in the pocket of time between my last therapy session and my parents' visit, I noticed the nurses acting strangely. They were checking in on me a lot more than normal. They kept asking me if I had gotten any phone calls, making sure I was still in my bed. *Nope I'm cool—no phone calls, and as long as my legs are opting not to cooperate, I am pretty sure I'll be in this bed for a long time.* It was as though those nurses knew something important I didn't. My imagination had been running wild for the last several weeks, thinking about what was happening in the world outside my hospital room. Suddenly, I was wondering what was going on inside my own hospital room.

It was a mid-November afternoon, and deep gray clouds covered the sky, threatening rain. I imagined it was probably pretty cold out there too. In real life I had no idea what it felt like outside. It was just a yucky day—the kind of day that used to make me shiver at my desk and dream of being back in my apartment with a blanket pulled up to my chest, watching TV. It was hard to imagine I dreamed so much of doing just this. Well, be careful what you wish for, and all that. Right then I could only hope someday to be so tired and sick of being busy that I would actually crave being in my bed again. I wondered if I was building up a reserve of rest so I would never be sleepy again. Like, if I had a big night out I wouldn't need to go home and rest because I could just dip into my savings account of energy. I had been making some serious deposits in the last couple of months. Just as I was contemplating what the rates on a rest/sleep bank would be and if I would need an ASM card (automatic sleep machine), three nurses came into my room together and told me I should plan on transferring to my wheelchair. This was unprecedented. We never veered from the schedule.

Once in my chair, the nurses placed a blanket over my legs so I wouldn't get cold on the little excursion we were about to embark upon. They wheeled me into the hallway and there were all these old ladies in the hall with nurses behind their wheelchairs. Something was clearly going on, and it looked like the nurses had kept it a secret from everyone because all the ladies were gabbing to one another, wondering if anyone knew what was happening. The nurses just smiled and wouldn't answer any questions. I didn't ask either. I loved the suspense too much.

Then I saw four men in black walking down the hallway. I couldn't quite make out their outfits or what they were holding, but my ears solved the mystery. I heard the first few lines of "Guantanamera" as they pulled musical instruments from behind their backs and walked toward me. It was a full mariachi band, wearing the bolero suits and sombreros. My nurses backed me into my hospital room as these four strangers followed me in. I was shocked, laughing and crying all at once. I stared at them in complete wonder. They were here for me— they were playing just for me. I felt like I was on the subway going downtown on a Saturday afternoon. I let myself forget where I was, and I was transported to the 2 train—the fake wood interior, the plastic brown-and-orange seats, the subway poles. I pretended they were playing for dollars and not just to entertain me.

I tried to keep myself from laughing because I knew how much it would hurt if I did, but I felt so joyful, I could barely contain it. *Who did this?* I wondered. *Who would have thought of this brilliant gift of joy?* They played three more songs as my hallmates crept closer and closer to the door, watching and listening, some of them clapping along. When they were finished, everyone applauded, and then the men said in thick Spanish accents, "Feel better, Mackers. We love you. Love, Malesy and Scrub."

They made their good-byes rather stoically; I think because they were still a little confused by the whole setting and maybe because I had no money to tip them with, but it didn't matter—Malesy and Scrub. For fuck's sake. I would have never guessed it was them in a million years. Chris Male and Michael (Scrub) MacGilpin were my two best guy friends from college. They were the guys I would go to when I wanted to drink a beer at eleven a.m. and the guys I went to when my heart was broken. They were equal parts hilarious and kind. I was completely amazed at this unbelievable stunt. A card and a phone call would have been more than enough, but not for those dudes.

It had been a long time since I had cried tears of pure joy. They felt so different. They even tasted different—not as salty, a little sweeter. I asked the nurses if I could have some time to myself before I got back into my bed, so they left me in my chair and closed the door. As soon as it was shut, I let myself laugh and clap, and I just looked upward toward the God that let all of these things happen, and I said thank you. Thank you for these boys. Thank you for this joy. Thank you for this pain, and even thank you for this accident—because without it I wouldn't have known how wonderful it feels to have a break in the gray sky and for the sun to shine directly on my face. I wouldn't realize the true power being loved has on a person. Something like this, a surprise mariachi band performance, would not have affected me as much in my old life. Sure, it would have made me smile, but it wouldn't have had the transformative power that this little miracle had. It made me fall back in love with living.

My relationship with joy had been much more fleeting before the truck ran over me. This new feeling lived in me now—to the right of my appendix—and maybe I could use it like my sleep bank account. All I had to do was place the things that made me happy in that little bank and pull one up and out whenever I was feeling sad. Malesy and Scrub had just made the first deposit. I heard it inside me like a coin dropping to the

bottom of a ceramic piggy bank. It sounded like the tambou-
rine in the mariachi band.

# CHAPTER TWENTY-TWO

# Lean On Me,
# When I'm Kinda Strong

I've never been great at taking care of myself. Not like being responsible enough to wash myself, but with things like resting when I was sick, or paying attention to aches, or being kind to myself when I needed to be. I thought it was cool to be tough. It made me feel strong like my brothers and my dad. When I thought about being caring, I thought about caring for others, like my mother, who gave every single part of herself to the people she loved. I wanted more from myself than I ever asked from other people. To be a successful person, I thought I needed to be superhuman. Because I consistently made the choice to put others' needs before my own, it became what was expected of me. I thought it was what made me likeable. I was afraid if I stopped doing it, if I wasn't always giving one hundred and ten percent, then people would stop loving me.

During my recovery I didn't have a choice—I had to put myself first. I had to rest and eat and be kind to my body.

Suddenly I couldn't take care of other people the way I used to. I couldn't rush to them when they broke up with their boyfriend. I couldn't meet them for a drink when something wonderful happened in their lives. I couldn't go to my parents' house when things were tough and make awkward jokes in hopes of lightening the mood. It was beyond my physical ability to care for people in the arms-around-their-shoulder way I used to. I mentally and physically couldn't be there for them. I was so consumed with trying to keep my own spirits up and my will strong that I had no room in my heart for other people's worries and heartaches. I was full. I had never been full before. It had always seemed there was space for everyone else's hurts and needs. I could always somehow squeeze them into any open places I had in myself. Now, though, there were no more open spaces.

I'm not proud to say it, but during my recovery it felt nice to be thought of first. To have my favorite foods brought to you. People calling just to talk about me felt indulgent and kinda great. Everyone telling me I looked good, and being proud of even my smallest accomplishments: *You ate a whole sandwich! Yay for you! I am so proud!* It was addictive to have so much positive thoughtful energy focused on me.

At the same time, it frightened me because I was unsure of what to do with all of the attention. There was a part of me that didn't know how to function when I wasn't giving. Who was I when I wasn't the person supporting and loving others? What would happen to me when people realized I had so little to offer them? Would they get bored with me? Was I being annoying? They must be so resentful of me, getting all this attention and not giving anything back to them. I was afraid everyone would stop loving me because I couldn't offer them the love and support I usually did.

I knew that I was a terrible girlfriend too. The balance of who takes care of whom was so lopsided. There was absolutely no part of this that was a partnership. When Warren came to visit, I could barely keep up my side of the conversation, let alone love and support him the way a girlfriend should.

The longer I spent at Glen Cove, the better I felt, though. A bit of solid ground had started to form where quicksand used to be. I made steps toward being a person who could connect with others on a real level. I was getting closer to being a person who could start giving again. On the nights I was aware enough to say prayers, I would say the prayer of St. Francis after my Hail Mary:

*Lord, make me an instrument of your peace;*
*Where there is hatred let me sow love*
*Where there is injury, pardon*
*Where there is doubt, faith*
*Where there is despair, hope*
*Where there is darkness, light*
*And where there is sadness, joy*
*O divine Master*
*Grant that I may not so much seek to be consoled as to*
*console;*
*To be understood, as to understand*
*To be loved, as to love*
*For it is in giving that we receive,*
*It is in pardoning that we are pardoned,*
*And it is in dying that we are born to eternal life*
*Amen.*

That had been the prayer I said every night before I went to bed—it was how I had thought the world worked. If I was feeling down and no one was making me feel better the way I wanted them to, I would refer back to this prayer and I would love other people the way I wanted to be loved. I did this with the hope that someday they would love me back in the same way. My brother had once told me that kindness was born of selfishness: we do it because it makes us feel good, and we do it because we want someone else to be as kind to us. I didn't agree with him. I thought the reason we are kind to people is because it's the right thing to do. It isn't about selfishness as much as it is human nature to help others when they are down. He asked me if I felt happy when I helped someone, and I said that I did. He said again that was the real reason I did it—because of the payoff of a positive feeling after I did something kind. No matter how many times we argued about this I refused to believe that my brother was right.

After a few weeks of physical therapy my loved ones noticed I was getting better, and they noticed I was asking more questions about them. They looked relieved when they were allowed to talk about themselves again. I got to hear about work woes and about little fights with significant others, difficult school papers and the trials of a new puppy. They asked me for advice, brought me their grief, their sorrow, their happiness, their laughter. It was as if I had been living in a foreign country for months without a telephone or e-mail, and suddenly I found a way to communicate with everyone I had been separated from. Being more physically active left me less time to feel sorry for myself, and in the place of feeling sorry for myself I started to think about other people again.

One night, over plastic cups of undercover red wine, I heard my weak but confident voice give advice to one of my best friends about her job situation—and I felt absolutely thrilled. I was helping someone! I was making them feel important and loved. I was making them feel heard and cared for. The person on the other side of my hospital bed wasn't feeling sorry for me! She was processing what I had to say and thinking about how to apply that advice to her situation.

As with most things in my life, though, I overdid it. I kept pushing myself to be a good friend, to be a good daughter, to be a good girlfriend and a good sister. I kept telling myself it was good to think about other people. But before I knew it, I started losing the energy I needed to take care of myself. I would talk too long on the phone, have too many visitors. I was exhausted, and because of that I found myself being resentful of my friends and family for coming to me with their problems. I was irritated at them for doing what I had invited them to do, but I didn't know how to tell them I wasn't able to help them right then.

One night after two very strenuous physical therapy sessions, I was lying in bed praying for the pain to stop. I was slowly breathing in and out, trying to manage the growing fear that this feeling would never ever go away, when my phone started to ring. A lot of people in that moment would have let it ring. They would have taken that time to care for themselves, but I was not that person. I picked up the phone to hear my friend crying. Other friends had hurt her feelings, because they had been reckless with their words and it had upset her so much that she was hysterical. I did what I could to calm her, but she was inconsolable. I stayed on the phone with her, not letting her know how much pain I was in. When we finally said good-bye and I hung up the phone, I started to cry. Was this what I had been doing to myself for my entire life? Ignoring everything my body told me in order to help someone else? I cried myself to sleep.

When I awoke for my finger prick the next day, instead of falling back to sleep until breakfast came, I couldn't stop thinking about why I did what I did. Why was it that I thought other people needed and deserved more than me? Why didn't I just

say I was tired, or I had a bad day (or say YOUR FUCKING
PROBLEM IS NOTHING IN COMPARISON TO WHAT I
HAVE BEEN THROUGH SO SHUT UP!!!!)?

Maybe it was gratitude. Maybe it was because I understood that the people in my life had been worried and stressed
out for me for the last two months. Or maybe it was an internal
realization that they had been sad for me for a long time and
giving up their time for me, and I felt this was the least I could
do. That I could listen to their problems, be there for them. I
hadn't been there for them in so long. Or maybe it was because
I wanted to—needed to—be needed. Whatever it was, it was
making me feel bad.

***

Enter Andrea: Andrea was one of the nurse's aides. She was
Latin American, tiny, enthusiastic, and completely adorable. I
loved when she was working. She was so thoughtful and kind
and would just chat with me like we were besties. She was
the type of person who made you feel as if you were the most
important person in the world. Andrea was quick to laugh
and animated when she spoke. I could feel life just vibrating
off her. I liked the way the world looked through her eyes—
so I would always ask her a million questions. She had come
from Colombia and had met her husband at a club in the city.
She was wildly in love with him. She would talk to me about
the clubs she had been to on the weekends and how she was
decorating her apartment. I loved that she would tell me these
things while she was changing my catheter bag or helping me
dress. I was grateful that she never flinched when she saw my
body and that she always looked happy to see me.

One day as she was helping me pick out what I was going
to wear that day, I sobbed that I was embarrassed I couldn't

help myself. She took a tissue from the box that was always on the left of my bed and clucked at me as she wiped the tears from my eyes.

"You don't know how well you are doing. There was a girl who was here a few months ago. She was about twenty-one years old, and she had an accident like yours, but not as bad. This girl wouldn't even brush her own teeth. She would make her mother brush them for her. But you, you want to be well. You want to do things for yourself—that is why it is easy for me to help you. I am happy to help you. You will get better. You'll see."

I couldn't believe there was a person who wouldn't want to be better, to do things on her own. It made me feel strong and proud. That morning I brushed my teeth with renewed vigor. I got every tooth, even the way-back molars, just to show myself I could. I washed my own damn face too—total grown-up.

Andrea always asked me about my boyfriend, and then I would ask about her husband. I would ask about her family in Colombia, and she would ask about mine. It felt like a ray of sunshine every time she walked into the room. It made me feel special knowing that she spent more time with me than with the other patients—mind you, many of the other patients were in their seventies and pretty cranky. I didn't care about the level of the competition as long as I was winning.

One afternoon we were talking, and I could tell she was sad. When I asked her if anything was wrong, she said today would have been her baby's second birthday. She and her husband were so excited when she had been pregnant, and now she felt that it was the only thing missing from her life. She just wanted a beautiful little baby who looked like her and acted like her husband. When she miscarried in her fourth month, they were devastated. It was impossible for her to even get out of bed, to face people, to get out of the house. It took her six months of fighting through her depression to be comfortable with herself again. It broke her heart and her spirit.

"I never talk about this to anyone, because it hurts me to think that God had forgotten me and my husband, but I feel like I can talk to you, Katie. You understand loss, and yet you are still fighting to be happy—it inspires me."

It was different to be on the other side of hurt. I saw her pain and I felt it, and I wanted to hug her, but Roberto got in the way.

"Andrea, could you come over here so I could hug your arm?"

We both started to laugh as she walked over with tears in her eyes and held out her arm for me to hug. We stayed like that for a few minutes, me embracing her left arm. When she was leaving, I touched her face in the way that always made me feel comforted.

# CHAPTER TWENTY-THREE

# Dr. Belkin

Dr. Belkin was one of my doctors at Glen Cove. When I met her, I was struck by how much she looked like Olivia Benson from *Law & Order: SVU* and was just about to tell her so when she introduced herself. She had a thick Russian accent, and like a total idiot I grew nervous. I blame all those James Bond movies I watched at an impressionable age. I was afraid she was going to be mean to me. I was scared that she was going to tell me to toughen up, or at the very least, she'd prove to be a secret agent working for the KGB.

But I also knew that Dr. Sheehey would never entrust my care to any nefarious characters. He was, after all, the reason I was even at Glen Cove. My godfather's brother-in-law, Dr. Sheehey was a pediatrician at the hospital, and he had pulled strings to get me there. He had a kind face and such a sweet way about him that he always put me at ease. I imagined he was the kind of pediatrician who is so good at distracting a child with conversation and magic tricks that they don't even know they're getting a shot. And this was not even the first time Dr. Sheehey had come to my rescue. After graduating from college, I decided I wanted to move to Dublin, and Dr. Sheehey introduced me to his sister, Anne. She lived in Dublin and became my guardian angel. She found me a flat to live in, interviewed my future roommate to make sure she wasn't a weirdo (this roommate turned out to be one of the best people I have ever met), and took me to lunch at the café where I wound up working for six months. Anne and her husband and two beautiful and charming sons were my surrogate Irish family. They invited me over for dinner on Sunday or for tea after work and basically adopted me into their wonderful lives. Whenever I thought of Anne, I thought of open hands, warm loving embraces, and the smell of lavender.

So, when I thought about it, I knew that Dr. Sheehey wanted to help take care of me. If he had connected me to a woman like his sister, there was no reason for me to be afraid of Dr. Belkin.

As I spent more and more time with her, I realized she was one of the sweetest people and best doctors I had ever met. She was so kind and so careful. Being around her made me feel like I was being covered in cashmere: everything was soft and comfortable—but also strong and well made. I actually looked forward to seeing her. She was open and honest about what was happening to me, and she was never harsh about it. I know that sounds like a little thing, but it wasn't. It was huge to be in the care of someone who realized the power of the information they were going to give me. Dr. Belkin presented the new medical challenges I was going through honestly but thoughtfully.

In Elmhurst, I felt as though I had done something wrong every time I had to have a new procedure. It was as though I was a pain in the ass for having to get a stent put into my belly to keep the blood clots from moving to my heart. The staff there made me feel scared and burdensome. Dr. Belkin was the first to tell me I had been disrespected at that hospital. She always made a point of telling me what was going to happen and then asking me how I felt about it. Can you imagine that? Taking the time to ask someone how they feel about a procedure that was about to happen to their already-mangled body. She explained how much I was going to have to go through in physical therapy; she let me know when they had to do X-rays; and she told me when they were worried about my weight. When she asked me how I felt and I told her truthfully, she did whatever the situation called for. If I was scared or sad or angry, she talked me through it and told me the reasons why something needed to happen and how they were going to do it. There was so much transparency it made it almost impossible for me to be afraid.

Dr. Belkin gave me the impression that she was invested in my recovery. I knew she wanted me to be well. I loved that she was so smart and capable, and I felt so lucky to have her as my doctor. All the hospital staff seemed to respect her, and they listened when she told them what to do.

I also got the feeling she kind of liked me. This became apparent during one weekend when Dr. Belkin was away and another doctor was doing her rounds. When this new doctor came in to check on me, he was still wearing his street clothes. He wore jeans that looked like they were fashionable circa 1998, a crimson sweater, and a brown leather bomber jacket. I didn't realize who he was, but I immediately thought he was a huge creep. He introduced himself as the on-call doctor and told me he'd come in to see me because Dr. Belkin had asked him to. I said hello, but I was not in the most awesome of moods. It was a Saturday night and weekend nights were especially hard for me, even when I had company. I spent the whole evening just wondering what everyone else was doing. Without fail, from Thursday night to Saturday night I would torture myself by imagining everything I was missing. I would fixate on how much it sucked to be in this stupid room, in this stupid bed, with this awful overhead lighting. I may have been missing a lot of parties, but I was a regular at my own pity parties. If you'd added some chocolate ice cream and an English accent, I am quite sure I was a dead ringer for a crippled Bridget Jones.

Luckily, my brother Conor was spending this Saturday night with me. He had traded the candlelight of Manhattan bars for the fluorescent lights of Glen Cove. Usually Saturday nights were Warren's and my "date nights." He would come in from Brooklyn with a bottle of wine and some fancy take-out, and we would pretend like we were out for a real dinner. Sometimes he would even bring those fake candles so we could dine without the dreaded institutional lighting. He was really incredible that way. He tried so hard to make me feel special and to make this time more bearable in any way he could. He was the one person outside of my family who I spent the most time with. Warren, more than anyone else, had been exposed to how intense all this was, and he was incredibly brave in the face of all of it. Where other people would have run away, he doubled down—coming to visit more, texting me all the time, finding out everything he could about my situation from the doctors, being so kind and understanding. This Saturday night a friend was having a birthday dinner he didn't want to miss, so he and Conor had switched their visits to make sure I didn't have to spend my Saturday night alone.

Even though we were grown-ups now, there was still that little sister part of me that felt really special to be thought of as Conor's friend. It didn't matter that we were in the hospital and not somewhere slightly cooler, like anywhere else.

Conor and I were talking when the doctor with the bomber jacket came back in, and his vibe felt off. He didn't do anything to build any rapport or to make me feel confident in his medical capabilities. In fact, he made me feel like I was a thorn in his side. As though I was the one who was keeping him from the Barry Manilow concert he was just dying to get to. I didn't pick your profession, bucko—don't get mad at me. I tried to make conversation with him as he was taking all my vitals. I asked him a few questions about what he thought about my prognosis and how I was doing. It was just a general question—one I hoped he would answer with something uplifting, a "Yay for Katie!" kind of thing. Perhaps it was silly, but a girl needs something on a Saturday night.

He started to talk, and it became pretty clear he was a really huge fan of the sound of his own voice. It was also obvious that he was not going to give me what I wanted: reassurance, even a little incredulity at my amazing recovery. Instead, unbelievably, he took it on himself to tell me I was not going to make a full recovery and that a lot of things were not going to go back to the way they were before.

Conor tried to interrupt him, to stop him from saying what he was saying. He tried to signal to this dreadful doctor that we didn't need this information, but the guy couldn't seem to stop himself. He went into a full spiel about what my recovery would be like, and how my expectations shouldn't be too high. This prognosis included the direst possible situation: I was never going to be able to conceive a child.

I felt as though I had been sucker punched.

*What is it inside a person that makes them do something like that? Where does that sort of meanness live? What was it about me, twenty-five years old, lying in a hospital bed on a Saturday night, that made this guy want to kick me? Didn't he think I had enough heartache? Enough hurt?*

Apparently not.

Conor later told me that he thought the idiot was giving me his full "cover his ass" story. Whatever the reason, the information he gave me that night was not anything I needed to know at that moment. What would possess a person to drop that kind of knowledge when he had so little background information on me?

*Why is everyone telling me I can't have babies? They must all be right—he's a doctor. Of course he knows. He must have read my chart. I'll bet that it says it right there on the chart—no babies.* With that realization, I started to think about everything else I wouldn't be able to do. I couldn't run, jump, play soccer, wear a bikini, do a somersault, climb Mt. Everest, or even go through a metal detector without setting it off. Why hadn't I done all those things before!?!?! Why didn't I do them? Now I will never be able to do anything. I am a cripple and I am barren and I will be alone and unhappy for the rest of my life.

*Nevernevernevernevernevernevernevernevernevernevernevernevernevernevernever* was what kept scrolling through my mind on a constant loop. I started to sob at the weight of it. I cried for my loss, for the loss of all these things and for the loss of time. I cried for the time I was spending in this bed, in this room, around a creep like this, and there was nothing that I could fucking do about it. *I will never get this time back. I will never be normal. I will never be okay.* I cried for the loss of those things, and I did some preemptive crying for the things I would later find out I had lost. Apparently the doctor didn't expect this response. He looked flustered and unsure of what to do about the mess he had made.

"You and I have to leave right now."

I wished that my brother was talking to me, but he was talking to the doctor. The man looked scared, and I told Conor it was fine, that it was no big deal. I lied to try to make things okay—I didn't want to make waves, but they left my room anyway, Conor closing the door behind him.

I didn't even try to quiet my sobs enough to hear what they were saying; I didn't care. I was too busy grieving for my loss. I didn't want to know what was being said. I just wanted my life back.

On the other side of the door my brother, in his best business-school voice, said, "You have no idea what you are doing to her right now. What you are saying may or may not be true; you have not spent enough time with my sister to know this. You just spoke to her in a way that implies that she could process what you told her logically. There is no room for logic when you are twenty-five and you can't move your legs. This is a daily process, and you can't make overarching statements about the future when you have no clue what's going on. To be clear, this just got very serious, and you will hear about this again. Also, if you come near my sister again, you and I will have a real problem, because I will kick your ass."

When they came back into the room, Conor's face was red, and the doctor looked as if he had just danced with a steamroller. He looked at the ground and then looked at me and apologized for what he had just told me. He said it wasn't something definitive but was just his opinion and that he could be wrong. I said okay. But the damage was done; you can't take that shit back.

After he'd left, tail between his legs, Conor squatted by my bed so his face was level with mine, chin just above the rail that protected me from falling on the ground in my sleep. "Katie, he doesn't know anything about you. He doesn't know anything at all. Do not give any weight to what he said, okay? He is just a punk doctor who got his ass kicked in high school and is so insecure that he needs to be an asshole to someone like you. He doesn't know how strong you are. He doesn't know how determined you are. He is coming out of left field and thinks because he has an MD at the end of his name he actually knows something. He doesn't know what you are capable of. Also, I told him if he ever came near you again I was going to beat the shit out of him. If you see him again, Katie, you tell me and I will take care of it."

I nodded, but I kept crying. I couldn't stop myself. I knew this fear and this feeling weren't going anywhere. Even though that doctor had gotten his ass handed to him by my brother, it couldn't take away what he said. It couldn't make this newfound hurt go away. It wasn't going to fix anything. Although I will say having my brother tell this pompous douche in no uncertain terms that his behavior was reprehensible was so fucking gratifying. Having Conor there to tell this guy he couldn't speak to me like that was such a relief. It was nice not to have to stand up to him myself. I felt less alone in that moment than I had since I had been admitted to any hospital.

Conor pulled up a chair, and we started to talk shit about the doctor to make me feel better. We decided that he looked like he was a fat extra from *Friends*. We told each other the reason why he was so mean was because his girlfriend wouldn't get the Rachel haircut. I laughed to keep from crying. We watched something on TV, probably some silly movie we had both seen a million times. We were both quiet—the heaviness of what had happened was still hanging in the air. My mind would be blank as we watched TV and then suddenly the nevernevernevernevernevernevernevernever would come scrolling through, and the tears would begin all over again. Conor held my hand and watched me as I cried. He didn't look away, which would have made me feel ashamed. He acknowledged my hurt and made it his as well. Then one of us would say something funny about the doctor, and we would both laugh again—the way we had been only a few minutes ago, when things were a little less sad.

Conor left to get water and a diet Shasta, and before he came back I had gotten an enraged call from my dad. He was so mad about what happened. He promised me the man would never be allowed to come near me again and that he was going to take care of it. I wasn't sure what "taking care of it" was exactly, but it did make me feel better. When visiting hours were over, Conor gathered up his things and made sure everything was where it should be in my room. The water was close by, I had the remote, my blankie was tucked up under my chin, and my cell phone was nearby so that Conor was just a phone call away from kicking that doctor's ass in case he tried to come in and talk to me again.

*** 

On Monday morning Dr. Belkin came in to see me. The corners of her mouth were turned down and she looked upset. She crossed to the end of my bed and leaned on the rail.

"Katya, I heard what happened this weekend, and I am so sorry," she said in her thick Russian accent.

"It's all right, Dr. Belkin," I lied. "It wasn't a big deal."

"No, Katya, it is a very big deal. That was not something he should have said to you. Not only was it not something he could say definitively, but it was also not his place. He knows nothing about you and has no right to say anything like that."

"So, does that mean I could still have children?"

"We can't say yes for sure; we won't know until you try. You will do that worrying when the time comes. Until then *no one* can say what will or won't happen to your body. We can only make educated guesses, but many things happen. Look at you now! No one would have thought you would have made so much progress in this short amount of time. I do want to tell you that this young man will be reprimanded for what he said to you, and he is not allowed to come to your room again."

Under normal circumstances I would feel very bad about getting someone in so much trouble. I don't like to make waves or make other people's lives uncomfortable—the tit-for-tat thing was just never my jam. In this case I made an exception. I was okay with the idea of him getting in trouble, of being punished, of being forced to feel sorry about how he hurt me.

Because I have the self-control of a cranky two-year-old, I started to cry again. Dr. Belkin brought over the box of tissues and pulled a few out for me to wipe my face and blow my nose. She leaned in and took my hand and said she was going to take care of it; there wouldn't be anything to cry about. She said I didn't need to worry about it today. I knew she was right. Now was not the time to be grieving about everything I didn't have. Instead, it was a day to concentrate on how to become well enough that I could get out of the hospital. I wiped my face and thanked Dr. Belkin.

I later found out that Dr. Belkin spoke to the doctor herself and ripped him a new one. My dad went after him with everything but the kitchen sink. He tried to get his fellowship revoked, have him suspended without pay, make sure he didn't work on the wing I had been in because he was deemed too insensitive to work with people who had been through a trauma.

My relationship with doctors up to that point had been one where they talked and I listened. I didn't have much of a choice but to take to heart everything they said. Because I had no context in my past life for what had been happening to me, I was willing to believe everything they told me. It didn't matter if what they were saying was wrong or mean or unkind. When I interacted with the doctors, I was usually on my own and I was scared and I wanted them to like me. In my mind, they would work harder to fix me if they liked me. Having my brother witness how I was treated, and watching him get mad in a way that I hadn't been able to, made me feel so much stronger. It reminded me of how I used to feel before the accident when people did something to me that was wrong: I used to be incensed as opposed to being crushed.

Having Dr. Belkin fight for me reminded me I was someone who was worth caring about—and it also reminded me of the humanity of most doctors. They aren't mind readers, they aren't fortune-tellers, and they aren't geniuses. They aren't any better than I am. They can just give out meds and get to park in places that I can't.

And that schmuck made me realize I can never again trust anyone in a bomber jacket.

# CHAPTER TWENTY-FOUR

## Heel to Toe

Lynn looked at me expectantly. It was our last day together, and I knew what she wanted me to do. It had been seven and a half weeks since I had been run over by the truck, and I had been working with Lynn for the last three weeks. This was the culmination of all our hard work. It was what was supposed to happen, like a kiss after a really good second date. How could I have thought this wouldn't be the moment? Of course she was going to want me to walk. Everyone wanted me to walk. It was like watching a seedling grow from a pile of dirt; everyone was waiting for a little flower to bloom. It was why you had been pouring sunshine, love, and water on that tiny little shoot of a plant. It was why you couldn't help but talk to the little seedling; everything that was good in life was supposed to come from those little sprouts. We all needed a little blossom, one pinprick of beauty in this indifferent world of mud.

It wasn't as though I didn't want to walk. I had been praying for this moment. My goal each and every day was to get closer and closer to walking. Unlike everyone else who was in my corner, I was the only one who knew how difficult this really was. Plus, the fear that Dr. Goldberg's initial prognosis was correct. I had finally told my parents about what he said when I came to Glen Cove. They said that he was jumping to conclusions and wasn't taking who I was into consideration. "He doesn't know how strong and determined you are. We know you can do this. Don't worry, Katie, this will happen." Easy words to say from a standing position. I knew what they didn't realize: there hadn't been an easy moment in this entire process. I had felt my muscles snap with shock at every exercise. It had been *my* teeth clenched in pain as I struggled to lift my leg from the bed. I was the one who felt the burning ache after each PT session. I alone felt the weight of the sadness of not having control over a body that used to be so uncomplicated. I was the one who was really living this. Of course I wanted the hope of that flower. I hated living my life as mud. I wanted the walking, but unreasonably, I wanted it the way it had been before—easy, free-flowing, and simple.

I was petrified that when I walked now, if I walked now, I wouldn't even be able to recognize myself. I was fearful that the feeling of walking would be so painful and so unlike what I had experienced in my past life that every step would be a reminder that I had changed. I was afraid of coming to terms with the fact that this awkward, limping person was who I was now. It scared me to death. At least in the chair I was safe, just like I had been safe in the bed. While I was in the chair, I could still be in transition. It was a stopgap until I was strong enough to just jump out of the chair and start running. In the chair I didn't have to show the world I couldn't walk or what had happened to me. When I started to walk, I would have to accept that this person, with a slow shuffle and a noticeable limp, was me.

This was how I felt but not what I told Lynn. There was no way I would let any of the old people in PT see me being a baby. I had a rep to protect.

Lynn had me sit in a very high chair, my feet dangling a few inches above the floor. The walker I had been using in therapy was right in front of me, waiting for me to walk, just like Lynn. It had been acting more like a tool to keep me balanced than an actual walking aid, but I think we both knew this day would come.

It was odd to be so afraid of something I wanted so badly. It was as if I had just gotten my dream job, and then as soon as I reached my office I just sat there, frozen. Completely incapable of doing anything for fear I would fuck it all up. I didn't want to ruin this. I didn't want to fail. I didn't want to know that after all my hard work and faith I was, in actuality, a cripple. While I was in my chair there was still hope I could "someday" walk. If I tried to walk and I couldn't, the hope would disappear into the ether. I wasn't sure I was capable of coming back from that.

On the flip side, if I didn't try, I would be giving in. I knew if I said I couldn't do this or I was scared or if I used the word I hated more than all other words—*no*—I wouldn't only be giving up on myself but also on my family—on every person who loved me. If I didn't try, I would be pushing the responsibility of taking care of myself onto them.

In the moments I felt the most like giving up, the only thing that seemed to pull me through to the other side of the fear was my family. More than being afraid of being a cripple, I was afraid of letting them down. I could be anything in this world in their eyes, except a quitter. That title I couldn't swallow.

Lynn was about six feet away from where I was sitting, and I stared at her, hard. I burned her face into my memory. I became really conscious that my life was about to change. Usually those moments sneak up on you, but not this one. It made itself known. *Things are about to get real.* I finally made my move. I thrust my bony hands toward the walker, wrapping them around the gray handles and lifting myself from my chair. At this point my arms were really strong and I was able to lift my entire body without letting my feet touch the ground. I hovered over my walker for about ten seconds, breathed in, and so, so gently placed my feet on the mat. Step one complete. That wasn't so hard. I am totally brave. I can do this.

Lynn and I had talked about how to handle the mechanics of walking. This conversation had seriously happened. Seven and a half weeks ago something I had done without thinking now warranted a very technical conversation. The way one walks is with your heel going down first and then rolling into your big toe. It seems simple enough, but I was so nervous I was sure I would forget how to do it. It was as though I was in a play and struggling to remember my simple lines: heel, toe, heel, toe.

The pain reared up, and I felt the full weight of Roberto tearing into my belly—I knew if I didn't get on with it, I would have to stop because it would hurt too much. I bent my knee a little bit, and willed my right foot to move forward . . . and it did! It did! My right foot moved! It moved for me, because I asked!!!! I asked it to lift just a little off the ground, and it did it! Gravity did the rest for me. Lovely, lovely gravity took my lifted foot and landed it on the floor. I stared at that foot and smiled. I wasn't there yet; I would need to do the left foot to make it walking, and if I didn't, it would just have been a step. More than one step made it a walk. I repeated my new right foot ritual with my left foot, AND IT DID IT TOO!!!!! I walked! Me! I walked! The walker still hadn't moved yet (these were like baby doll steps), and I could tell it was just itching to make it happen, and who I am to deny a walker its destiny? I went heel-toe on my right foot, then heel-toe on my left foot—and the walker rolled forward. I had only moved the walker forward a few inches—but it didn't seem to matter. I had moved those inches forward, by myself.

I kept going, neither Lynn nor I talking, not even making eye contact, afraid to break the spell of my slow shuffle toward my new life. When I reached Lynn six feet away from where I had been sitting only a few minutes ago, I felt a ridiculous grin spread across my face. It was huge; it was as though everything good inside of me was trying to make itself known through my lips. We hugged, and I started to cry and laugh at the same time. I couldn't believe what just happened. I had just faced my fear, and in a weird way that fear had been realized. I didn't walk the way I used to. I did look different. I wasn't who I was before—but I didn't give a fuck. All my worries seemed so trivial in comparison to the immense joy I felt right at that moment. How could I have almost given up?

There is nothing in life that turns out exactly the way you want it to, but does that make it any less beautiful? Does it make it any less amazing? My reintroduction to the mobile world was not romantic, or miraculous, or dramatic, but it was absolutely perfect. I wondered at the legs I had thought betrayed me, and I welcomed them like prodigal sons who had returned home again. It felt as though another puzzle piece had been fit into the picture of this new life. It was a different picture, but it was one much more precious than the one that had been there before.

# CHAPTER TWENTY-FIVE

# Home

Every time I say the word *home*, an image of my parents' house pops into my head. I've lived in Ohio, London, Dublin, and in my own apartment in Brooklyn, but that house on Hunt Lane in Manhasset is where I have always considered home. I had every square inch of that house memorized, but during those final days at Glen Cove I forgot what color the throw pillows were, which floors were carpeted, and which were hardwood. Not remembering where the colander was would get me very worked up.

I wasn't really worried about finding everything if I needed to throw together a dinner party for fifteen guests; it was that I wanted to be as prepared as possible for this next known/ unknown. I didn't want to admit it—to myself or to anyone else—but I knew the next leg of this journey was going to be a difficult one. For the first time it wasn't because I was lonely or because I was afraid, but because it was going to be really surreal to come into the place that I always felt so at ease in and not feel like my old self. I was a completely different person now compared to who I was when I had walked out of that blue front door a few months ago. Facing that kind of stunning reality, the life that unfolded outside of these hospital walls scared me. If I couldn't remember how the house looked and where everything was, how would I have any sense of where *I* belonged?

In some secret place inside myself I hoped that maybe I would magically become well as soon as I arrived home. I thought that somehow my home would heal me. Like it had when I was sick at school, or heartbroken in the city, or when I simply needed to feel there was a place where I was understood. I wanted this house to take my broken bones and mend them, to find my splintered pieces and somehow make me whole again. I wanted to be in my own four-bedroom Oz where I could click my heels and everything would be right again. I don't know what I was thinking, especially because I could barely bring my heels together at this point, let alone click them three times.

I let myself live in those hopes for part of the time, but the emotion I felt most acutely was trepidation about how I was going to live as an injured person in a place that wasn't a hospital. I had never been so vulnerable. As opposed to its being a place of safety and comfort, I was suddenly aware of the danger that lurked in every corner. Scarier than monsters under my bed or sneaking in after curfew was the thought of not being able to save myself if there was an emergency.

When we pulled up to my parents' house, I was struck immediately by the slick, black ramp that was now covering the gray slate stairs that led up to the house. *This doesn't belong there!* I thought. *Why did we get that? Is it for Aunt Marleen for Thanksgiving?* I had completely forgotten that it wasn't Auntie Mar who needed the ramp now. This house definitely did have magical powers; for a moment it had made me forget that I wasn't a healthy girl in my twenties. Instead, I was someone else entirely—someone who couldn't even handle going up four small steps. My dad carefully pushed me up the ramp as my mom held the storm door open. I couldn't help but scream out in pain as I bumped across the threshold like an unwilling bride.

I scanned the front hallway for a moment, amazed to find everything was the same as I'd remembered it—just a lot higher up (you don't realize how much height you lose when you're sitting in a wheelchair). All the chairs in the dining room were where I remembered them. All the china was placed perfectly in the china cabinet. Everything was the way it should be. We passed by the kitchen, and nothing was really any different, and I even remembered where the colander was (bottom left-hand drawer in the island). As we went down the hall, my dad had some difficulty maneuvering the turn—it was more a three-point turn than a curve to the left, but we managed. As we approached the family room, my favorite room in the house, my mouth dropped. The chairs in front of the window had been replaced with a hospital bed. I had completely forgotten that of course I wouldn't be able to sleep in my own room. It was up a million steps. I must have had some romantic idea that my dad or my boyfriend would carry me up to bed every night.

My mom had put fresh sheets in bright colors on the bed, brought down my favorite duvet, and set up my books on the hospital table. For a hospital bed in the middle of a family room it looked downright cozy. I was already exhausted and wanted to lie down, but I felt ashamed asking my dad to spot me as I went from my chair into my bed. It had always been hospital staff who had been there to do it with me. This felt more intimate and much sadder. As though I was admitting defeat in front of my family. Like saying out loud, "This is who

I have become, and I can't pretend that I can get into bed by myself, and I can't believe you assumed that I could do this on my own. I am the person behind the curtain; I am not as strong as I wanted you to believe."

But my dad gently and slowly helped me transfer to my bed, as my mom stood nearby as a second line of defense, and with tears in my eyes I let him help me. I sat on the edge of the bed as he lifted my feet and rotated my tiny body so that my head was near the pillow. I nervously tilted my body back toward the bed, not wanting to make Roberto mad. My mom and dad kissed me and told me that I had been brave and that they loved me. Looking at their hopeful, caring faces, I saw that they were my constants. With them there, I was sure everything would fall into place.

# CHAPTER TWENTY-SIX

## Removing Your Own Catheter (A Twentysomething's Guide)

The nuances of the life of a healing person were never something I thought about; they hadn't been brought to my attention. The little stuff doesn't get broken down on *ER*. There aren't any close-ups of patients asking how to go to the bathroom if they can't walk, or what happens to your muscles if you aren't moving. It's the rushing of gurneys and the cutting open and bleeding that gets all the airtime.

Suddenly these questions were very important to me. While I was in the first part of my recovery, the doctors and the nurses took care of everything; I was cut out of the peeing process completely. They had inserted a catheter into my lady parts. It was a tube that started in my bladder, exited through my hoo-ha, and arrived at a bag that hung on the side of my bed. Because my bladder had gotten mangled during the accident, I also had something called a suprapubic tube. This tube was inserted about three inches to the left of my belly button and took out the more grody stuff—the non-pee fluids. It was transparent, so I could see everything that was coming out of my body. What was coming out was completely gross. What made the situation worse was that it also looked a little like I was peeing out of my stomach, which was nothing short of awkward. Actually it was shockingly disgusting, but endlessly fascinating. I couldn't help but look at what was coming out of me. I'd stare at the tube waiting for something really gross to appear—like a brown blob or a clot of blood—and for some reason I thought other people should see it too. They came to visit and I would tell them to take a gander at what's exiting my body this morning.

When most of the nasty stuff had been removed via the suprapubic tube, they took it out, leaving me with the regular catheter. When I started physical therapy, they gave me a mobile pee-pee bag. It was the sleeker version, smaller, sportier—for the cripple on the go. For some reason it was really embarrassing when they had to put on my mobile catheter, which was still the same tube in my lady parts, just another receptacle for the waste to go in. To be honest, I had thought by then that I had no pride left. More people had seen me naked than Jenna Jameson. Doctors talked about me as though I wasn't even there, and I hadn't taken a shower in six weeks—but having a bag of my own urine Velcroed to my leg as I was trying to rebuild muscle mass in a room full of old people made me blush.

There was one thing I liked about this catheter business, though: for the first time in my adult life I actually stopped thinking about peeing. In my real life, I'd thought about it constantly. I'd walk into a bar, restaurant, concert hall, or sporting event and automatically scan the place for the closest bathroom. This wasn't just because I had a small bladder, but also because I am obsessed with beverages. Doesn't matter what

kind, I love them, in an almost manic way. My dad had always
stressed the importance of hydration. He drinks about two gal-
lons of water a day. Also, when I was about fourteen I read in
*Seventeen* that you could burn ten calories with every glass of
ice water you drank. So from then on, whenever I was feeling
fat and lazy, instead of working out I would just drink as many
glasses of ice water as I could choke down. It did nothing for
me physically, but it did make me feel better. My love of beer
also played a role. I would spend a good slice of my Saturday
nights waiting in line for the bathroom.

With my new peeing apparatus, all the stress of wondering
if I would have to leave in the middle of talking to someone
to go to the bathroom was gone. In its place was the general
mortification that any time I did pee, someone would have to
come in, comment on the color of my pee, and drain it. Still I
continued to drink three pitchers of water a day, plagued by
the irrational fear that all my drinking was going to cause the
bag to overflow. Or worse, the pee would creep back up my
urethra and I would pee-poison myself. I wasn't sure exactly
how that would happen, but the mind makes up some ridiculous stuff when it has all the time in the world to think. To the
extreme chagrin of the nursing staff, I would press the call button and say, "Hi, hi, um, I think my catheter bag is overflowing.
I'm sorry, could you empty it?" Then when they came into my
room, there wasn't even anything in there. I was the little girl
who cried pee.

As I was getting ready to leave the hospital and go back to
my parents' house, the thing that frightened me the most was
the catheter business. It was the most medical thing that had to
be taken care of more than once every day. The bigger events,
like wound cleaning and monitoring my progress, would happen every other day when the home care nurse came. The hospital nurse gave my mom training on the process of changing

my catheter. Mom brought in a yellow legal pad that was usually kept in the kitchen by her desk to take notes, and she wrote down everything the nurse said. She asked so many questions, looking about as worried as I was. When I had told her my theory on pee-poisoning, she'd said I was being silly. As she looked at her notes that afternoon, it seemed she might be starting to think it was a possibility.

And then there was the fact that I had been hanging around with the same tube in my lady parts twenty-four hours a day, seven days a week for almost two months. That seemed really wrong to me. I requested a new one before I left, and they were kind enough to schedule a change. It wasn't a big deal. It wasn't even a surgery; it was just a *procedure.* It could be done in my hospital room. Still it was scary for me, because something was going to be changed inside me, and I had become very protective of my insides. They had been battered enough, and any change, even a good one, even one I requested, seemed bad.

The nurse assigned to this particular procedure was a woman who had been working with me for the last month. She was a really sassy lady in her midsixties who regularly confided to me about her granddaughter and all the problems she was having in junior high. I was still pretty strongly connected to my inner awkward preteen, so I readily doled out advice about what to tell her granddaughter and how I would have handled a few of the situations (which usually amounted to crying alone in a bathroom stall).

She and two other nurses came in, just casually chatting away. They were talking about random things: the weather, her granddaughter, hospital gossip. Part of me hoped they were doing this to make me feel better, to emphasize that this wasn't a huge deal. They were calm and breezy. I was not calm *or* breezy—I was flipping the fuck out, peppering them with questions as they removed and reinserted the new catheter.

"What are you doing right now?"

"I am removing the tube that was in your bladder."

"Is it disgusting?"

"It isn't bad."

"Can I see it?"

"No."

"What size is the catheter?"

"Six."

"What does that mean?"

"What size are you putting in?"

"A 6, but it is a French 6; it is a little slimmer—it is better for women."

"But the regular 6 was working fine for all those weeks."

"Trust me, this one will be better."

Even though the grandma nurse in charge answered all my questions, she was pretty dismissive, as though I was asking about things I didn't need to know. I felt really silly, but whatever, it was my biz, and I did need to know what was happening. The whole French thing made me feel uneasy; the other-size tube was fine before—why wouldn't it be fine now? But then again, the people at the last hospital weren't always the sharpest, so maybe I was just lucky something bad hadn't happened already. She was a nice woman, but even nice people make mistakes, so I asked her how I would remove the catheter in an emergency.

Turns out a catheter stays in your bladder because there is a tiny little balloon at the top of the tube. When the catheter is placed in your biz, the balloon is inflated with water that is injected into it with a syringe. The water in the balloon makes it impossible for the catheter to slip out. If the catheter needs to be removed, there is a little knob thing just below my biz that I could cut, then the water from the balloon would drip out, and the catheter tube can be removed.

I left Glen Cove with a lot of trepidation. I hated being in the hospital, but I felt somewhat safe there. I am not a careful person (please note the beginning of this book), so I was sure I would do something irresponsible at home. I worried I would somehow make myself worse, thereby having to return to the hospital to start healing all over again.

But Glen Cove was having none of it; my time had come. I'd graduated, and it was time to get the hell out of there. The day I was to be released, my nurses and doctors came to say good-bye. They hugged me and wished me luck. They covered me in blankets for the five minutes of cold I would have to endure between the exit and the ambulance. They swaddled me from head to toe. Each blanket was tucked in so carefully, not too tight around my middle, closing all the gaps so no cold air could rush in. The afternoon was crisp, and the sky was bright and blue. The cold air rushed in through the places that the tucked-in blankets missed. It felt incredible.

I was riding solo, because only my dad had been able to come to the hospital that day, and he had to drive himself home. So it was just me and the ambulance driver on the trip from Glen Cove to Manhasset. The driver was very careful and kind as he locked the wheels of the gurney into the floor of the ambulance. There were no windows in the back of the ambulance so I didn't know how far we were from home. I asked the driver to tell me what landmarks he saw as we passed them.

"We're on Glen Cove Road now. So what happened to you?"

"I was run over by a truck."

"For real?"

"Yeah, for real."

"Like a whole truck, like a full one? Were you in a car or something?"

"I was on a bike."

"Holy shit, that's crazy."

"I know, right?"

We were silent for a while.

It was so simple to break it down like that; it was all that had happened. I had been run over by a truck, a full one, on a bike. I was alive, and, yeah, it was fucking crazy. That was it.

"Um, we are on Northern Boulevard."

"Did we pass the Barefoot Peddler?"

"Yeah, just a second ago."

"I used to work there. I was a hostess, and they have the best turkey clubs. Have you ever been?"

"I have—I like their wings."

"Me too!"

He turned around in his seat when we were stopped at a light.

"We're going over the viaduct in a second."

"Almost home."

"Yeah, almost. Hey, I have these movies that my friend got for me; they're bootleg copies, but they're really good. I was going to watch them, but I guess you won't be able to get to the movies anytime soon. Do you want them?"

There is so much good in people that sometimes I get overwhelmed and feel like my heart is going to burst with love for complete strangers.

"Are you sure?" He nodded. "That is so nice of you—I would love them. Thank you!"

He smiled and turned back around.

When he looked back again, it was to say that I was home.

***

On my second night at my parents' house, in our makeshift hospital in the family room, something inside me shifted. I wasn't sure what it was; I just knew there was something going on in my nether regions. *This is different* suddenly turned into *This is NOT awesome*. I tried to think about what it could be: maybe it was because it was the new catheter? I was sure it had just shifted momentarily, and it would readjust itself in a little bit. Because of the amount of drugs in my system, I wasn't sure when the pain had really started. It could have been hours ago, but it was only when the drugs started to wear off that I became hyperaware of the burning. Everything that had any connection to peeing felt like it was being cut with razor blades by mean little body trolls. I was pretty certain it had finally happened: pee-poisoning.

There was no slow build to this pain. There was no time to say, "Hey, I'm not feeling so well." It went big immediately, and I started screaming and speaking in tongues. It hurt so much more because I didn't understand it. I had become acquainted with the pain in my belly and my back; it was the devil I knew. This new feeling was the devil I didn't know, and it scared the shit out of me.

My body was on fire from the inside, and the only way to put out the fire was to pee. But I couldn't do that. It wasn't possible. I was in agony, and worse, I was helpless again. My screams brought the entire household to my bed, not knowing what to do because I wasn't able to give them any cogent information. I was just yelling a stuttering mixture of "catheter," "pee-poisoning," and "ow ow fuck ow, why?" My dad called an ambulance to come and take me back to the hospital. They told me to be patient. The ambulance would be here soon, and everything was going to be fine.

I didn't believe them. I didn't want to be patient. I knew the ambulance wasn't going to be here soon enough, and for fuck's sake, things hadn't been fine in months. I was not going to be fine. I was so sick of waiting. I was going to take care of myself.

I told my parents to bring over the commode and to bring me a pair of scissors. The looks on their faces made it very clear they did not want to bring me either of these things. But at this point I was shaking from the pain, and I was incapable of stopping my teeth from chattering. I had been the nervous one. I was the one who was afraid of dying. I had asked all the questions in the hospital. I had an idea of what to do and they didn't. They reluctantly brought the commode over to my hospital bed and then helped me to transfer onto it.

I was scared of cutting off some of my lady parts trying to do this, but I was feeling emboldened by the idea that I was taking my life back into my own hands. I sat down on the commode and asked my parents to leave. If I was going to cut my vagina, I'd really prefer to do it alone. I found the plastic safety valve on the catheter; I grasped it gently between my index finger and my thumb. I took a very deep breath, said a quick "Help me, Jesus," and snipped the valve. I put my hand underneath where I had cut and felt drops of liquid. Either it was blood from my now-mutilated lady parts, or the water that had been keeping the catheter in place was leaking out. I crossed my fingers for the latter. It felt like the catheter was starting to slip out. I carefully tugged on the tube and felt it slacken. So I took a deep breath and pulled harder. It gave way and slipped out, like a large splinter finally removed.

I peed like a big girl on my own for the first time in two months. There was no joy in it, no pride—mostly because I wasn't two years old, and I knew I wasn't going to get a cookie. All I kept thinking was that my being broken was never going to end. I was going to feel like this forever. The ambulance arrived with its sirens blaring, and two EMTs came barreling into the family room. I could feel the frosty evening air rushing in from the open front door. The EMTs smelled like cold and cotton T-shirts. They made like they were going to try to lift me onto the gurney, but at this juncture I had had enough of being jostled about without my permission. I had just removed my own catheter, and I felt I could do whatever I wanted. I told them I was going to do it myself. I didn't need their help.

In the ambulance I kept asking for morphine, again, and again they said no. I had thought that maybe the Long Island EMTs would be a little more understanding of my need for morphine than the Brooklyn ones. I was incorrect. On the way to the hospital, I felt every bump, every crack in the road, every pothole. How, with Nassau County's high taxes, was it possible that there was this much road damage—and would it kill the Manhasset-Lakeville EMS service to put in new shocks?

When I got to the hospital, all the night-shift nurses who had taken care of me were there to greet me. They cooed over me, attending to my every need. It turned out that I had a kidney infection. It wasn't pee-poisoning, to my huge relief, and I was right to have been worried; the infection had been caused by the French catheter. It had been too small. Because it was so small there was room for infection to get into my urinary tract and then go straight to my bladder and kidneys.

My days of taking the word of doctors and nurses as law were over. I had actually been right to question them. I should have known not to trust a sassy nurse or anything French. I'll know better next time—no sass, no France.

I used to be pretty capable of taking care of myself when I was a real girl. I trusted myself. But when I was in the hospital, I had no confidence. I didn't understand anything that was happening to me, so I deferred to the opinions of others. But when that infection hit me at home, I took full control of my life for the very first time since the accident. I had needed to remove the catheter myself because I was in horrible pain, and I was not at the hospital, and I was so tired of not being able to do anything about it. The pain had been my prison, but this time I was afforded the opportunity to escape—and in the process, I reminded myself that I was the one who held the keys.

# CHAPTER TWENTY-SEVEN

## The Giving of Thanks

Eating is awesome. I love eating until I am sick. I love giving myself huge portions. I love saying I'm stuffed and then cramming in just one more bite. This is very American of me—but it's true. That is why I love Thanksgiving so much. I know, I know—family, gratitude, blah blah blah. I like those things too, but what really makes me excited for that Thursday in November is eating. Which is gross, I realize.

Yet being at my parents' house that Thanksgiving didn't make me as happy as usual. Eating had lost its appeal. Food no longer held the fascination it once did. It wasn't something I looked forward to; it was just something I had to do. When I looked at food that used to make me so joyful—sandwiches, cookies, chips—I'd just hear *You've lost that loving feeling* looping through my head. I knew there were things about food that used to make me so happy; I just couldn't remember what they were. It was like the end of a relationship: I knew I still loved food—I just wasn't *in love* with it. But how do you explain that to a turkey leg, to a slice of pumpkin pie, or to your loving family who wants so badly for you to be the happy, hungry girl you were before?

I was also really nervous. I wasn't sure of myself in this house, as this person. Who I was before the accident and who I was now were so far away from each other. I had no idea how the two would ever meet. Was I the girl in the photographs with the big smile and the open heart? Or was I the girl in the mirror with the weak laugh and the skinny wrists? I didn't know, and I didn't particularly want to think about it.

\*\*\*

At the family parties my parents threw when we were children, I would play the little hostess. Trying to get four kids showered, dressed, and looking relatively good was a huge challenge for any parent—mine especially. My father had to work out every day, for at least an hour—it was just how he rolled. And for some reason he always seemed to work out right before company was expected. My mom would be hustling around the kitchen, unshowered, getting things together, putting meat into the oven, stirring pots, and my dad would be on the stair machine. My brothers and sister would be watching TV or outside making mud castles, or really anything that would be either difficult to pull us away from or wildly messy. Usually about thirty-five minutes before relatives were scheduled to arrive, my mother would yell from the kitchen.

"Conor, are you showered?"

"No."

"Callie, what about you? Are you showered?"

"No, not yet."

"James, have you showered?"

"No, I haven't."

"Katie? Katie, did you shower?"

"Yes, Mom—I did."

"Oh, thank God. I'm going to run upstairs and get ready. Conor, Callie, James, go upstairs and get ready."

Dad was still on the StairMaster.

The reason why I was always showered and ready wasn't because I was a good kid or because I was really into being clean—it was because I knew if I wasn't ready no one else would be. People would come to the house and there would actually be no one there to greet them. It had happened before—the doorbell had rung and six separate voices said *Hold on, hold on.* I HATE rushing, and I HATED making people wait, so I was usually ready for our family's three p.m. parties at around ten a.m. Well into my twenties, I couldn't find my own apartment keys in my purse, but I was organized enough to be dressed and ready for any event five hours in advance.

I also quite enjoyed playing hostess. I loved greeting people and taking their jackets and hanging them in the front closet. Even at age twelve, I knew how to make drinks for all the guests (I made the first one strong to get them loosened up and then went lighter after that). It certainly wasn't something I could write on my college applications, but I was pretty proud of my bartending talents. I would spend the morning before the party thinking of things to ask our guests. I would ask my grandmother about the Mercy League and her beach club. I would divulge details about my teenage life and give her sound bites about the fam for future fodder with her friends. With my uncle Pete, I boned up on local sports news and asked as many questions as I could about my wonderful cousins. With my aunt Lois, I took any opportunity to cuddle next to her because she made me feel so loved and perfect. It was pretty awesome to sit with all the adults and talk about grown-up things. I liked that my parents could entrust me to be their stand-in entertainer.

Now, in my wheelchair, it was difficult to get around the sharp corners on the first floor of my parents' house. This fact alone would have made it hard for me to be the hostess I was used to being. Why weren't more homes built with banked, rounded corners? Builders certainly lacked foresight. Didn't they know there was the potential for residents to get into near-fatal accidents with trucks?

So, with my first big family party since the accident approaching, I wrestled with whether I should be feeling happy or sad. It wasn't an easy fight. Both sides were well represented and had done their research.

The sad side of me had a vested interest in feeling very sorry for herself. She talked about pain and flashbacks. "The people who are coming over for Thanksgiving don't even realize how much they have to be thankful for," she said. "THEY DON'T UNDERSTAND THE MEANING OF THE WORD *THANKFUL!*" she yelled. "You, Katie, you understand." She also showed me pictures of myself on the gravel right after the accident and pictures of my roommates at Elmhurst and a close-up picture of my stomach with the staples in it crusted in blood. "Do you think all the people who are going to be here tomorrow with their smooth bellies know anything about what you have been through? They don't understand you. You're too much of a wounded creature for anyone to ever understand where you are coming from. For that very reason I think a deep dark depression should be the forecast for at least another year or two."

The happy side didn't look the way I thought she would. I had assumed she would be laid-back and smiley, but she was much fiercer, like a warrior. Her teeth were clenched, and she was actually angry at the sad side. "Look around you," she began, and, being a good judge and jury, I did as I was asked. I looked around the room my parents had transformed into a makeshift hospital room. I saw the green carpet I had helped my mom pick out when we were redecorating ten years ago. I saw the stereo system that was now covered by pill bottles. I saw the table that had been placed next to my hospital bed and always had treats and books and notes on it. I saw a fire in the fireplace and the way my family had rearranged the entire room so no one would ever have their back to me. "These are the reasons why you should be happy. What happened to you before was bad—no one is denying that, but think about all the things that have happened since then. Think about all you've been through and see this time as a gift. Sure, no one understands your pain, but, Katie, you don't understand theirs. The more you laugh and the more you smile—the more grateful you are—the happier you will make the people around you. The happier they are, the more they will try to keep your spirits up. If you keep giving in to the idea that you are a desperate, sad person, everyone will believe it. And they will give up on you. Does this suck? Fuck yeah, it sucks. But can you do anything about it? Fuck no, you can't. What you can do is think about what is in your life that you love, and you can smile about that. Be grateful you can still think. Your mind can still bring up these thoughts and memories, and you have people who want to be kind to you, to love you and support you. After a tragedy, happiness doesn't just come to you the way it might have in the past—now you have to fight for it."

I considered both arguments carefully. The sad side felt good because it meant I wouldn't have to do anything except feel sorry for myself, which I had become exceptional at. I could sulk with the best of them. I had made feeling sorry for myself into an art form. The happy side had a compelling case, though. I liked fighting. I liked the idea of fighting tooth and nail, fists and fingers, for my own happiness. It made sense to

me. What good is anything if you don't fight for it? Anything I
had ever gotten easily I hadn't cared about as much.

So, that night before Thanksgiving, as judge and jury of my
own emotions, I decided that fighting for happiness was going
to be my MO for the next twenty-four hours. If it didn't work
out, sulking like a big fat baby would be my plan B.

The night before Thanksgiving has to be the biggest bar
night of the year. It's the night when almost everyone comes
back to their hometown for the holidays and then has nothing
else to do but get shitfaced and tell people who are now strangers their deepest darkest high school secrets. It was always one
of my favorite nights. This is mostly because it was the night
when guys I had crushes on in high school would slurringly
tell me that I "got hot" and then, very romantically, ask me
if I would like to make out with them behind the pizza place
around the corner. The answer was usually no, but sometimes
it was yes—just to say I had finally kissed the captain of the
football team and also because I loved making out.

In years past my friends would come over to my parents'
house to preparty, aka drink as many beers as possible before
getting to the bar so as not to A. have to spend as much money
at the bar and B. be at least a little buzzed while waiting for
a drink that takes thirty minutes to arrive. My crazy parents
and my lovely friends didn't want to leave me out this time just
because I wasn't mobile, so they all came over before they went
out. I put on my size-large black velour tracksuit and my fanciest polo shirt in a size extra large to cover Roberto, and I put
on some eyeliner—which was harder than you would think, as
my wheelchair made it difficult to get close to the table. The
makeup mirror was about two feet away from my face, and I
didn't have the steadiest hand, so I wound up looking like an
early-nineties Courtney Love. My eyeliner was about a quarter of an inch thick below my eyes. As the pièce de résistance

I doused myself with honeysuckle body splash in case I still smelled like stale corn chips.

My friends looked beautiful, though. Their hair was perfect, and they were wearing tall, spike-heeled boots and tight sweaters in dark colors. They greeted me with smiles on their faces and tears in their eyes, and in that moment I put up my fists and I punched sad in the face. I smiled and hugged them and made sure my wonderful friends knew how happy I was that they were there.

My dad looked at me and at all my friends together in one room and opened up a bottle of champagne and said "Girls, never forget—life is a celebration." And he smiled as he poured out a glass for everyone. I asked what their plan of attack was for the evening. What bar was going to be first? I forced them to drink beers as fast as they could to make sure they were buzzed enough to talk to people they hadn't seen in about a year. They talked and giggled, and I did my best to keep up, but my body ached from sitting up for so long. When it was time for them to hit the Plandome Road strip, I was just about ready for bed. They kissed me good-bye, and I smelled each of their perfumes as they left. The sweetness of it lingered with me for the rest of the night.

My parents wheeled me into "my bathroom," where they had laid out my pj's, a bowl of warm water for me to wash my face with, and my toothbrush and toothpaste. I wondered if my friends were thinking about me. Were they feeling sorry for me? What did the conversation sound like when they got into the cab? Were they surprised at how I looked? Was it as weird for them as it was for me to have everything look the same, except for me? Would they have a drink for me?

Whenever I had seen a young person in a wheelchair in the past, it broke my heart. It made me feel so sad that something bad had happened to someone so young. Did my friends feel achy after they left me? Did they know how happy I had been to see them? To feel as though I was still a part of that life, and how good it was to put on my fancy black sweatsuit and to feel like a real girl, even if it was just for an hour?

"Do you know how much your friends love you, Katie?" my mom asked as she took my evening pills out of their bottles. "I know, Momma, I know," I said out of habit—I said I knew things all the time now.

"You are so special, little girl," she said as she handed me my pills. "All those times you felt as though your friends didn't appreciate you, or you were afraid they didn't like you anymore, or you weren't important to them; erase those feelings from your memory. Your friends love you so deeply."

"Ahh, Mom, I know they love me, but it's also because it's the right thing to do. It's the holidays, it's what is supposed to happen: feed the homeless, hang out with a cripple, you know."

"No, Katie, it is because of you. If this had happened to me when I was your age, I don't know that the friends I had would have been there for me through everything you've been through. You must have done something really right."

"Thanks, Momma," I said before I swallowed my evening's dose of tranquilizers and blood thinners. She asked me if I wanted the TV on; I said I did and asked that she leave the remote on my little hospital table. She pulled out my evening diaper from the storage space under my hospital bed and placed it within arm's reach for me to take care of privately. Everything else everyone could see, but I was pretty serious about not letting anyone be around when I put on my diaper. Change my bedpan, sure! Diaper, I would prefer some privacy.

"Hey, Mom, did you know that I love you?"

"Yes, I did know that actually," she replied, smiling.

"Good. I was just checking."

The idea of being with my friends had scared me so much that I hadn't thought about how awesome it would be to be in a room with all of them. I decided to fold up the last hour and put it somewhere in my memory bank, so I could take it out, unfold it, and be reminded when I really needed it how much I was loved. I watched an old sitcom on *Nick at Night* as the sleeping pills got to work. I closed my eyelids and didn't think of uneaten turkey or about how different I looked. Instead, I carefully pulled my blanket up to my chin and allowed myself to feel the warmth of the love that had been given to me over the last hour, and I knew what I was truly thankful for.

# CHAPTER TWENTY-EIGHT

## Momma

The first morning at home I slept past 6:30 in the morning. I didn't have to get my finger pricked to give blood or have to be woken up for whatever random reason the hospital people seemed to come up with. My face felt heavy and warm—and then I panicked and felt as if I was late for the job I hadn't had in two months. I was confused about why it was light out and I hadn't been awake for a few hours already. It was so foreign, and I felt scared.

"Mom! Mom!"

"What, Katie? What's the matter, are you all right?"

"Am I allowed to sleep this late? Is this okay? Did the doctors say this was allowed?"

"Yes, Katie, it's fine. You can sleep as late as you want. You're home now. You are fine. Everything is okay. Do you want to go back to sleep? Are you hungry? I'll make you tea and toast."

I lay there blinking at this new life. Was this the way it used to be? Now that I was at home it felt like I was having a sick day instead of being really hurt, and except for the pain part, it felt wonderful.

There were so many things my mom hadn't been able to do when I was in the hospital. She wasn't in charge there. She had to follow other people's rules. She could only come to visit me when they said it was okay, leave when they told her to, only touch me there. She also had to hear the stories of what had happened and know she hadn't been there to stop it and couldn't protect me from the hurt.

Now we were playing by my mom's house rules and everything was so much better. She would leave me cookies and tea with the saucer on top of the cup to keep it hot. It would just be waiting there for me when I woke up. Cookies . . . FOR BREAKFAST! My mom offered me everything I wanted, but more important, she offered up herself, wholly unconditionally. Her main focus was what was going to make me happy. It was so overwhelming to be loved that way. Overwhelming in the way that Uncle Scrooge probably felt when he went into his vault during *DuckTales* and saw all that money. I am sure that he just stood there sometimes and thought, *All of this is mine? All of this is for me? How did this happen?* Well, maybe Uncle Scrooge wasn't supergrateful, but I was. I had forgotten what it was like to be loved full-time. I couldn't believe I hadn't realized how amazing this was earlier. How had I not known how lucky I was to have someone who loved me like this?

After a few days, a certain routine had formed. Following breakfast and a washup on my commode/shower seat, we would begin our day. We would usually have one event on the agenda. Maybe it was washing my hair or ordering a movie off cable; maybe a person would come over, or there would be a visiting nurse or the physical therapist or the occupational therapist. Washing my hair was an interesting process, just because most of my hair had fallen out. I had very thick curly hair before my accident, but because of the medications and the stress most of it had fallen out. The first time my hair was washed was three weeks after the truck ran over me. Maribeth and my mom took on the herculean task while I was still in bed at Elmhurst. They brought the water in from the bathroom in a bucket and used pitchers of warm water to wash out the soap. At first we were laughing about how silly it was that they were washing my hair when I was a grown-up, but as they poured the pitchers of water over my soapy scalp they both stopped giggling at the same time.

"Is everything ok?" I asked because I couldn't see them behind the bed. They said, "Yeah, yeah Katie, everything is fine. It's just that a little bit of your hair is coming out."

"Is it a lot?"

"No, no it's fine."

They later told me my hair had come out in chunks as they had run their fingers through it. She had never seen anything like it. By the time I was done with my first hair-washing about half my hair was gone. I could feel when I put my hair up into a ponytail that it was thinner, but I had no clue by how much, and that was probably a good thing.

Now that we were at home, my mom was able to get to water more easily, and we could make a mess and then clean it up ourselves. We wheeled me into the kitchen, and we would MacGyver a way to make the seat on my wheelchair higher so my head could reach the sink. It wasn't the most pleasurable experience. Any position that wasn't lying down and not moving at all was still excruciatingly painful. But it was something I had to do. Clean hair was cool, and the amount of perfume I had been putting on to mask what I still believed to be the "corn chip" smell was getting out of control.

My mom would take the extendable faucet and tilt me toward the sink. The feeling of that stream of water on my scalp was incredible. I had forgotten that my head could be covered in that kind of warmth. It was like tiny little water blankets were being placed on every single square centimeter of my head. I looked up at my mom and smiled—knowing how hard it must be for her to do this, your grown-up daughter needing you to wash her hair. The girl you already brought up needing you to clean her commode and bring her meals. Seeing her so helpless and knowing you are the one who has to help her.

While I was in the hospital, I so badly wanted the people who were caring for me to treat me like family. There, I was completely exposed, naked literally and figuratively in front of these people to whom I was just another body in a bed. It felt so good to know that my mom knew when I was falling apart— she just knew. She could tell when I was about to drown in the pain. It was the way it felt, like I was drowning in a black oil of pain, and she would just lie right there with me. I had almost forgotten what that was like, to have the luxury of time. There was no place she had to go, there were no rules saying she couldn't get into bed with me, there was nothing that said she couldn't do anything she wanted. We were back to making our own rules. It was such a relief to not have to do it myself, to not feel lonely in my pain. Someone else was there to see and acknowledge what was happening to me. She saw it all day from morning to night, not just during visiting hours, and that made me feel so much better.

The visiting physical therapist came to see me about twice a week, and we did exercises and stretching and lifting and all the things that would help me to get closer to the person I remembered being. The therapist was a very encouraging woman who was okay with me pushing myself. If I felt well enough to do it, then I should. I latched on to that idea and decided I was going to push myself as hard as I possibly could. My mom would put weights on my ankles before we started the day so I could do my exercises before even getting out of bed. When I told her I wanted to do more weight the next day, she didn't try to stop me or tell me I would overexert myself. Instead she asked me if I felt I was really ready for it, and when I answered yes, she would put the extra quarter of a pound into the ankle weight.

As the in-home therapy continued, my physical therapist would try to get me to walk a little farther than I had during the last visit. On the days she wasn't there my mom would stand next to me and we would walk together, like two old ladies at the mall. I found myself pushing a little harder with my mom. I would endure a little more, partly because I wanted her to be proud of me and partly because I felt as if she needed to see that all she was giving up wasn't for nothing. I wanted to do what I could to reassure her I was going to work as hard as I could to get back to where I was before. At this point the only way I knew how to comfort her was to show her I was going to work my balls off until I was better.

One day in mid-December it started to snow. It was twilight, and the clouds were colored a light purply-blue as the flurries fluttered down to the ground. From the time I was little until I was way too old for it to be normal, I would freak out when it snowed. I would scream. I would jump. And then I would go outside and run around with my mouth open, trying to get snowflakes on my tongue. On this particular day, I was staring out at the clumps of snowflakes as they fell like feathers from the sky when I felt my mom looking at me.

"Do you want to go out and dance?"

"What? You are crazy!"

"No, no, let's go outside. We'll just go for a minute. You're already in your wheelchair! Come on! It will be fun."

A light was shining in her eyes, and I saw her—not as my mom, not as my friend, but as a little girl who wanted to bring joy into my life.

"Okay. . . . Okay, let's go."

She put blankets over me and said, "See, look, here you are all toasty and warm." And she wheeled me down the ramp and there we were out in the front yard—a mother and her daughter. My mother stood there laughing, her tongue stuck out, trying to catch snowflakes. Clapping, I smiled at my mother with her mouth open, beckoning the snowflakes onto her tongue. My mother was the one who reminded me what it was like to enjoy the good things about being a child—that it was good to let go. If I ever forgot that joy was close by, she was right there to bring me to it. Either by taking me outside to play in the snow or by placing our little dog, Cassidy, into my arms while I was lying down or even by buying us matching shirts from an expensive store just because we had seen them on *Oprah*. She taught me how to swim through my heartache, instead of just treading water and gasping for air.

# CHAPTER TWENTY-NINE

# The Blame Game—Rules and Regulations

Okay, so maybe about now you're wondering whatever happened to the driver of the truck. That's usually the case when the victim is out of immediate danger. Well, you're not the first, nor did it take this long for the question to bubble up to the surface. Way back at Elmhurst, over a month or more ago, one of my friends had just settled herself into the official visitors chair when the inevitable question first came up (at least in my presence).

"Katie, I've been wondering something: Has he tried to contact you?"

"Who?"

"The driver."

"I don't know. I don't think so." If he had, his visit would have probably been lost on me. Since I'd been in the hospital, everything had sort of just been slipping by me. I knew there were always fresh flowers and candy in my room. I saw smiling faces and heard stories, and I felt hands on my forehead. But I depended on my parents to remember the comings and goings of room 403B.

"Has he tried to contact me, Mom?"

"He came the day after the accident. He wanted to apologize, but you were still in the ICU, and your father and I didn't want to see him."

"What an asshole," my friend said angrily. "How dare he come here after what he did to you? He makes me sick. I hate that guy."

I understood her anger. I understood why she felt the way she did. But I couldn't get there. I didn't hate him. He didn't make me sick. My mind was too stuck on having lost control of my life. Being sick was what was making me sick.

I didn't think about the truck driver at all when I was in the hospital. It wasn't something I wanted to do. To hate this nameless, faceless man felt like a waste of energy. It would only make me angry, plus I was aware the guy hadn't done it on purpose. He hadn't gotten up that morning with the intention of running me over. I was sure he didn't want to live with the guilt. I had seen on *Oprah* that when you do something like this, and you have a soul, it never leaves you. Adding blame to the guilt I was sure he was feeling was not something I needed to do. Making him feel worse wasn't going to make me feel better.

Part of the reason why I was reluctant to say it was all his fault was because I wasn't sure I wasn't partly to blame. I tortured myself with whys. Why did I need to ride my bike? Why didn't I realize it was dangerous? It was New York City (okay, a borough, but still), not the back roads of a Vermont village. Why couldn't I have just slept in and gone to work like a normal person? Why hadn't I just sucked it up and joined a gym? It only costs an extra sixty bucks a month—that's like two dollars a day. Why couldn't I have just been like everyone else?! Everyone else was safe, living their normal lives, and here I was—broken.

When I allowed myself to be rational, I could see that there were a lot of good reasons why I had done what I did. I had to ride my bike that early because you couldn't see sunrises in the gym. I couldn't sleep in because like an overenthusiastic motivational speaker, I liked to wake up and take the day by the horns. It was how I lived. It was who I was. I couldn't blame myself for wanting what I wanted.

When the police report was filed, it said I wasn't at fault. I was so relieved. I didn't do it. The pain my family had to go through, the hours spent at the hospital, the tears that fell from friends' eyes were not my fault. That made me feel better . . . sorta.

I still had questions: If getting run over by a truck wasn't something I was responsible for, why did it happen to me? I thought of myself as a pretty good person. Weren't there tons of douchebags who deserved this more than me? There were people who kicked puppies, who shoved on the subway, who yelled at babies. I was relatively nice to be around. I was kind to people, I remembered birthdays. I hugged people a lot. But somehow I was the one who'd been run over in the street. It was me in the hospital. It was me not being able to use my legs. It was me who'd been broken.

While I was at home recovering, a friend asked if I thought my accident and suffering were my penance for having lived such a blessed life. That made me cry, even more than usual, because I was afraid it was true. Was this the price I was going to have to pay for having such a lucky and beautiful life? Was this the price I had to pay to even the score? There are thoughtful, smart, kind, good people who have to root through garbage to get their meals, and I had always had three square meals a day, plus snacks, anytime I wanted. There are people stricken with illnesses and disabilities I had been blessed to avoid. Was it just my turn? I forced myself to think about it honestly, and the truth was my life had been pretty fucking sweet. Wonderful, in fact, compared to people in many other places, but also in comparison to the people in my own home. When my dad introduced me to his friends, he would say, *This is my daughter Katie; she's the pick of the litter.*

I got good grades. I was on varsity teams from the time I was a freshman. I was a captain in three of the sports I played. I made friends easily. I could drink a beer faster than most men I knew. And I got a scholarship to go to college.

When I complained about how I felt pressure to do well, to be the best, my brothers and sister would tease me. "Wow, Katie, it must be so hard for you to be perfect. It must be so tough to always do everything right. Too many parties to go to? You don't have enough time to call back all your friends?" I wanted to fight back, but I didn't. What did I really have to complain about? It was my job to make jokes, to hold hands, to be rational and reasonable. It was my responsibility in the family to bind up wounds with soothing words.

I couldn't admit to my family that I still felt like that fifth grader who got Milk-Bone biscuits thrown at her on the school bus. I couldn't tell them how, by the time I was twenty-four years old, the weight of my expected perfection hung around my neck like a yoke. This pressure woke me up in the middle of the night, with my heart beating out of my chest. I was never good enough for myself. I never deserved the accolades. I believed the compliments were lies, everyone was wrong, my friends were deluded. In fact, I didn't deserve this beautiful life. I didn't deserve to have so much that so many others never had. Rationally, I knew the universe didn't have a checklist of who deserved happiness and who didn't. Rationally, I knew what had happened to me wasn't my fault. The fear that it was my fault still lived inside me, though—hiding in the dark corners reason couldn't reach.

\*\*\*

By Christmastime, thirteen weeks after the accident, I had been out of the hospital for about a month. I was living in my parents' house, the house I grew up in, sleeping in a hospital bed that had been shipped in just for me. It was different from my bed upstairs, which was a big-girl bed in the middle of my yellow, sun-filled room. This hospital bed was a single—black, plastic, slippery, and adjustable. The only good thing about it was the triangle thing hanging over it. It looked like the triangle that farmers' wives would DING A LING LING to call people in from the field for supper. Instead of signaling mealtime, I used it to pull myself up and shift my body if I needed to. This triangle was my most favorite thing in the world. I would wrap my bony hands around the bottom part, and take control of my uncontrollable body. For the first time in many weeks, if I wanted to move my body I could use my own strength to do it—I didn't have to call anyone. It was magical.

My parents' empty nest had become my one-woman hospital. Aside from the aforementioned hospital bed, on top of the stereo playing Christmas carols there was a pharmacy's worth of painkillers, and there were boxes of bandages and balms underneath the family computer. My wheelchair was where the rocking chair used to be.

The most amazing conversion was of the living room right next door. My parents had turned that space into my own personal bathroom/changing room. This was the room we kids had never been allowed to enter as children. Even at twenty-four, I had been afraid to bring anything but a glass of water into that room. Apparently, if you almost die, the rules of the living room can be bent. Suddenly, the Persian rugs weren't so important, and it was okay if there were dirty washcloths on my great-grandmother's rosewood desk.

I felt extreme affection for that room, and I also felt an intense hatred. It was where I went to the bathroom, which was painful, awful, and unfortunately necessary. At this point my bladder was about the size of a postage stamp, and the process of peeing was not only time-consuming but also irritating. It begins with having to transfer my body from bed to wheelchair. Then, I wheel myself over to the commode (that is fancy talk for freestanding nonflushing toilet that family members, who apparently love you so much that they will take your bodily waste out of the little bucket and then take it to the actual flushable toilet, have to deal with for you). I then transfer my body from wheelchair onto commode. Then, with one hand, I pull the elastic waistband of the sweatpants I am wearing down to my midthigh, while using the other hand to keep my body upright. Then there is the actual voiding (there's that sexy doctor talk again). Next, I repeat the balancing with the pants, but now in reverse—pulling up instead of down. Then I transfer myself back onto wheelchair, maneuver myself back to bed, and scream for someone to come spot me while I transfer body back onto bed. It all ends with flopping down onto bed, sweating, exhausted, in pain, and with the very small feeling of satisfaction that I will not have to do that for at least another half an hour.

The living room/changing room/bathroom was also where I took my sponge baths. The sponge bath was a very different form of torture. It was just as involved as the voiding, only much sadder. Like many other young women, I had always said how much I hated my body. I thought it was disgusting, so fat, pale, flabby, mushy. Really whatever negative adjective I could conjure up.

Then my pretty, smooth, perfect little body was replaced with a body I did not recognize. This new body was cut with a scalpel from my lady parts up to the top of my rib cage and then sealed back up with staples that stayed in my tummy for months. Roberto, the fixator that was fusing my shattered pelvic bones back together, was like something from a horror movie. He stuck out six inches from my body and went flat across my stomach and imprisoned my belly button. My right side, where my bicycle's gearshift had dug in, looked like a shark had taken a bite out of the curve of my hip. In its place there were angry purple scars, screaming red scabs, and new skin that was just trying to figure out what color it would like to be.

I would sit on the commode before I started to wash and stare at my naked body and weep. I would weep as I took the washcloths that had been laid out for me by my loving parents, and as I dipped them into the red bowl of warm water on the card table to my right. I swirled the cloths around in the water until they felt like they could make me clean again. I would cry as I took one and rubbed it with the white soap, knowing what was next. I had to wash around the metal lodged in my body. I had to watch and be careful how I cleaned myself—trying to avoid shifting Roberto—knowing the pain that would ensue if he was disrupted.

It was so hard to stare at myself. This broken body, which was all skin and bones and metal and scars, was mine now. This was the physical evidence of what had happened to me. I could spend all day forgetting—making jokes, seeing friends in the house, watching TV, making phone calls, eating sandwiches—but every time I stripped off my clothes, I was assaulted with the remembering, and it hurt.

Roberto was not a happy character. He must have missed his family, in whatever country I had decided he was from, because he was screaming all the time. If I moved in a way he didn't like, every nerve ending would be set off. And he had reach! He was touching my hipbone, he was stuck through the skin that was covering my belly, and he was intertwined in all my core muscles. If there was a nerve to hit, Roberto was going to find it and punch it in the throat.

My body had gone from being something that gave me comfort to something so foreign that it scared me. I didn't understand this body; it was torn up and incredibly fragile. I felt if I made a wrong move my entire being would shatter.

***

Every member of my family reconfigured their holiday for me, and it made me hate myself. My younger brother, James, was home for his first Christmas break from college. This break should have been about hanging out with friends, drinking his parents' beer, regaling us with freshman year stories, complaining about the curfews and rules he was being forced to follow at home. Instead, he was getting me tea, lifting me from my chair onto my bed, and running errands for my parents. James and I hadn't really seen each other while I was in the hospital. He had been at college learning how to acclimate himself to a new life five hours away. When he came home he was faced with a very different sister from the one he was used to having. Instead of me making jokes and grilled cheeses, I was lying in bed immobile, grimacing in pain.

My younger sister, Callie, was home for two months before she went off to Australia for her semester abroad. She should have been consulting guidebooks, asking me for advice on foreign men, working, and saving money. Instead, this twenty-year-old child was emptying my bedpans, bringing me pain pills, holding my hand as I sobbed, and crying with me for moral support.

Conor was on his Christmas break from business school. This time was critical for him in his search for a postschool job. He should have been able to lock himself in his apartment on the Upper West Side and just research and prep and get ready for this next big phase of his life. Unfortunately, he was needed at home, so he stayed at my parents' house and helped as much as he could, doing his own work in between taking care of everyone else, particularly me.

This wasn't their fault; they didn't deserve this. And I felt terrible, on top of the normal terrible I was used to.

Every Christmas Eve in the McKenna household, my brothers and sister and I exchange gifts, and we also give our Christmas gifts to our parents. I always thought of it as the cocktail hour before the big feast of Christmas morning. This year, my family did two shifts of Christmas Eve Mass. No one wanted me to be alone, so my dad and Conor went to church first, and my mom and Callie and James stayed with me and went together later. When they came home, my whole family got together in the family room and my parents suggested that instead of opening presents around the tree like we always did we should open them around my hospital bed. My eyes filled up with tears for the sacrifices my family had made for me in the last few months, and I begged them not to. I didn't want it. Enough for me . . . Please, enough.

They opened presents around the tree, and I opened mine in my bed. I liked seeing them there, at the base of the tree with all the colored lights. The ripping of wrapping paper, the expectant faces of the givers, the happy squeals of the receivers. I had never realized how beautiful the process was—taking something from your heart and wrapping it up and giving it to someone you love. Watching them all together was so pretty. It was so normal. This Christmas I had thought the mall crowds would just be a little too overwhelming in a wheelchair, so I ordered all my presents online from the comfort of my hospital bed. My presents weren't as thoughtful as they had been in past years, but I felt very proud I had actually managed it at all.

After the presents, we watched the *Christmas Story* marathon on TBS. Each family member took turns sitting in the wheelchair next to my bed, and they would hold my hand as we watched. I drank red wine out of a water glass. When I thought something was funny, I would fake laugh with my mouth wide open, but I wouldn't allow any noise to come out. If I real-laughed, it shook my stomach too much. Roberto, like an abusive stepfather, would get angry at my happiness and make me hurt. It just wasn't worth it. Even though I was on two hundred milligrams of OxyContin a day, I was still in so much pain that every part of my body that wasn't numb felt as if it was on fire. I would take my pain pills at the recommended intervals, but it didn't help. I was actually taking as much as a two-hundred-pound man would take in a day, but there was still breakthrough pain. And, recently, the sleep had stopped coming. No matter how many pills I took or how many sheep I counted, I would lie awake until four or five a.m., semiconscious, with nothing else to do but wait for sleep or the next wave of hurt to come.

After the first *Christmas Story* was over, my family went up to bed one by one, kissing me on the forehead as they went. They wished me Merry Christmas and hoped I'd sleep well.

After everyone had gone to bed, it was time for me to put on my adult diapers. I had to wear them because my bladder wasn't strong enough to make it through the night. If we are going to talk about a heartbreaking experience, putting on your own diapers as a grown woman is high on the list. This evening I was having trouble conjuring up the strength to lift my tushy up high enough with my magic triangle to actually get my diaper on. My family had gone to sleep, and this was one of the last things I wanted to wake them up to help me with, especially on Christmas Eve. As I struggled, I heard *A Christmas Story* in the background, and I stared at the fire as it burned down to red-hot coals. Finally I was able to get my fucking diaper on. By that time my body had shifted around so much that Roberto had become loose. I could feel him just wiggling in there. It felt as though he wasn't connected to anything, so then—like a crippled Encyclopedia Brown—I decided I should investigate. I wanted to touch Roberto. I pushed that fixator with my index finger and watched as it moved with the pressure. I was terrified. Did that mean it was going to fall out? Were my bones going to crumble? Was my belly going to collapse? As I took my finger off the bar, another thought hit me: I just moved that. Sweet Jesus, this is going to hurt.

The pain ripped through my body. It felt as though every one of my bones had been frozen and was now beginning to thaw. You know the pain—where you watch your hands go from white to red and then back to skin color. It was an undulating, burning ache, and it felt as though it was turning my entire body inside out.

I thought about the truck driver then. I thought about his family. I imagined them around the Christmas tree. All of them opening presents together, hugging and being hugged, sitting, eating, drinking, laughing with the sound coming out, and in that moment I hated him. I hated him for doing this to me. I thought, *He is an irresponsible, selfish asshole. I'll bet I am not even a thought that is itching at the back of his mind. His life is too full of joy and family and light to think about me in this hospital bed where I haven't been able to turn on my side in two months.* And I said to him in my head, *Here, my family has to suffer because you were a reckless driver.*

I blamed him then. I blamed him for everything. He did this, he broke me, and he was the one who deserved all this distress, not me. I wanted him to have this hurt. I wanted him to have all of it. I wanted to go to his home and break every single thing in it. Injure everyone he had ever loved, and then look him in the eye and tell him to start all over again. Then after he rebuilt, I wanted him to live with the fear that I would just come back and break it all over again. I wanted him to think God had forgotten him. I wanted him to think he wasn't good enough, that he was wrong and bad and stupid. I wanted his family to be in the waiting room, planning a funeral, begging God to take them instead. I wanted him to live with tubes and fear and hurt. I wanted him to live in a nightmare, where every night he begs and pleads for it to end, and then every single morning he opens his eyes and sees what has become of his life, and the horror starts all over again.

*I blame you. You did this, truck driver. I hate you.*

The sobbing started then, and it hurt. But, for the first time, I wanted it to hurt. I wanted to be in pain because now I could push it onto this man I had never seen. My rationale was that if I hurt more, he would have to hurt more. Not exactly what Jesus was trying to teach us, I realize, but this seemed like an extenuating circumstance. Plus, I was pretty sure Jesus was too busy helping Santa get all those presents around the world to worry about my angry thoughts.

I exhausted myself with the sobbing and the hating after about forty-five minutes. I fell asleep as Ralphie's family was having dinner at the Chinese restaurant. Chinese food makes me sleepy, even if I am not eating it.

I woke up, and somehow Santa had visited our house without me seeing him, even though I was RIGHT THERE. Blame had been placed on someone, but I felt no different. I didn't pass Go. I didn't collect $200. I didn't get a Get-out-of-being-crippled-free card. I was just puffy, dehydrated, and still angry.

A little while after I had woken up, my dad came downstairs and pushed the hair away from my forehead and wished me a Merry Christmas. I didn't find it necessary to tell him about my revelation. I thought I would keep the blame game to myself. He helped transfer me from my bed to the wheelchair and rolled me into my makeshift ladies' room. As I was trying to sit down on the commode, I miscalculated where my body was in relationship to the arm of the commode and Roberto hit the corner. What that meant to me was that my fixator went up about two centimeters very quickly. It ripped through the skin and muscle tissue that had just been attacked by my curiosity the evening before. I felt every part of it. I bit my lip and tried not to scream, because I knew it would just bring my dad running and wake up the rest of the family. And, at this point, there was nothing they could do. There was no way to undo what had been done.

The only thing they could really do anymore was to look at me, coo, and pet me. Now, I wish I could be tough and say I hated being pet and loved on . . . but in truth, I am really into it. Regardless of how much I love to be loved on, I knew if I were to scream and cry it would just make them upset, and I was going to hurt anyway. I decided to just try to suck it up. And suck it up I did.

The real problem with sucking it up is that at some point you are going to have to spit it out. It seemed at that moment I was full of everything I had been swallowing. All the pain and hurt suddenly voided via my mouth, and I started making some deals with God. They were not really good deals; I didn't promise God to give up anything like my nana did. It was more of a prayer/favor/deal:

*Dear God,*
*If I have to hurt like this for much longer, I don't think*
*that I will be able to live. Please please please please,*
*God, I can't do this anymore—please make it stop. I*
*need it to stop. I know that I won't make it.*
*Katie*

After purging myself with some more *please God*s, and some serious keening, I went to wash up. I got to the side table and reached for the red bowl and the washcloths, but there weren't any. I had to call to my dad like a kid without toilet paper. "Daaaaad, I need a waaaaaaasssssssssshhhcloth." As I heard him bound down the stairs, I felt a mix of gratitude for his speed and care, and jealousy that I couldn't do that. After some serious searching in the linen closets, bathrooms, and laundry room, he finally came to the conclusion there were no washcloths to be found. And on that Christmas morning my father woke up the entire household with his screaming (the screams that I had selflessly held in, mind you). He said he was upset about washcloths . . . but I don't think it was really about the washcloths.

He yelled at my mother for not having them washed and ready. He yelled at my brothers for not helping to clean the house. He yelled at my sister for not helping my mom with the cooking, because if she had, then my mom wouldn't have forgotten to do the laundry. The only person he didn't yell at was me. But I was why he was angry. I was the reason why everyone was on edge. I was why my mom didn't have time to wash the washcloths. I was the reason why my brothers hadn't been helping to clean; they were busy entertaining me. The reason why my sister hadn't been helping with the cooking was because she had been helping me wrap my presents. They all got blamed for what was my fault. It was easier to blame them than it was to blame me. No one wanted to blame me, but I did. I knew that it was me; it was all my fault.

After my dad was done yelling, my older brother told him the best thing he could do was to go to church. While he was gone the five of us cleaned and washed and cooked until he got back. (Okay, really the four of them did all that stuff. I tried to help by taking my extender arm, which was like a thumb and an index finger made of plastic, which could grab stuff on the floor. I honestly picked up probably eight things in an hour and a half. James had found the extender helpful when he didn't feel like getting up from the couch to grab his soda off the coffee table.)

By the time my dad came back from church, the house was a little cleaner, the tears had dried, and there was a stack of clean washcloths next to my red bowl. Conor and Callie in their infinite wisdom broke out the champagne that had been chilling in the garage. They put out Solo cups on the side table next to my hospital bed, and as my dad walked in the front door, they opened the bottles of champagne. They poured out six cups—one for each of us—and it wasn't even ten a.m.

No one really said anything, but we clinked our plastic glasses. My father apologized and so did we. I looked around at their five faces that looked just like mine and said, "Sláinte." Everyone mumbled cheers to one other, and somehow everything was forgiven. Everything was all right, and we still loved one another.

The truth was there was no one to blame. I realized my accident was an unfortunate confluence of events. In every situation you have choices. You can ache from it, you can accept it, or you can choose to fester in it. If you let yourself fester, it doesn't change the fact that your world just got fucked up. It doesn't make you well or happy or okay, it just makes you angrier because the cause of your pain has a face and a name and is still living in a way that you can't anymore . . . as if nothing ever happened.

At the end of the day, when there is hurt, someone needs to be blamed, someone needs to say I'm sorry, and then that someone needs to be forgiven. Sometimes it matters who those people are. Other times it doesn't. The anger needs to seep out. It can happen with your family, or it can happen with a complete stranger. Regardless of who it is, I recommend always having a spare bottle of champagne chilling.

\*\*\*

The best thing about having a really rough morning is it can only get better from there. The champagne relaxed us and together we watched the James Bond marathon on FX. This Christmas was the first one we were having at our own house instead of at my aunt and uncle's in New Jersey. I wasn't the most mobile kid, and the idea of the potholes on the Cross Bronx Expressway was enough to make me want to take nine OxyContins and call it a day. So we planned a more low-key Christmas at home than my aunt Lois and uncle Pete threw. When they did Christmas, it was an event. Their house was decorated so beautifully it could have been in a magazine—all sparkly golds and maroons, a gorgeous open fireplace—and enough delicious food to feed an army. There was homemade mozzarella and stromboli, and that was just for starters. My aunt and uncle somehow were able to make five courses' worth of food for about thirty people. Seeing them in the kitchen was like watching superheroes whose power was to prepare amazing food and make everyone feel full and loved.

Being at home was going to be a new experience for us, but, the fight notwithstanding, we were all just really happy to be together—everything else was gravy. Most of our family was in New Jersey, but other family and friends stopped in intermittently to say hello and have a drink. It was so comfortable and easy. The way I could tell everything was okay with the fam was that as soon as guests came in, they were greeted with a breakdown of the fight we had earlier that morning.

That Christmas was a blur of family coming in the front door, friends coming in the side door, and neighbors coming through the back door. It seemed that every fifteen minutes there was a reason to open another bottle of champagne, and I definitely drank more than my share. After dinner the house was full of people, and everyone was in the family room/my bedroom, but I couldn't stay up anymore. So my mom helped me into my jammies and then was with me as I transferred into my bed. She pulled my blankets up to my chin and placed the silky part of the blanket near my fingers. She gave me my meds and started to shoo everyone into another room to let me sleep.

"Please don't go," I said. "I like hearing everyone, it's so nice. Don't go. Stay and talk, play Christmas music—please."

Everyone stayed in the room, and it made me smile to feel so many warm bodies all around me, so much happiness and so much love in the room with me. It felt like a slumber party where it was okay for me to fall asleep first. It was all stories and giggles and fun. My eyelids started to lose their fight against sleep, and the room became a blurry haze of candlelight and colored Christmas lights. Before I closed my eyes, I heard my dad say, "Doesn't she look like an angel? Truly, she looks just like an angel."

After my eyes had closed, the party went on around me. I felt the same way I did when I was four years old and my parents would have a party and I would purposefully fall asleep under the coffee table so that I wouldn't miss out on anything.

This Christmas I didn't miss a thing.

# CHAPTER THIRTY

# BFF

My best friend Maribeth did more than just horrify me about being naked in front of my family, my friends, and medical personnel; she was also my main medical contact. She had already been a nurse at Sloan Kettering, the best cancer hospital in New York City, for two years when I got into my accident. As a family, we McKennas were never terribly scientific. I understood cough syrup and that Pepto-Bismol made everything feel better. I knew vegetables were good for me and drinking a lot of water was a great idea. Other than that, my working medical knowledge was nil.

Maribeth made herself available for every question my parents or I had. I called her about itches, random aches, and hospital politics. Anytime I worried about anything, Maribeth was supposed to know what it was and judge if I was okay or not. She was supposed to know all of this without even seeing me. It was her job.

What one would not guess by looking at Maribeth is that she is sort of hard-core. She is five foot five inches and weighs one hundred pounds soaking wet, but I wouldn't fuck with her. Of course, everything you can surmise about Maribeth physically would make you think the opposite. She's a blonde-haired, blue-eyed girl with the face of a cherub. She has that "all-American girl" sweetness that makes you want to take her home to your parents.

During my stint in Elmhurst there were a lot of times when I was denied basic care. Times when they wouldn't bring me meals, when I pressed my call button and no one would answer, and even, in my worst moments, when they would deny me pain medication. The most egregious incident occurred on my return to Elmhurst, five weeks after I had been released from Glen Cove. I had to go back to Elmhurst to have Roberto removed. Dr. Joseph, the doctor who put Roberto in, had to be the one to take him out. I was terrified of going back to that hospital. I had nightmares about it every night that week, but there was no other way. It was the only place I could get it removed, and I knew in the end it would be worth it. I couldn't wait to be done with Roberto once and for all. So I put on my brave face and my big-girl sweatpants, and my parents and I returned to Elmhurst.

The surgery was in the morning, and when I came out of the anesthesia my parents were there to hold my hands and make sure I got into my room okay. By now I was sort of a hospital pro, and I was sure I wouldn't need them to stay with me any longer. My great aunt had died a few days before, and the funeral Mass was set for that afternoon. I already felt such guilt and sadness for not being able to say good-bye to such a beautiful woman that the idea of keeping my family away from saying their own good-byes would have killed me. I told my parents I'd be fine. After all, this was only a removal—I could handle that shit in my sleep. But what I hadn't counted on was the fact that I didn't have my forty milligrams of OxyContin being placed into my hand every two hours, with an extra ten if the pain got too bad. As the anesthesia began to wear off, the pain started in, and I pressed the call button.

"What do you want?" the voice inside the wall asked.

"Can I have some pain medication, please?"

"There is no prescription for any pain medication on your chart."

"I just got out of surgery; the doctor said I would be on a morphine pump. I need to be hooked up to one. It must be there on the chart."

"There is nothing there—you don't have a prescription. I can't do anything without the doctor saying so."

"I just got out of surgery. Why wouldn't I get any pain medication? Could you please call Dr. Joseph? He said that he called it in."

There was radio silence. After that the voice in the wall stopped answering my calls.

This was when things got serious. I was still in pain from the initial trauma of the accident, but now I also had this intense burning feeling at the site where they had to fuse my skin back together, where Roberto had been. On top of that, I was starting to go through withdrawal from the OxyContin, and the shakes had started. The fear of dying crept back into my mind. I didn't think a body could handle the pain, the withdrawal, and now this aggressive neglect on the part of the nursing staff.

Every one of my family members was at my aunt's funeral, so I called Maribeth. Before I even finished telling her what had happened, she was in a cab on the way to the hospital. She walked into my room and peeled off her cocoon of a jacket—the kind that made a person look as if they were walking around in a sleeping bag—pushed up her sleeves, and grabbed my chart. At this point I couldn't stop itching, and I was writhing in pain. My anger was getting bigger and bigger with every passing moment. I thought about cutting myself, making myself bleed so I could make the pain seep out. It was the only thing I could think of that would make it stop. What I really wanted to do was run away from there, somehow, some way. I took Maribeth's arm and held it in what had to be the most desperate grip. "Please fix it, Maribeth. Fix it."

She stood next to me and held my hand as I called the nurses' station again and asked for pain medication. Maribeth heard the nurse tell me no, again. Then she marched down to the nurses' station with my chart in hand. I could hear her yelling from down the hall.

"Are you fucking serious? You are denying this girl medication? Did you not read her chart (insert medical jargon here)? Of course she needs morphine. Call the doctor. Call him now."

"Who are you?"

"I am her friend, and I am also her nurse. Call the doctor. I know you can. I am not leaving until you do."

She came back flushed, forehead crinkled, spitting curse words as verbs, nouns, and adjectives. It was wonderful.

Finally one of the nurses came in with a morphine pump and hooked me up. That cold rush of morphine going into my veins was one of the loveliest feelings I had felt in a long time. Knowing the hurt was going to subside just because of what was in that needle was like a hug from someone you hadn't seen in a long time. It was comforting, soothing, and something that you never wanted to end. I touched Maribeth's face and said thank you.

She stayed with me until my parents returned, and because the nurses were not my biggest fans, she took care of me. She got me ice chips and bought me a candy bar I couldn't eat. Maribeth held my hand, made jokes, and cursed about the nurses in this hysterical endless cycle. When I pressed the call button for the nurses to take away my bedpan, she took care of it herself.

Now, let's break this down for a moment shall we: best friend cleans up other best friend's pee, and neither of them is drunk. I am not sure that it belongs on a Hallmark card, or if it is something one would ever talk about during a bridesmaid speech, but the care and selflessness that action took induces in me a feeling I can only describe as wonder. I wonder at her strength, at her being able to stand tall for me when all I had to offer up was weakness, fragility, and desperation.

And I learned that it is better than any BFF necklace, any well-chosen card, or any expensive gift to know you can be loved when you feel like you are so worthless. It is a miracle I would have never have experienced if I hadn't been run over by a truck.

# CHAPTER THIRTY-ONE

# Jump and the Net Will Appear

It wasn't like I hadn't been practicing at home. I had. It wasn't as though it was the first time I'd walked. I had been doing it around the house with my walker like a good girl. My family or boyfriend would spot me, making sure I was always covered, always steady. I didn't need to be brave when they were there. They wouldn't let me fall.

I was sans Roberto. He had been removed the previous day, and already I felt lighter. Interestingly enough, I also felt a lot less like RoboLady, which was refreshing. Not having to see the inside of my flesh was also a huge bonus, because now my skin was fused together. The pain was just so different. There was still the undulating ache of bones mending themselves and of my body trying to make itself whole again, but the fear of knocking Roberto out of alignment no longer existed. I wasn't as scared of moving because I knew the repercussions wouldn't be as serious. Before the removal, I was caught in a constant tug-of-war between what I wanted to do and what I thought I could do without really hurting myself. Suddenly, after the surgery, it was as if one of the teams dropped their end of the rope and walked away.

The doctors at Elmhurst said I needed to be in the hospital for a few more days after the surgery. My parents and boyfriend were in the room keeping me company and shooting the shit. This was my first time being in the hospital sans catheter, and I was now able to walk to the bathroom on my own, like a big girl—which was fine, but time-consuming because I had to pee every eighteen minutes.

My hands were gripping the walker as I emerged from the bathroom for what felt like the ninth time in the last hour. I felt myself push the walker forward and let the handles go, just a little bit. I loosened my grip enough so there was air in between my hands and the plastic. The sweat that had been accumulating on my palms felt markedly cooler, and I liked it. As I walked, I realized I didn't need to lean on the walker as much as I thought I did. I was actually kind of balanced. I took another step and allowed my hands even more breathing room. Then my fingertips just barely touched the walker. Even though the whole fam and Warren were there, no one was watching this unfold, and it was kind of a relief. If I failed, there were no consequences.

It seemed only natural that the next step would be without my walker—no one supporting me, no one egging me on— just me, my totes socks, and a little bit of boldness. I didn't give myself the time to be afraid. *Jump and the net will appear, jump and the net will appear, jump and the net will appear* is what I said to myself as I pushed the walker a few feet in front of my body. I stared at it the same way I used to stare at the finish line at the end of a fifteen-hundred-meter race. It was all I wanted. The sweet success of finishing was what I deserved for working as hard as I had, and nothing was going to stop me from getting there. I placed one foot down, but I didn't know what to do with my hands. I hadn't walked without gripping something for a long time, so I held them out like a zombie. That was when everyone in the room took notice.

My dad's eyes grew really wide, and everyone else took in a very deep, collective breath—but no one said a word as I walked like the undead toward my end point. I didn't look at them. I was just focused on the walker, my feet slow and shuffling. When I was close enough to death-grip my walker, I started to laugh. A deep belly laugh, one I hadn't had the pleasure of since my accident. Laughing aggressively was so much easier without Roberto. I felt in those seconds the same way I did during the last one hundred meters of the run: ebullient, overwhelmed, and exhausted. My family and boyfriend rushed up to me, shouting a chorus of "I can't believe that you did that!" and "Why did you do that?!" and "Do you know how dangerous that was?" In the mix of anger and glee, I stood smiling. I had created my own miracle, and for the first time in a long time I had done it without fear.

# CHAPTER THIRTY-TWO

# Becoming a Real Girl

My sister and I were five years apart, so that meant we didn't really spend much time together growing up. We were never in the same age bracket to really be able to fully relate to each other. I tried to be a good older sister, but I was pretty sure I wasn't great. I would give advice when asked, and I gave her all my old clothes, but I wasn't as awesome as some other big sisters I knew. I never took her out with my friends; she didn't drink her first beer with me. But she did tell me about the first time she went to a party.

It wasn't easy for Callie to pave her own way in high school, because everyone around her knew me or one of my brothers in a six-degrees-of-separation way. It was hard for Callie to find something that any of us hadn't done before her—it was tougher for her to find her own thing.

We loved each other, but before my accident we related to each other like a Venn diagram—two separate circles that overlap, making it impossible for one to function without the other. After October 2, our relationship changed drastically.

I went from being the big sister who was there when Callie needed me—for a late-night piece of advice, to buy her beer when she was underage, to give her money if she was short on cash—to me asking more from her than any person ever had.

If it had been the year before, she and I would have probably seen each other about six times before she left for Australia, but now we spent every single day together. Callie became my constant companion, whether she liked it or not.

Callie was used to me asking for things, but it usually had to do with sibling hazing, aka *Make me a sandwich, get me a Popsicle from the ice cream man, hand me the remote.* Now, it was more like, "Cal, could you bring me a bucket? I think I'm going to throw up," or "Would you mind holding on to me while I transfer?" or "Would you hand me those pills?" My sister did everything I asked of her, and she was shockingly happy doing it. She was the perfect sister: sweet, funny, and strong, and somehow she made it all look effortless.

My relationship with the bathroom biz during this time was so awkward I had stopped really thinking about it. I just dealt with it as it came, literally. My boyfriend and I had been together for about two years when I got in the accident, and we had been best friends since I was sixteen years old, so we had very few secrets. After my accident we had even fewer. If a person can watch you vomit on yourself in a hospital gown with your hair falling out and still love you . . . things are pretty solid. Through all the disgusting stuff he had to witness, I swore to myself that I would do everything I could to avoid him coming in contact with me going to the bathroom in front of his eyes.

One afternoon there was no avoiding it. I had removed my catheter a week before and was still not really in charge of my bladder yet. Warren had come over to watch the Giants game with me, and when he got up during the commercial to get another beer, I realized I had started to pee into my bedpan.

I did everything I could to stop it. I imagined what it felt like when I used to try to hold it. I thought of deserts and other things that were dry—but my bladder had a mind of its own. All those muscles had atrophied, and you can't tell a worm to start acting like a boa constrictor—it just wasn't going to happen. "Callie, Callie," I whisper-shouted to my sister across the family room.

"What, Katie?" she said, without pulling her eyes away from the TV.

"I just peed—and I can't let Warren see it. Can you take the bedpan?"

What she did next was nothing short of heroic.

"Hey, Warren," she called into the kitchen. "Would you mind getting Katie and me a bottle of champagne from the garage?"

"Callie, there's a bottle in the fridge. Can I bring that one?"

"No, you can't—Katie likes the ones from the garage better. They're colder and make her feel more in touch with nature. Right, Katie?" The girl was brilliant, totally and utterly brilliant.

"Yes, I definitely like the champagne from the garage better. It's a totally different taste sensation. . . . The bubbles are just better." I ran farther with the lie than I needed to because I am an awful liar, and when I lied I would just keep talking. I thought saying a lot made everything much more believable.

When we heard the back door close, Callie ran over to my bed, as I lifted the lower part of my body by holding on to the trapeze over my hospital bed, so that my little sister could reach under my ass and remove the bedpan I had just peed in. She hustled it over to the bathroom, poured it out into the toilet, and then placed it back under me before Warren even returned to the kitchen. I was so grateful, but I couldn't let Warren know what had just happened. All I could do was stare into her eyes as I mouthed, "Thank you!" hoping by some sort of secret sister power she could feel my gratitude and love. She looked back at me and smiled and nodded her head. I believed she knew.

There were days when things were harder for her to fix, though. Times when I woke up and was so devastated about what had happened that I couldn't let it go. I couldn't think of anything else all day, except for the fact that I was not walking and that I was in an insane amount of pain. One morning in my parents' family room after a Christmas Hess truck commercial sent me into a tailspin of flashbacks, Callie held my hand and said, "Squeeze. Squeeze my hand, to make it hurt less."

"I don't want to. It won't make it hurt any less. It will just make you hurt more, and I don't want that either."

"I would like it if we were just a little closer to even."

"Not gonna happen, kiddo. Truck v. hand squeeze—truck is going to win every time."

"Bitch, you always get to win," she whispered with fake anger, which made me smile through my tears.

She was ridiculous and fantastic. She let me ask her about a million times why she thought this had happened to me, and she didn't once get annoyed with me. *Why me?* is the most annoying question in the entire English language, because there is no good way to answer it. If you say, *It's because you were an asshole*, the asker gets their feelings hurt. Plus it's a self-indulgent question, but somehow Callie was willing to indulge me and only answered, "I don't know, Katie, I just know it isn't your fault."

Spending my days with Callie felt like training for when I was a real girl again. It was great to be with another girl, giggling (even if no noise came out), watching YouTube videos of hilariously adorable babies. I love hilarious baby videos, and my sister made it her mission to find me as many of them as possible. She would sidle up to my bed, put her laptop on my hospital table, and play me the gem of a video she had found on the Internet that day. We would watch and rewatch it. We would spend the rest of the evening either imitating the video or forcing everyone who came into the room to watch it. No one ever found the videos as funny as we did, but I kind of liked it that way.

When we were younger, I was afraid that Callie and I wouldn't have the closeness some sisters had. I wanted for us to be sisters but also friends, and we hadn't gotten there yet. During the two months we spent together, I saw this incredible side of her. She was so careful with me, so kind and unselfish; it made me want to be a better sister to her. I was more interested in what was happening in her life and more capable of understanding her because now I actually knew her. From my hospital bed I couldn't take her out drinking, but I could have happy hour with her every night. I could help her root through the clothes I hadn't worn in months to find the perfect outfit for her Friday night out. When she got into a fight with one of her friends, I was there to listen to her as she talked out how hurt she felt. I was also able to be there to coach her on the phone when she confronted those friends. We were able to be more open with each other than we ever had been, and it felt good.

Taking care of other people looked good on Callie. For the first time she didn't feel as though she was in anyone's shadow. Now she was the light.

# CHAPTER THIRTY-THREE

## Dance Dance Dance

I got kicked out of ballet. Okay, that isn't exactly true, but it sounds so much more dramatic than saying I was a shitty five-year-old ballerina. It carries more weight than *I couldn't follow directions and I didn't really know my left from my right.* (To be honest, I still kind of don't. I thank God that *left* begins with an *L.* When I was learning to drive, I drove with my hands in an L formation at all times for this very reason.) This lack of coordination made it very difficult for me to be a positive addition to my ballet classes. These were not fancy classes. There were no French instructors or those aggressive time-keeping poles. The lessons were held in the American Legion next door to the fire station in my town. When the instructor told us to turn left, I would just stand there dumbfounded, unsure of what to do, except to turn in whatever way seemed to be the correct way. Unfortunately, I was wrong 50 percent of the time, usually knocking the little girl who was correct over into the next little girl; you can see where this is going. It became so embarrassing that I had to quit. This being said, I have never been much of a dancer, but I motherfucking loved it and I missed shaking it.

I had gotten an iPod for Christmas, and Callie had been spending the majority of her mornings going to and from the library to pick up CDs for me. It was a brilliant move, actually; she would go to the library, take out a CD, and then we would upload music to our iPods and she would return the CDs the next day. I was wowed by her genius and thrift. Callie picked up music she thought I would like, and she would also make her own recommendations.

As I became more and more confident on my feet, I would take my iPod and put it in the elastic waistband of my velour tracksuit, and I would listen as I walked with my canes. It felt nice to shut out the world with music. Everything that had happened to me in the last few months made me so transparent. I felt like I rarely had any privacy. Being able to keep something to myself, even if it was just a song in my headphones, felt good.

One morning in early February, I woke up feeling bold. I decided today was going to be a day I was going to wear underwear AND jeans. I had been refraining from the underoos for the last few months. This was not an homage to my accident experience, but for more logical reasons. Having one more thing to pull up and down was difficult and labor intensive. Today I felt ready to rise to that challenge. Plus, as awful as this is, my mom had bought me a pair of jeans for my wasted-away self that was a smaller waist size than I had ever been. I wanted to know what it felt like to put on a pair of 26s and not be twelve years old. I don't think that my family or friends had really realized how skinny I had gotten until I was able to stand up, and we all saw my ass had literally disappeared. It was bad. I would not have been shocked if I had seen a picture of my ass on the back of a milk carton. Even my dad, who does not like to talk about the human anatomy at all, said, "Wow, you really have no fanny, do you, Katie?"

So that morning I put on my undies AND my jeans and was feeling pretty good about myself. My dad was upstairs, and I yelled up to him that I was going to get myself a Diet Coke.

"Are you going to do it by yourself?"

"Yes, Dad, I will." I didn't think it would be appropriate to yell up to him, "DON'T WORRY, DAD, I'M FEELING GOOD ABOUT THIS. I AM WEARING PANTIES AND JEANS. . . . IT'S A NEW DAY!"

The last concert I had been to before my accident was for a singer named Feist. Her most recent album was so fun and uplifting. I had been nuts about it before the accident. One morning Callie went to get it for me, but the library only had her first album. It was sweeter, slower, and sadder, but Callie brought it home, and I wanted to keep it. These older songs felt as though they fit me a little better now. One of the songs I loved was "Mushaboom." It was about dressing her children in snowsuits and a one-story house in the country. It was so basic and so pretty; it sounded hopeful.

I put my iPod in my back pocket, the headphones in my ears, and I hit Feist on my playlist. I took my canes in my hands and walked to the kitchen. *Left foot, right cane, right foot, left cane,* I told myself as I walked. In the beginning I had some trouble getting started—I would use my left cane and my left foot and would almost lose my balance; it was awkward for everyone.

I got into the kitchen, and I leaned my canes on the island and used my left hand to steady myself as I opened the refrigerator with my right hand. Everything had to be thought about carefully. I needed to be sure to support my body with my arms at all times. We still weren't sure if I was steady enough to balance on my own. I took out the Diet Coke and reveled in

how nice it was to get something for myself. I wanted a drink.
I got a drink. I wanted to wear underwear. I wore underwear. I
couldn't remember what it was like when I started to be more
independent as a child. There was no memory of walking or
of getting my first snack, but I was sure it had to be a lot like
this. So exciting, so much like what grown-ups do. The only
difference was as a little tyke I had no fear of what would happen next. I wasn't worried about falling down or of what it was
going to mean to be able to do things myself, of how to not
have my parents take care of me anymore. But on Underwear-
and-jeans Day there wasn't a whole lot of fear, just happiness at
doing things I used to be able to do. All I could think about was
how good the Diet Coke tasted that morning. It was a good
bottle—the syrup-to-carbonation ratio was outstanding, and
it tickled my upper lip and made me smile in spite of myself.

I had been steadying my body on the island with my
canes leaning by my side, there just in case I needed them.
"Mushaboom" came on my mix, and I was feeling so happy, so
confident, that my hips started to sway a little bit. Just gently
side to side, and then I felt my feet moving—a little shuffle in
place in time with the music. I lifted my feet one at a time off
the ground and moved them with my hips, and I saw myself in
the window, and I was *dancing*. I wasn't dancing well, but I was
dancing on my own. I clapped my hands at my reflection like
a child excited about what she saw. I could only move like that
until the chorus kicked in, but it felt incredible.

I stood there as the music faded, letting the reverberation
of the piano's exit notes ring in my head. I smiled at myself and
looked down at my skinny legs and my feet that still didn't feel
right on the floor. I felt so proud of my little body. So amazed at
how hard it had worked after all that it had been through and
how it could still dance—at how there was enough strength
and energy and fucking joy in it to dance. Even after surgeries

and immobility and crushing pain, there was still something so pure and so good inside of this fragile thing that it fearlessly moved its legs and swung itself out of its safe space and into the place it wanted to be. I felt so happy and so good that I didn't want to move. I wanted to live in that triumph for as long as I possibly could.

But my back started to ache, so I gathered up my canes and walked, left arm, right foot, right arm, left foot, back to my bed. I kissed each leg for being so strong and so brave, and then I took off my jeans and put my velour trackpants back on. We had had enough jeans-and-underwear excitement for one day.

# CHAPTER THIRTY-FOUR

## First Day of Work Mix

I love a good mixtape. They have been important in many aspects of my life. Whether they were created for a road trip, a person I liked, or a way to commemorate a breakup, they were always amazing. They seem to encapsulate periods of my life into a tiny little rectangle that would play on command. It didn't need to be a tape; I wasn't a purist. I also loved the next incarnation: the mix CD. My friends and I would burn them for each other and then listen to them before we went out. They became a soundtrack to dance to while we got dressed and spackled on makeup. The playlists of the iPod generation were even more instantly gratifying; all you had to do was drag a song across your computer screen, and you were immediately creating a keepsake, one you could access whenever you needed to be brought back to that moment. It was fantastic.

I started to see a therapist that January to help me to deal with the post-traumatic stress. The flashbacks were happening at least fifteen times a day. They would sneak up on me with no rhyme or reason, with nothing around to remind me of bikes or trucks. *What would happen when I actually went into the city for the first time?* I knew that the avenues were choked with large cars and trucks, and I wasn't going to be able to stop every few feet to have an episode.

All my time with doctors made me very comfortable saying exactly what I wanted. At my first meeting with Dr. Gordon I got straight to the point:

"Dr. Gordon, here is my problem; I am reliving my accident at least fifteen times a day. I want you to give me the tools to make that stop. I am also really afraid of a lot of things, and I need you to help me deal with these fears and move past them. I don't need to talk about my feelings. I am cool with my feelings—I just need you to give me an idea of how to fix myself. I don't want to have to see you every week for the rest of my life just to feel okay. Does that make sense?"

He seemed a little taken aback by my candor but said he understood, and we went from there.

Dr. Gordon was smart and sweet, but he didn't put up with my bullshit, and he told corny jokes that made me laugh, to boot. I liked that I could talk to him about the things that were bothering me and he gave me a way to fix them. It wasn't just me talking about myself—we were talking about solutions. My flashbacks decreased after I started to see him. I was still having around ten a day, but progress was progress. Of course, the true test would be when I went back into the city.

I had my finance job waiting for me—the one I had had for all of a month before I got run over. The basic plan was I was going to be the office assistant while I studied for the Series 7, and after I passed, I would get promoted to internal wholesaler, and then I would be able to call up financial advisors and sell them financial products. At the time I didn't really understand what the job was going to entail, but I knew the test I was going to have to take was based on the financial markets, which I knew almost nothing about. In my previous jobs I had been an event planner/salesperson—about as far away from finance as a person could get. Oh, and did I mention I was a theater major in college? As an aside, my math skills kept me in the math lab for the majority of my mornings throughout high school. Who wants me to get after their retirement portfolio? Luckily, I was a good saleswoman and I had sold my fantastic manager, Matt Witschel, on the idea that I was a fast learner and that I really wanted this job. I had made a promise to Matt when I interviewed that I would become a great internal wholesaler. He put his faith in me. And truck or no truck, I had a promise to keep. I started to study for the Series 7 test while I was at home. I was trying to somehow make up for the time I lost. It was a way for me to feel in control, like I was getting closer to being the person I could have been if I hadn't been run over.

As I became healthier and healthier I let Matt know that I was chomping at the bit to get back to work, even though I was terrified. I needed to tell him I was excited so I would believe it myself. When Matt asked me when I thought I'd be coming back into the office, I told him, "March 1st is the day I would like to come in."

"Are you sure, Katie? Will you be okay?"

"Yup, totally sure!" What the fuck was I saying? There was no way I could do it. I hadn't worked a full day in four months! I only had four weeks to relearn how to be a contributing member of society.

"Okay, well, if you're sure, then we will see you on March 1st. I'll let HR know, and we will get everything set up. Really looking forward to it!"

"Oh, yeah, me too! Can't wait!"

Seriously, was I on glue? Why did I just say that? There was no way I was going to be ready, but I couldn't take it back now. My boss had only known me for—literally—thirty days, and my company had been working to keep me covered by medical insurance for the whole time I was in the hospital. I owed them. Whether I was crippled or not, these people had been good to me, and it was time for me to start returning the favor.

The next time I saw Dr. Gordon, I told him about the decision I had made to go back to work in a month, and all my "giving back" bravado faded as soon as the words left my mouth. The reality of how unbelievably shitty and hard this was going to be set in. I hadn't gone a full day without a nap in months. How was I going to be a normal working person? I started to freak out about everything I hadn't done in so long, and I started to sputter out *what ifs* until my breath couldn't keep up with my words. Dr. Gordon let me cry through my fears, and when I calmed down enough to notice he was still in the room, he said, "All these things you are getting upset about are things you can't control. You don't know if any of these bad things will actually happen. What about the factors you can control? What are a few things you know you can take care of before you go to work, so you won't have to worry about them?"

"I can plan my outfit."

"There you go. What else?"

"I can study for the 7, and I've already started to do that."

"Great, you're already on the right track with that one."

"I could find out what train and subway I need to take to get into work."

"Perfect. What else? What made you excited to get to work—something that kind of pumped you up?"

"Music. I really like listening to music on my commute."

"Why don't you plan what music you're going to listen to on your first day?"

"Like a first-day-of-work mix?"

"Yeah, something like that."

I loved the idea! As soon as I got home from my appointment with the good doctor, I caned myself over to the couch and asked my mom to bring over my laptop. I was going to create a sound track to the first day of the rest of my life. I pored over the songs I had in my iTunes library, dragging each song I deemed worthy of "First Day of Work Mix" status. Anytime I was feeling anxious about my first day, I would stare at the suit that had been hanging so patiently on the back door of my closet, and I would work on my first-day-of-work mix. The songs I chose were a jumble—some from my past, some from my present, some I hoped would be a part of my future.

March 1 arrived and I put on the suit. I pulled out the train ticket I had bought a week before, I held tightly to my two canes, and I tucked my iPod into my purse. My brother and my dad accompanied me on the train into the city that morning. We did everything we could not to talk about how scared all of us were about what was going to happen. New York is not known for being particularly friendly—period. If you are a disabled person, the city gets even meaner. The three of us chitchatted on the Long Island Railroad, and I ate my buttered roll and drank my Diet Coke (breakfast of champions), wishing I could listen to my mix.

The New York City skyline started to come into view, and it took my breath away as it always did, and I felt my eyes fill with tears. Then the train dipped under the East River, and we crossed from Long Island into Manhattan. As we pulled into Penn Station, I saw my brother's and dad's faces tense and their shoulders square up; they were ready to be my bodyguards. They each took one side of me and ushered me carefully through the throngs of people rushing to leave the bowels of the station. It was overwhelming and intimidating, and I was so grateful to have them right next to me, protecting me from the mob. We took the two subways that we needed to get to Grand Central. My office was three blocks away, and as we were getting onto the escalator to leave the subway station I asked my brother and dad to stop for a minute while I put my headphones in. I placed the little white buds in my ears and turned the volume up as loud as it would go. The reverberating bass of Kanye West's "Stronger" filled my head.

The music pulsing in my ears, I took my two canes in my right hand and let the escalator do the work as I moved closer and closer to the light streaming in from the exit onto Park Avenue.

My heart (and Kanye) knew what my head had been afraid to say: this is what I had to do. There was never going to be a time that was more right or more wrong for me to start this new life, but no matter what happened in my life from that day forward, it would make me stronger.

If a truck couldn't kill me, I'm pretty sure that my first day of work wasn't going to.

# PART III

# Old Katie Meets New Katie

# CHAPTER THIRTY-FIVE

## Miss Dependent

After my accident my parents went from having a twenty-four-year-old independent woman for a daughter to having the equivalent of a large talking baby with major health issues and a serious Diet Coke addiction. When I was first in the hospital, I struggled to understand what the doctors were saying to me about my prognosis and where I was in the healing process. I tried to keep track of myself, to stay motivated to be better, but I could never seem to wrap my brain around what was happening. The constant pain, and the drugs I took to keep the pain at bay, made me feel so fuzzy I didn't have the mental ability to take in what was being said to me most of the time. In the few moments of clarity I did have, I would spend much of my mental energy searching my memory banks to remind me of what had brought me there. After I lived through it all over again, I would inevitably fixate on what the road ahead of me looked like. My thoughts would begin to spiral, and I would yearn to walk around to alleviate my stress. When I was reminded that I couldn't walk, I would start to freak out and become even more anxious. Then I would need an anti-anxiety pill to get me back to the place I was before I started to think about myself. For self-preservation purposes, I had to let it all go. I gave myself over to the confusing comfort of being completely cared for.

I had been fighting against my natural inclination to be dependent on my parents since I was a small girl. My parents like to recount the story of when I was three or four and on a walk to the duck pond with my brother and them. Apparently, I was so excited to go to the duck pond, and I thought they were going too slow, that during the entire half-mile walk I would run about thirty feet in front of them, look back to make sure they were still there, and then start running again, full speed, toward the pond. My mom would cap off the story by saying, "We knew right then that we didn't have to worry about you never leaving the nest. You would be just fine."

I wanted to do it all on my own but with the full and certain knowledge that my family was still there, somewhere, behind me.

This time, I didn't have the option of running ahead. Instead I was holding on to my parents for dear life. Not only did they take care of everything that was happening to me medically and financially, but they also did what they could to keep fear away. I trusted my parents to know why I was getting X-rays, what the results of my blood tests were, when the surgery to implant the stent in my side was going to happen. I expected them to know everything and to synthesize it into digestible bites for me. They, for better or worse, protected me from the really scary things. I'd had my fill of being frightened already.

In the very few times I was alone and had a choice to make, I didn't trust myself to know what the right answer was. I was so unsure of myself that I called my parents with all kinds of questions: What should I eat for breakfast? Should my friends come to see me? What was my favorite color? At this point I felt as though they knew me better than I did. They were so much more certain of things. They were a steady dock to my sinking dinghy.

More than just everyday choices, I felt I needed them to handle living. Without them nearby I became acutely aware that I didn't know what to do with myself. I was unsure of my next step. I was constantly afraid I was only one fall away from dying. When they weren't close by, this body I now inhabited became even more foreign, and I didn't understand how to interact with it. I didn't know where I belonged in the world without my parents; they made me feel safe, understood, and less afraid.

The question I would always ask them, and I asked it all the time, was if it was going to be okay. I wasn't even sure of what "it" was; I just needed reassurance. I needed to know someone had faith that everything was going to be all right. My mom and dad did that for me—they were hopeful, so I was hopeful; they were sure, so I was sure. Without them I would have fallen into the dark side of my fear. They pulled me into the light of a better future.

In late January, two months after being back home, I had become self-sufficient enough to be left alone. I was still sleeping in the family room, and the stairs and I weren't best friends yet, but I didn't need as much monitoring as I once did. It was decided that if I was placed on the sofa with my walker, the remote control, my cell phone, a glass of water, a snack, and an emergency bedpan, I could be left by myself. When my dad did leave me alone for the first time he didn't make a big deal of it— he just set me up with my rations and said he was running into town and would be back in an hour. I smiled and said, "Sure, of course, Dadda. I'll be just fine. See you soon!" I was scared out of my mind. I bit the inside of my cheek to keep from crying. I thought if I focused on the pain in my mouth I wouldn't think about how lost I felt as I watched him walk out of the family room. As I heard the front door close, I unclenched my molars and tasted blood.

I sat there and blubbered loudly in my parents' empty house, the echoes of my self-pity ringing through the halls. After about ten minutes, I blinked myself back to reality, and I breathed. No one had come to soothe me out of my sadness. I felt like a baby who had been left in her crib to cry herself to exhaustion. It was time for me to deal with the fact that I was alone, and even though I was crying my lungs out, no one was going to come for me.

The idea of independence was one I used to cherish, and now, just a small taste of it had turned me into a total mess. I had become so used to my parents always being there—loving me wholly and deeply—that I never thought about the day when they wouldn't be able to care for me full-time. On some level I believe I knew that this day would come, but I didn't expect I would feel as lost as I did without them nearby. Nothing felt right until they returned to me.

My dad's trip to the drugstore was my first unmonitored hour in three months, and it was the first time I felt my fingers loosen their death grip on my fear of being alone. I leaned back into the couch and wiped my face with the sleeve of my velour zip-up. "What is a good thing to do when by yourself?" I wondered out loud. I grabbed the remote control and put on really trashy, stupid daytime TV, the kind my dad would never be caught dead watching. I looked around and turned the volume up on a talk show that was dealing with the riveting topic of "My Sister Slept with My Husband—and I Don't Care!" I felt like I used to when my siblings and I would jump on our beds as soon as my parents left the house—we knew it was wrong, but being bad was so fun! I knew I wasn't being specifically bad, but this small thing felt like rebellion, and I liked it.

It was good to remember the things that were fantastic about being alone. I could do what I wanted (as long as it didn't include anything that involved a lot of walking). I could listen to very loud music. I could make phone calls to anyone I wanted. I could watch what I wanted on television, or I could just sit in the silence. It was nice to be the boss of these small slivers of my day.

When my dad went back to work in early February, I had become much more mobile and was having my physical therapy appointments at an actual office, so my aunt Carol took care of my day-to-day out-of-the-house pursuits. She became my parent placebo. Aunt Carol is the person I would like to be when I grow up. She has the most incredible laugh and a way of making the most mundane activities a celebration. When I think of her, I think of laughing, champagne, and mink coats. She took over the responsibility of taking me to and from physical therapy, throwing in an additional side trip (The drug store! The nail salon! ADVENTURE!), making me lunch, and then tucking me into bed until my mom got back from work. Aunt Carol made me feel loved and cared for, but she also treated me like the grown-up I truly was, not the confused child I had been behaving like.

I now had mornings and late afternoons to myself. The house was so quiet without anyone in it. I tried to wean myself off my parents by resisting the temptation to call them all the time. I wrote down what I would have said to them instead. I started to ask myself the questions I would have asked them. I took my time answering myself. No need to rush figuring out the who-the-fuck-am-I? process. I realized I was now much more honest with myself than I had been in my past life. I didn't try to soothe myself with the idea that somehow it was all going to work out. I didn't have the patience for rose-colored glasses—now was the time for truth and a very fierce sense of hopefulness. I started to feel more like myself and to take comfort in the idea that I was strong enough to handle this next chapter of my life. I started to tell *myself* I was going to be okay. My parents gave me the space I needed to kick my parental love addiction, and they didn't push to get back to the codependent relationship we had before. They let me put some distance between us but were willing to come and close that gap when I was feeling too weak and broken to go without.

On one of these afternoons by myself I decided that I was going to move back into my Williamsburg apartment in April. It didn't matter to me that I was still rocking two canes and wasn't very steady on my feet—I had promised myself, so I had to make it happen. I told my parents it was time. I wanted to see what the life I had fought for looked like outside of my childhood home. My parents were hesitant to let me go, but they respected my decision. They also knew I had amazing roommates and Warren to help take care of me. They knew I would be okay.

*** 

It was a Saturday afternoon in mid-April when I walked into my old room—left cane, right foot, right cane, left foot—and looked around. My room, but it didn't smell like me anymore. Nothing felt familiar, everything was in places it didn't belong, and I couldn't remember where it was supposed to go. As I stood there and took in the space, my back began to seize up, and I started to feel panicked. The pain triggered my deep fear that I wasn't capable of doing this. Trying to start again was too big a feat. The pain and the loneliness would always be too much. I wouldn't be able to conquer them alone. I needed my parents. I felt myself starting to hyperventilate. I spiraled into flashbacks of the last time I was in my room and how easily I had moved around. I remembered what I was wearing when I walked out the door on that October morning. I saw everything happen all over again. I felt it shudder through my body. As the tears started, my parents entered my room carrying cardboard boxes full of my books and tchotchkes. Without saying anything, they put the boxes down and held me close until I was breathing normally.

"Katie, is this too much? Do you want to come home with us? You can move in another day, when you're a little more ready."

"Dadda, it's always going to be too much. Seriously. You know that. I know that. I'm never going to be ready. It's either I get through it today, or I get through it a week or a month from now—and it will be just as hard then, you know?"

My parents nodded. They knew.

The easy thing would have been to go home with them. It would have been really nice to live under the protective eaves of their love for another night. But this new life wasn't about easy; it was about making my life the happiest it could be. To be happy, I had to reclaim my independence and start to build a new life for myself, and I needed to do that alone.

After my mom and dad left, I lay on my bed and stared at the ceiling, trying to ignore the burning in my back and legs. I struggled to remember what I used to think about when I was on this bed. I looked up and wondered what this new life was going to look like, what it was going to feel like. I felt excited but fearful. I reached for the phone and called my parents. They picked up and put me on speakerphone.

"Hi, it's me. Everything is going to be okay. Right, guys?"

"Yes, baby girl, everything is going to be okay."

"Yeah, I thought so too. It's going to be okay. I love you, Momma. I love you, Dadda."

"We love you too."

I hung up and smiled. That night I fell asleep with the lights on, in my clothes, over my covers. I was a grown-up girl who could do what she wanted, and that was okay.

# CHAPTER THIRTY-SIX

## Angry Little Grown-up

By June almost all my pieces were back together. I looked like me. I sounded like me. I even almost moved like me. I had been using my canes less and less. I wasn't totally unaided but I was closer than I was before. I was shuffle-walking my way through my life, and it was amazing! Everything was in place. I should have been happy. Like really, extremely happy. I finally had everything I wanted. I was back in the city in my own apartment; I was back at work, and I was desperate to leave "Katie Who Got Run Over by a Truck" far behind. You would think I would be ecstatic, right? Nope, instead, I was incredibly angry. I was the kind of angry where I always wanted to kick something or hit something with my canes. It was an angry that was just bubbling inside of me and could be set off at any moment, with absolutely no warning.

I had little outbursts every now and again throughout my recovery, but these became more frequent and intense as I started to really dig into my Series 7 studying and work full-time. My days looked like this: wake up at five a.m, study for two hours, get in the shower, and get dressed. Get my two canes and head out of my apartment to the subway. I would then take two flights of stairs, one step at a time, down to the L train. The L took me to Union Square, and then I walked up three flights of stairs and down two flights to the 4/5. I'd take the 4/5 to Grand Central, go up three more flights of stairs, gripping for dear life on to the banister with my left hand, using my right hand to hold my canes and support me. I spent all my time on the stairs being shoved and harrumphed because everyone around me didn't realize the reason why I was going so slowly. In my cute business suit, I didn't look injured. All they were aware of was that there was an obstacle in their way. I was the thing they were going to complain about while getting their morning coffee. *And there was this girl just taking her sweet-ass time. Who does she think she is?*

By the time I got to work, I was exhausted, and I couldn't wait to take some pain meds and sit in my padded chair so my back could recuperate. I didn't want anyone to feel sorry for me, so I didn't complain. I sat at my desk quietly and plastered a smile on my face and tried to look like I knew what was going on. I smiled as I answered phones, ordered office supplies, stuffed envelopes. I was a happy office assistant! At lunchtime I would whip out my books and take practice Series 7 tests for an hour. After that I would go back to phone answering, office upkeeping, and being positive.

When five o'clock rolled around and my coworkers started to leave the office, I took another pain pill, bought myself a fountain Diet Coke, and studied in the office until nine. On my way home I did all those stairs and all those transfers again, before walking that last flight of stairs up to my Williamsburg apartment. I gave myself a half an hour to eat dinner and watch a sitcom, and then I forced myself to go back into my room and study until I passed out from exhaustion. Needless to say, a couple of months of this routine made me a cranky, cranky woman.

I knew I was pushing myself way too hard. But no one could tell me there was another way to do it. I felt like a greyhound chasing a robotic rabbit at the track. A part of me knew I was never going to catch it, but there was no way I could just watch it go by. I was tired, I was overworked, and I was in excruciating pain most of the time. The amount of wear and tear I put on my frail body was insane, but I couldn't stop.

While I was living the hell I had created for myself, I was a complete bitch to anyone who tried to love me. To people I knew socially or didn't relate to in a real way I was sweet as pie. To them I was this little miracle who had overcome the greatest odds and was still kind. To my family, friends, and boyfriend I was a bitch on wheels. I was mad at the world. I felt some sort of anger toward everyone for a myriad of reasons. I was livid at them for not understanding me, for not getting my pain, for not seeing that I needed love and care and attention. I wanted to be treated as though I was special, even though I limped around telling everyone I just wanted to be normal. I needed other people to think I was special so I knew who I was. If they didn't think I was special, I felt spurned and hurt, wanting to say, "Do you know who I am? I'm Katie McKenna, and I was run over by a truck. Look at me now! Don't I look fabulous?"

When the strangers didn't respond in kind, and my social acquaintances were tired of talking about how amazing I was, I felt hurt, which quickly turned into anger. Suddenly the world I had promised to love and cherish, I hated. And this anger and hate just built and built and built, until I barely recognized myself. I was a bubbling cauldron of complaints and misdirected anger. I would talk to Dr. Gordon about it, but the therapy wasn't helping. I kept going back every week, talking about my feelings, taking his thoughtful advice, but I couldn't seem to fix it. And while I knew I was being ridiculous and unfair, I couldn't let go of how wounded I felt by everyone. I would wish awful, childish, petty things on others and feel desperately sorry for my little miracle self.

When I finally took my Series 7 test, in early June, I passed by 1.3%—and I was elated! I hoped passing this test would free me from the angry prison I had locked myself in. Unfortunately it wasn't that easy. I couldn't shake this feeling that I had suffered so much more than anyone else in the world and that every person I met for the rest of my life owed me something. I didn't know what I felt they owed me, but I was pretty sure it was something big, like a lifetime supply of milkshakes or a dishwasher or something.

This feeling stayed with me for a few more weeks, until right before the Fourth of July. I was walking up Metropolitan Avenue toward my apartment at twilight, completely cane-free, feeling the most normal a girl could feel. I was listening to a Regina Spektor song as loudly as my headphones would allow, and I stopped at the crosswalk at the corner of Metropolitan and Humboldt, and as I turned to cross the street, I saw fireworks going off downtown. I stood there on the corner and watched as they exploded across the sky, like dandelion seeds in the wind. In that moment the world looked truly beautiful.

It became very clear to me that the world was not only beautiful, but it was really, really big. I looked around for what felt like the first time in a very long time, and I saw all the other people around me: fathers carrying crying children, lovers kissing, old women pushing their grocery carts to their empty apartments, boys with broken hearts tucked inside their undershirts. Every single one of them had their own joys and their own heartaches. And it didn't have anything to do with me. How could I be angry with people who have their own crosses to bear? How could I be angry at all when there are fireworks and the air is heavy with the scent of fresh-cut grass and cigarette smoke from those brokenhearted boys?

I wish I could have stayed in that moment forever, rooted in joy and gratitude, looking around at the world I lived in and feeling a bond with my fellow human beings. But the fireworks display ended and the traffic light changed to green, and I had to get home. Luckily the feeling of understanding stayed with me and, happily, it grew. The anger was still there, but it stopped being the star of the show; it was demoted to a supporting role. After a few more weeks it only made an occasional guest appearance on a couple of episodes and then left as quickly as it had appeared. When I let the anger seep out, there was a lot more room for the things I liked feeling: joy, kindness, and compassion. I hadn't wanted to be angry, but at the time it had seemed as though it was the easiest option. Now, anytime I find myself slipping into the dark and easy place of anger, I try to remember standing on that corner with my mouth open and my eyes filling with tears of gratitude and love—and I feel my anger dissolve like those bursts of fireworks over the East River.

# CHAPTER THIRTY-SEVEN

## Warren

Warren and I had been dating for over two years when I was run over. Part of the reason why I always hoped we would end up together was because our story sounded so perfect. We had been the best of friends for eight years, throughout high school and college. After college I moved to Ireland for a few months, and when I got back something changed for Warren. Suddenly he saw me differently. I wasn't just one of the guys; I had suddenly become a girl he wanted to kiss. I didn't feel the same way at first and was overwhelmed at the prospect of dating my best guy friend. I immediately feared the worst-case scenario: What would happen if we stopped dating? Would we still be friends? What if we hated each other? How could I live my life without my best friend?

After thinking it over I realized I couldn't live in a world of *what if*s, especially *what if*s about a really good guy, one who really cared about me. He said we would never hate each other. "There's no way," he promised. "We know one another too well to ever hate each other."

We spent the next two years figuring out how amazing and difficult it is to date someone you have known for years. Everything you think you know about someone when they are your friend changes entirely when you start dating them. On the upside, we both just *got* each other; there was no falsity, no pretending. On the downside, my social-butterfly tendencies made me really fun to be friends with at a party but made me tough to date. And his need to sometimes be quiet and stay at home didn't gel with my need to be out and experiencing everything New York City had to offer. Right before my accident I had been getting more and more frustrated with him. I knew that I loved him and that he was a fantastic person and a great friend, but I couldn't seem to stop getting upset with him for small things. Although he wasn't telling me about it, I knew he was tired of me getting after him all the time. I wanted to be with him, because I loved him, but I knew something was off.

After my accident the Warren I had known for years became the man everyone should dream of becoming in times of crisis. He was strong, he was kind, he was good, and more than anything else he was always there. He was there for me in every instance; he never balked at my broken body or was embarrassed about how his girlfriend was a mess. He promised to stay with me and to love me no matter what. He came to the hospital every day, took days off work, brought me presents, answered every one of my phone calls. He supported me as much as my family did and was nothing short of heroic. He had always said he wanted to take care of me, to make me feel safe and protected, and that was just what he did. He dealt with things many people don't have to encounter in their entire lives, let alone when they are only twenty-five years old. Warren became the man he had always hoped he would be. Everyone in my world, and in his, marveled at his maturity and generosity.

As I started to heal, no one was more excited than Warren. He was so proud of me, so ready for me to be myself again. He wanted for us to start this new chapter of our lives together. I remember he once came to the hospital with pictures of different cars he was thinking about buying—asking my opinion because I was going to be the person who would ride in it the most. He would talk about what we would do when I came back to Brooklyn. He spent New Year's Eve in my hospital room while I was getting rehab after having Roberto removed, saying how much better 2008 was going to be. Holding my hand until I fell asleep, telling me how much he loved me. He told me that everything was going to be better soon. So soon.

I was overwhelmed at how good he was to me. How could anyone who wasn't my family be this unselfish and kind? He was the ideal boyfriend, and I couldn't have been more grateful for him . . . except for when I felt overwhelmed by him. His care was amazing, but sometimes it felt like it was too much. I would get frustrated but couldn't seem to find the words to say how I felt. So I swallowed the frustration, and without me being even conscious of it, the feeling grew.

As I continued to heal, I became more and more aware of the fact that Warren liked it when I was in the hospital. He was amazing when I was dependent on him, when he was my go-to for everything. This was where he thrived. He was incredible at being the strong man who took care of his little lady. The problem for him was that I was getting better and better every day. I was becoming more and more like my old self, and my old self was not really great at making herself vulnerable. I started to talk about my life after the hospital. When I brought it up to Warren, he also had some ideas about what my life would look like then. As it turned out, these ideas were different.

Warren had been doing a lot of hard work taking care of me, and in a way he felt that in his care I had written him a check that was going to have to get cashed at some point after I was all healed. He had been the good guy, the hero. He had given up a large part of his life for me, and he deserved something for his kindness. That something he deserved seemed to be my unending love and—above everything else—my devotion. It was as if he believed that after my little stint in the hospital I would start to really understand what was important to me. He believed the thing that was important to me should be him. I owed him. He knew it, and honestly, I knew it too.

How could I not marry this man? He did all the right things. He followed all the rules. He deserved the prize. I got back to being myself. I was back in Brooklyn, just a half mile away from his apartment, and then Warren exhaled. He thought everything would fall into place as it should. We would be normal people dating in their midtwenties. We would go out for dinners. We would go out on weekend trips. And we would spend nights in together watching movies and drinking wine. He was ready to settle down, and he assumed that after all I had been through, so was I. Unfortunately for both of us, I wasn't a normal person in my midtwenties anymore.

Now that I was back, I wanted everything, and I wanted it five minutes ago. Everything was in extremes—studying for the 7, working, going out, rediscovering New York City, drinking away my bad memories, laughing the way Old Katie did. I was reckless with myself, made myself crazy, cried as often as I laughed. I was living as if I was going to die tomorrow. As though the grim reaper was hovering above me, saying, "We missed you once, kiddo, but we won't miss you again." The distance between what Warren wanted and what I wanted became wider and wider. I would ask him if he would like to come out with me, and he would say no. Then he would ask me to stay in with him and make dinner, and I would rattle off all the plans I had made for that evening, saying it was impossible. I would be mad at him for not wanting to be a part of my life in fast forward, and he was resentful that I wasn't willing to slow mine down for him. We were in different places in our lives. But I couldn't break up with him. Who would I be without him?

We continued to see each other, but we lived almost completely separate lives. I wasn't happy. I knew he wasn't the person I could spend the rest of my life with—we were too different. I also needed to figure myself out. I was too fucked up to be honest, and I wasn't ready to be married. I didn't want to settle down, and I also didn't want to feel like I owed anyone anything. I was too busy believing that the world owed *me* something for me to feel any responsibility to anyone else. Our breaking point was reached when Warren had hit his limit and asked me to stop spending so much time with my friends and family. He needed me to make him more of a priority. It was a completely reasonable request. This is exactly what a person who loves someone wants. They want to be the other person's favorite, and I wasn't making him feel like that. Unfortunately, I was too much of a pussy to tell him I wasn't capable of being what he needed. I told him that I would try.

I pushed off my feelings and I kept partying and working until I reached my boiling point on a weekend away for his birthday. I broke up with a good, decent, kind man, in a car. In traffic. On his birthday.

Warren and I ran into each other two weeks later at a bar near my apartment. I had already had a few cocktails before I walked in and we saw each other, so I wasn't functioning at full speed. My stomach dropped, and I had no idea what to say or do. I was frozen in place and had to be pulled to a table inside the bar by one of my friends. She sat me down, got me a drink, and told me to stay put. When Warren approached the table and asked to talk, I ignored my friend's advice and followed him to the front of the bar, near the door. He had had a few drinks, and it probably wasn't the appropriate time for us to talk, but unfortunately we did anyway.

He told me that I was selfish, that I had taken advantage of him, and that I was a person he didn't recognize. He couldn't believe what I had done to him. He said he had been willing to be with me even though I was scarred, even though I probably couldn't have his children. He was still willing to be with me, even though I was a mess. "No one is ever going to love you the way I loved you," he threatened. "No one."

After he walked away from me, I felt my knees buckle, but I somehow made it back to the table. I thought about trying to drink away the feeling of self-hatred that was washing over me, but I knew it was a lost cause. This feeling wasn't going anywhere soon. Instead, I asked my friends to walk me home, and I tucked myself into bed. I curled myself into the smallest ball possible. I kept trying to make myself smaller and smaller until I disappeared. I wanted to crawl into a hole and not come out until I felt like a human being who deserved to be loved. All I could think about was that he was right. He had spoken the fears that lived deep in my heart. Actually, he hadn't just spoken them—he had yelled them, very, very clearly, making sure I heard every word. I was devastated. How was it possible for someone who "loved" me so much to feel this way about me? He knew me so well that I thought what he was saying must be true.

The thing that scared me the most was after all the time we spent together as friends, and as boyfriend and girlfriend, he was still only *willing* to be with me. Not that he wanted to be with me, but he was *willing*. It made me feel as if I was volunteer work, something you were willing to do if someone made you. I was so confused and unsure of myself at this point that a tiny part of me thought I should get back together with him. I was afraid he might be my only chance to ever be loved.

I fell asleep in the fetal position and woke up stretched out diagonally across the bed—my new favorite single-girl sleeping position. Staring at my feet at the lower-right corner of my bed, resting my hand on the cool spot on the pillow next to my head, I thought again about what Warren had said, and it made me feel sick. I had hoped the more I thought about it, the more I acknowledged it, the less it would affect me. It didn't work that way. It continued to make me feel as though I was the worst person in the world. I shocked myself with the strength of my guilt and fear, which made me realize there was a lot of hurt still living inside me. Hurt I wouldn't be able to drink away or party away or love away. If there wasn't something broken in me emotionally, I wouldn't have thought the best thing I could do to make myself happy would be to get back together with Warren—especially after all the awful things he had said to me. I owed myself this time to heal the hurt and to be better and to relearn how to love myself—selfishness, deformities, broken ovaries, and all.

This life wasn't created so I could live it unhappily, and it wasn't rebuilt so Warren could make me into something I wasn't. Although I owed Warren a lot, I owed myself more. I decided the debt I absolutely needed to pay was to myself.

# CHAPTER THIRTY-EIGHT

## Baggage

I had always been a girl who traveled pretty lightly in the emotional baggage department. No daddy issues. I loved to eat food. And if my boyfriend was hit on, I was more likely to give him a high five than get angry. After the accident and breakup with Warren, my packing needs became very different. There was just so much more I needed to carry with me emotionally . . . at all times.

Warren was the first man I had loved and who had loved me in return. Although we loved each other, I realized he was not the person I was meant to be with. It was incredibly difficult for me to break up with him, not only because I had been with him for three years and we were best friends—but also because I was afraid that no one else would ever love me again. I was damaged goods. I knew that. I was sure the world knew it too. When he said those things to me, in anger (or honesty), I wanted to throw them away, but they refused to leave—I had to fold them up and put them in my duffel bag.

When I thought about the prospect of dating anyone new, I was scared to death. There were so many things I was going to have to explain to this new dude that most people would never have to talk about—like why I shudder every time I see a truck, why I can't run/ice skate/stand for too long in one place, why I can't somersault or ski, and how the plastic tubes in green packages aren't actually Japanese lip glosses but self-catheters that I have to use because my bladder no longer functions properly. These were things I didn't even want to admit to myself, let alone to a person I was just starting to get to know. The thought of it made me want to stay in my room and watch *Will and Grace* reruns. I started to seriously think about growing up to be a person who refuses to date or get married and instead devotes her life to training seeing-eye dogs, quilting, and becoming the best aunt anyone has ever seen!

But as mentioned earlier, I like kissing a lot. Way too much to give up on men altogether. So, enter Mike. Luckily he was not a stranger. We had known each other since we were fifteen. He was actually a cousin of my very good friend Tim. In the incredibly tangled, fantastic web that is my life, Tim is my roommate and also amazing friend Leah's boyfriend. Mike grew up in the town right next to mine, and—beautifully enough—when he heard about my accident from Tim, he'd left work and come straight to the hospital.

He didn't really know anyone except for Tim and Leah, so my family and friends kept asking who the guy with the beard in the waiting room was. This fact alone saved me a lot of time in the explanation department. I had always thought he was very handsome, but I assumed I wasn't his type mostly because he was incredibly smart. He could talk about politics and World War I in deep detail and knew more about music than anyone I had ever met. And me? Well, I spoke in abbreviated words (for example: *obvi, totes, abbrevs*), rocked out to pop music, and struggled to keep up with world events, past or present. I thought Mike was out of my league. Even though I thought he was good-looking and cool, I didn't want to push it. I would just keep everything very friendly. However, after three years of being in a relationship, I had forgotten what it was like not to have the protective bubble of "taken" surrounding me. I didn't realize that my "friendly" now looked a lot like flirting.

After seeing him a few times at bars and house parties, I realized I was having real big-girl feelings for him. And after some serious eye contact and a few e-mail exchanges, I figured there was a chance that he might reciprocate those feelings. I was so excited! Like, nerdy teenage girl excited! Unfortunately, that feeling was quickly followed by sick-to-my-stomach-with-fear. The way things ended with Warren had left me feeling awful. I honestly didn't think I deserved to date anyone because I was so selfish and mean. I was also hesitant about the scars. Making yourself vulnerable in that way is difficult enough as it is, and if you compound that feeling with the dents and divots that were all over my midsection, you have got one insecure twenty-five-year-old. And then there was the bigger issue of the future. I didn't want to get into it on a first date, but out of fairness to the other person, I felt it needed to be said. How would Mike feel about the possibility of me not being able to have a baby? This was pretty aggressive, thinking about a relationship that hadn't even started yet. I contemplated outlining all this in a note, which would end with, "If you still want to date me after knowing this information, check the yes box. If you don't, please check no, then buy me a whiskey and walk away very quickly."

Actually it wasn't such a bad idea, but I decided to seek a little advice first. So, I sat my friend Alysa down over a large bottle of wine and asked her what she thought. Basically I wanted to know what the fuck I was going to do with these huge emotional duffel bags I was lugging around on my back.

"Be honest, but not aggressive," she said. "Think of your baggage as a gift. See it as a way of cutting through the bullshit of whether or not the other person likes you. If your scars freak him out, fuck him. If he can't handle the fact that you dated someone before him and it didn't end well, fuck him. And honestly, Katie, if he can't deal with the challenges you and this new body face then you are better off knowing it now than later. Just be honest and if he freaks out, he freaks out. There'll be someone who doesn't. You are fantastic, and you can only be you."

I stared at my glass of wine like it was a crystal ball and then took a large mouthful and nodded. She was right; this was who I was now. I could only be me.

I don't know how I got so lucky, but he was more than okay with my baggage—he actually helped me carry it. Still, when the time came for me to tell him about my scars, I wasn't really sure how to broach the subject.

"So you know I was in that accident, right?"

"Right."

"Well, you know how I went through surgery, and there was that thing with the gearshift, and Roberto and all that other stuff?"

"Yes?"

"Okay, because of that I don't really look like other girls in the tummy area. Sooo if you want for me not to show my stomach, or always wear a tank top, that is totally cool, and I totally understand." I said this with tears in my eyes, mortified that I had to say any of it, completely scared of what he would say.

"Katie, I am here with a pretty girl. I don't notice your scars. You are beautiful, so they are beautiful. Please, I seriously don't

even see them." Because he didn't see them, I tried to stop seeing them.

When I told him about my breakup with Warren, he
shrugged it off, saying, "People have bad breakups. Some take
it better than others. I understand."

He made everything seem so simple and easy to grasp. It
made me feel more comfortable with myself and my situation.

Many months later, when things were getting much more
serious, the subject of babies came up. I braced myself and told
him what I knew about my situation. "They don't know what
my deal is, but there have been some doctors who have said it
isn't possible, and there are some who say that it might be possible. The truth is I won't know until I am actually trying. So it
is really just a waiting game, but I needed to let you know, so
you never felt as though I was blindsiding you with this stuff.
I'm sorry."

Mike inhaled and calmly said, "We won't know what your
situation is until the time comes, so there is no reason to worry
about it now. Who knows, everything could be fine! And if it
isn't fine, we'll figure it out then. Right?"

He was right, and he was calm. Somehow Mike was able to
take the things I was afraid of, break them down into reasonable easy-to-comprehend pieces, and take away the fear that
had been crippling me just moments before.

Mike wanted a lot of the same things I did: to live an interesting life full of travel, books, music, and as much laughter as
possible. Just being around him made me feel as though I was
getting closer to the person I wanted to be. Somehow he made
me want to be a better person while at the same time still really
liking the person I already was.

One night a year or so after we started dating, Mike pulled
me close to him as he slept, and I realized how content I felt.
Everything that had made me anxious—guilt over my bad

breakup, my scars, my potential inability to have children—was no longer an issue. I had never imagined all these things would just unpack themselves the way they did. Every day we spent together, my bags became lighter and lighter, until one day, miraculously, they were small enough to fit in the overhead compartment.

# CHAPTER THIRTY-NINE

## Now

The summer after my senior year of college, I started to have panic attacks. They wouldn't just appear; they would build slowly—fear placed on top of fear with a thick layer of anxiety binding each brick together. The wall would grow and grow until nothing could get through it. Any new, positive thought would run full force toward the wall, only to get knocked down. All I was able to process was, *Holy shit, there isn't enough time; I can't do it all. I want more. I am wasting my life. I am a waste.* Then the bricks would land one on top of another. And my chest would hurt, breathing would become difficult, and my hands would go numb. This would happen to me about once a day until I started to take medication to control it. I took these meds until the day of my accident.

After the accident I didn't panic anymore. I had found out it was true. I was never going to get it all—never. Everything I wanted from my life was probably not going to happen.

\*\*\*

I had always known there would never be enough time, but I was definitely living on borrowed time now. Every single thing that happened after my accident was all just that cherry on top now. If I died today, if I didn't get it all in, I didn't give a fuck. What I had now was better than nothing. I was ready to take it and be happy. Anything more that the universe was willing to give me, I was going to accept gratefully. There was no time to freak out anymore.

I stopped fearing death, but more importantly, I stopped fearing life. I joked with my friends that I was bulletproof. I crossed Broadway without looking. I pushed myself too hard. I drank until four a.m. Everything I wanted I went for, regardless of the consequences. I didn't care about consequences—they were something the living would have to worry about; I wasn't one of them anymore.

A fearless life felt like my consolation prize for getting run over by a truck. It wasn't winning, but it was something. That following autumn, after I went back to work, the company I had been working for had been acquired by another firm, and I was offered either a job in Minneapolis or a few months' worth of severance. I was pretty sure that my bionic body would not fare well in subzero weather, so I opted for the paid time off.

Suddenly, there was time and money for the life I had always wanted to lead. There it was: my oyster, my pearl, and I chased after it with all the strength and voracity I could muster.

I found myself falling in love with my life at the same time I was falling in love with Mike. I was nervous but excited about all my future had to offer.

Then on March 15, a year and a half after my accident, I found myself afraid I was going to lose my life again. I was afraid the nightmare would return and I would get knocked down once more, and have to start all over.

I woke up on that particular morning, and things seemed different. I was uneasy, uncomfortable, and some of my old anxiety had returned. It felt as though there were spiders under my skin. I had recently begun a new job, which was great, but it had been a change, and change scared me now. I didn't know what to expect. I didn't know what might happen. I felt out of control and unhappy. This state of mind was where I had spent a good bit of time before my accident, but I hadn't felt this way in months. I wasn't even exactly sure how to handle it. So I did what had made me feel better in the past: I went for a walk.

The night before Mike had been sick. I brought him ginger ale and Pepto-Bismol, but he was just too ill to have me stay over. I understood, but I couldn't help but feel rejected. I thought I had done something wrong. I was sure I wasn't good enough, that if he really loved me he would want me to stay. Of course, it had nothing to do with love. When he has a stomachache, he just doesn't want someone in his bed with him. It's a reasonable thought, one that I would have totally understood if I had been in a less vulnerable place. Instead, I went home feeling lonely, dejected, and worthless.

My fastest way to accessing feelings of worth had always been running. If I was made fun of when I was an awkward teen, I would think to myself, *It doesn't matter. I can run faster than her.* I would get home, strap on my sneakers, let my feet hit the pavement, and feel like pure light. All my feelings of inferiority would disappear with each step.

I can't run anymore—the accident took that from me—but I can powerwalk. I am talking fierce, serious arm-pumping walking, for a maximum of thirty minutes. It isn't much, but it's better than before and for that I am grateful. I started to walk down my block when I saw the pink fingers of sunrise creep across the pale blue sky. The moon was still shining above the horizon, but I didn't want anything so subtle—I wanted big. I powerwalked myself toward the orange pink glow, like a moth who had forgotten how singed her wings had been by the flame the last time.

I heard the rumble of a truck whiz by me as I pumped my arms toward the light. I was there again, chasing sunrises to places I didn't belong. I turned on my heels and walked back to my apartment. As I walked back, my mind was blank, but I had a fearful feeling—one that I couldn't wrap my head around. I dressed in silence, not sure of what to do with this feeling of heaviness. What was the matter with me? Was it my job? Was it Mike? It felt bigger, but I couldn't get to it in the twenty-five minutes I had left to get ready for work.

The L train got stuck underground that morning because of train traffic ahead of us. My mind started to spin with what an asshole I was for being late for a position I had held for only eight days. I tried to think of what I could do. How could I fix it? I decided I would get out at the first stop in Manhattan and instead of taking the 6 to my office I would a take a cab uptown to save time.

There was not one cab heading uptown, no matter which avenue I powerwalked over to, so I had to walk the whole thirteen blocks to work. A stabbing pain started to creep into my lower back around my back plate. As I hobbled toward my office, I realized I couldn't explain this to my new bosses: *They don't know that I was in an accident, and I'll bet they don't care. I am late, like a serious twenty minutes late, and they won't care that I was run over by a truck a year and a half ago. It doesn't matter to them. I'm just like everyone else.*

Then I stepped in a puddle. Bits of things I couldn't identify were all over my foot and in my shoe. *Great, I probably have gangrene or something now,* I thought.

I arrived at work in a panic, only to find that my manager was totally understanding about my subway issues. My shoes had dried out and no visible signs of gangrene appeared. Suddenly, all was right with the world. My focus shifted to all the tangible things that needed my attention that day: learning about a new job, still meeting new people, learning new passwords. It felt as if everything was back to normal until I caught the 6 train home. I walked down the stairs, swiped my MetroCard through the turnstile, and stood and waited for the train. My mind was quiet for the first time since that morning, and it went back to my last important thought—I'm just like everyone else. That means my life could be taken away again.

I had just started a new job before the accident. I had been feeling weird about my boyfriend before the accident, and I had ridden my bike toward the sunrise the morning before the accident. It was going to happen again. This was too reminiscent, too coincidental. I started to cry before I could get my oversized sunglasses out of my bag. I tried to wipe away the tears that snuck down my cheeks below the tortoiseshell rims. I didn't want all the normies in the subway car catching me with my emotional pants down.

Before this moment, since coming back into the real world, I had felt invincible. I figured since I was broken once, I had paid my dues. I didn't have to be scared anymore. But I suddenly realized that being stronger and smarter didn't make me safe. I wasn't safe. I was never going to be safe. I hadn't been afraid of losing my life again, because I still wasn't whole. I had still been feeling that if something were to happen to me, I would only wind up losing two-thirds, because one third of me had already died.

The fear of dying that would come to me occasionally before I was run over by a truck is with me all the time now. That feeling can be scary and overwhelming, but it can also be wonderful. It makes me aware that my time on earth is limited, but it also forces me to remember how scared I was when I thought I would never get any more of that time. I think about rolling into surgery, the plastic mask around my face, my eyes closing with the anesthesia, and I remember that I hadn't cared then whether the next minute would be good or bad—I just wanted more minutes.

I have promised myself that I will squeeze as much goodness as I can out of all the minutes I have left. I am grateful for the heartache, the joy, the ugliness, and the beauty.

And it's the beauty and joy that take away my panic and replace it with gratitude. And now that I am back to what feels like Katie 2.0, I know I will always be afraid of the fall. And if that is the price I have to pay for living, I will happily write the check.

# EPILOGUE

## Eff the Tee

As soon as the weather gets colder, the days shorter, and the nights longer, I find myself waking up at three a.m., searching for the light of the alarm clock to tell me the darkness doesn't mean that I am dead. I find myself shuddering with the memories of my accident. I cry for reasons that don't make sense—an evening out with Mike not going exactly as I had planned, not being able to find the right suit for work, forgetting to DVR *New Girl*. These things all seem like normal reasons to cry myself into a little hysterical puddle.

There are also moments of intense joy and gratitude—unlike anything I have ever experienced. I stare at the setting sun until it burns itself into my retinas and the outline stays behind my eyelids. I want to hug every single person I see. I find beauty in the oil rainbows floating on the tops of dirty puddles. I feel like a five-year-old who has a lot of feelings and no idea how to control them. I ride each one like a roller coaster, unsure where the next turn will take me, feeling my stomach drop at every dip.

When I was still recovering at home in Manhasset, I would make tons of plans for my future life. I needed to have milestones—I needed ways to say I had won. This was when I came up with what I would do on the anniversary of my accident. I decided it would be the day that I would say, *Fuck the truck.* My plan was pretty simple. Everyone would come to the apartment, and we would all go to the spot where it happened, together, and we would drink champagne, and we would celebrate life and living. We would laugh, and we would cry, and most of all we would be grateful.

So, on October 2, 2010, I wake up at six a.m., and I put on a pair of jeans and a sweater. It's chillier out than it was three years ago. As I dress, I run though what I did that morning one thousand ninety-five days ago. I still live in the same apartment as I did before everything happened, and I look around and imagine myself getting ready for that bike ride as the sun was coming up. I put on a pot of coffee, and I wait for everyone to arrive. My parents, Conor, James, Callie, Mike, and my best friends, Alysa, Leah, and Tim. Alysa and Leah were my roommates three years ago when the accident happened, and they became my family when I moved back to Brooklyn. This is a gathering of people who feel the repercussions of my accident almost as acutely as I do. We're in this together. Even though it is the third time we've done this together, the emotion is as raw as it was the first year.

I kiss and hug each one of them as they arrive, and then I start to cry, as I am wont to do. After we have all gotten a little coffee, I pull out red Solo cups and the champagne that has been chilling in the refrigerator. I put everything into a bag that my sister so kindly holds, and we all make our way downstairs. The sun is rising as the group makes a right out of my apartment. Everyone is laughing and joking, a little delirious that they are up and out and drinking at 6:30 on a Saturday morning. Leah can't stop giggling. I keep a few feet behind them, trying to wrap my head around all that has happened in the last three years, and we make our way down three blocks to where I almost lost everything.

What is interesting is that on the walk there, my back doesn't hurt, and I don't think about my scars. All I can think about is how incredibly amazing it is to be alive. I watch some of the people I love the most in the world walking in front of me. I see their feet hit the pavement. I hear their witty banter. I notice the way the golden morning light reflects off their faces, and I realize I almost missed all this. I feel nothing but gratitude.

When we get to the corner, I stare at the road and point out where the truck was and where I was. I show everyone where the black Mazda was and the place where the pastor parked his Camry. The corner is incredibly busy, even this early on a Saturday morning. I show my parents what size the truck was that ran me over. It always makes me shake when I think about it—my body feels the pain all over again in small tremors that run right through me.

My dad opens a bottle of champagne, and my mom hugs me, and Mike holds my hand. We pour out cups for everyone, and we drink a toast to living, as the huge trucks whiz by. As everyone talks, I step away from them and I pour out some champagne onto the spot where I was run over. I pour it out for the girl I used to be. I know Old Katie gets thirsty too, and I wouldn't want her to be at a party where she didn't get a drink.

I wind up staring at the spot and imagine my old self sprawled out with bits of my bike lodged in my side. I relive that girl's fear, and I think about what she was afraid of. She was afraid of not having more, afraid that this was going to be it. She was scared she wasn't going to get to see another sunrise, that there wouldn't be any more crisp breezes or champagne or smiles. I hear her prayers in my head, and they scare me. In that moment I love her so fiercely for holding on, for not giving up, for being stronger than she thought she could be, that I can't breathe.

But then I do.

With the air going in and out of my lungs, I realize her prayers were answered. Someone was listening and didn't let me go. I am here. I am breathing. I got one more day and then another and then another and then another.

I stare up at the sky I was praying to three years ago, and I say thank you. I know it doesn't make sense that I survived, and I am so cognizant of the fact that I'm so insanely lucky to be here. I begged the universe to let me live, and the universe granted my wish. In this moment, I know I have been given a second life, and it's my responsibility to live it joyfully.

I have worked so hard, struggled so rigorously, revisited places I never want to go again, and I have tasted triumph and pride and a love for myself I didn't know existed.

I don't want to be scared of dying, and I sure as shit don't want to start over again, but Jesus Christ, I know I don't want to stop following sunrises either.

# ACKNOWLEDGMENTS

This memoir began in a hospital room years ago, and would have never become a real book without the faith, support, and encouragement of so many people that I am blessed to know.

First and foremost, I want to thank the doctors and nurses who were responsible for saving my life and for my continued care. I wouldn't be here without your skills and talent! I am also so thankful to Matthew Witschel and Colleen Mansfield for being such phenomenal human beings and incredible colleagues—thank you for being so caring to someone you barely knew.

I am grateful to my incredible family for their constant support of this book, and of me, in every aspect of my life. A huge thank you is owed to my aunt, Carol Edwards, for telling me that this was a story that needed to be told, and encouraging me every single step of the way. I owe a debt of gratitude to John Freeman for believing that I could write, even before I did. I am so thankful to Susan Heath for her thoughtful and insightful early edits, as well as her guidance. I am incredibly grateful to Geoff Boisi for his care, generosity of spirit, and especially for the laptop that made this book possible!

This book wouldn't have become the beautiful item you hold in your hands without the direction and thoughtfulness of Matt Kaye, Angela Melamud, Devon Fredericksen, and all of the wonderful people at Inkshares and Girl Friday Productions. Working with you has been a dream come true.

I am so overwhelmed by the kindness of the best friends a girl could ask for. I don't know what I did to earn your love, but I promise to keep doing it until I die. It is impossible for me to name everyone, but those who stand out are Tommy Hampton, Maribeth Smith, Michael O'Loughlin, Alysa Perez-Kalbfell, Annamaria Iakovou-Gabriel, Nadine Partridge, Scott Rohan, Jack Rodolico, Erica Fowler, Colleen Barrett, Linda Silver, Kerrin Prewett, Kelly McKenna, Whitney Pagani, Kristin Whiteford, Samantha Heller, Maggie Sunderland, Liz Homas, Emily Erwin, Michael MacGilpin, Christopher Male, Alan Klingler, Sai Mokhtari, Leah P. Johns, Janet Koh, Christine Femia, Sarah Fullen-Gregory, Ellie Jackson, Kerry Robinson, and Erin-Leigh Schmoyer.

Tim McDonough, you are a port in stormy weather, and are one of the best people I have ever known. Leah Bonvissuto, you never gave up on me, or this book. It didn't matter if I was dejected or elated, you were there with a drink, a hug, and a belief that all of this would happen. Because you had faith, I did too. Thanks to you both for always taking that long walk down Maspeth. I love you.

Patrick Conlon, your confidence and excitement about *How to Get Run Over by a Truck* is what made it possible for me to have the strength to put myself out there. Thank you for asking the right questions, for being the cheerleader of my dreams, for loving me. I am the luckiest.

# ABOUT THE AUTHOR

Katie McKenna is a professional fund-raiser and stand-up comedian living in Brooklyn. She runs a blog called *Small Bites and Little Victories* and is an expert on the best date spots in New York City. *How to Get Run Over by a Truck* is her first book.

# LIST OF PATRONS

This book was made possible in part by the following grand patrons who preordered the book on inkshares.com. Thank you.

Adam and Kara Altenhofen
Alan Klingler
Alexandra Mertens
Brian Burke
Brian Hughes
Brian Maher
Brian Nese
Brian Yuen
Caitlin McGlynn Scanlon
Catherine G. Male
Christopher R. Male
Dan Carmichael
David A. Vaala
Donna Di Pietro Leanza
D. Thomas Healey Jr.
Edward G. Hynes
Elana Davis

Eleanore Jackson
Erin E. Roberts
Francesca MacKie
Frank A. Shea III
Geoffrey T. Boisi
Helene M. Bowler
Jackie Quigley
Jane F. Narich
Jim and Mary Regan
João Luís Serrenho
Joaquin Rojas
Joel D. Cohn
John Welsh
Joseph Halaas
Kathleen A. Hampton
Katy J. Breazeale
Kay Jackson

Kelly E. McKenna

Kief Rosa

Kristin Lewis

Larry Fox

Leah Bonvissuto

Leah P. Johns

Lindsay Moore

Margo and Arthur McKenna

Margot S. Funke

Mark G. Muller

Mark and Stacy McCray

Mary C. McHugh

Mary Burnes

Maryjo Collins

Matt Kaye

Matthew Naclerio

Melissa Dooley

Michael D. Edmonds

Michael K. Bird

Michael S. Gross

Morgan and Luc
    DesGroseillers

Patrick Conlon

Peter J. Caulo

Richard A. De Long

Richard J. Duggan

Robert and Jo Ann Corti

Sally Mac Gilpin

Sam Berlin

Simone Celio Jr.

Susan Heath

The Silver Family

Thomas L. Potter

Timothy McDonough

Tom Fulgieri

# INKSHARES

 Inkshares is a crowdfunded book publisher. We democratize publishing by having readers select the books we publish—we edit, design, print, distribute, and market any book that meets a preorder threshold.

Interested in making a book idea come to life? Visit inkshares.com to find new book projects or start your own.